Development and Stagnation

Studies in Critical Social Sciences

VOLUME 327

The titles published in this series are listed at *brill.com/scss*

Development and Stagnation

The Debate between Developmentalists and Neoclassical Liberals

By

André Nassif

Translated by

Christine Wight

BRILL

LEIDEN | BOSTON

Cover illustration: © André Nassif, created using ChatGPT on January 28, 2025.

This book was originally published in Portuguese as *Desenvolvimento e Estagnação: o Debate entre Desenvolvimentistas e Liberais Neoclássicos*. São Paulo: Editora Contracorrente, 2023. The English edition was translated by Christine Jennifer Wight and reviewed by the author.

Library of Congress Cataloging-in-Publication Data

Names: Nassif, André author | Wight, Christine Jennifer translator
Title: Development and stagnation : the debate between developmentalists and neoclassical liberals / by André Nassif ; translated by Christine Wight.
Other titles: Desenvolvimento e estagnação. English
Description: Leiden ; Boston : Brill, [2025] | Series: Studies in critical social sciences, 1573-4234 ; volume 327 | Originally published in Portuguese as Desenvolvimento e estagnação: o debate entre desenvolvimentistas e liberais neoclássicos, 2023. | Includes bibliographical references and index.
Identifiers: LCCN 2025014704 (print) | LCCN 2025014705 (ebook) | ISBN 9789004734289 hardback | ISBN 9789004734296 ebook
Subjects: LCSH: Economic development | Stagnation (Economics)
Classification: LCC HD85 .N3313 2025 (print) | LCC HD85 (ebook) | DDC 338.9--dc23/eng/20250609
LC record available at https://lccn.loc.gov/2025014704
LC ebook record available at https://lccn.loc.gov/2025014705

Typeface for the Latin, Greek, and Cyrillic scripts: "Brill". See and download: brill.com/brill-typeface.

ISSN 1573-4234
ISBN 978-90-04-73428-9 (hardback)
ISBN 978-90-04-73429-6 (e-book)
DOI 10.1163/9789004734296

This book is printed on acid-free paper and produced in a sustainable manner.

To the memory of my parents, Morena and Alfredo, and my brother, José Luiz: all very much alive in me

The purpose of studying economics is not to acquire a set of ready-made answers to economic questions, but to learn how to avoid being deceived by economists.

JOAN ROBINSON, *In*: *Contributions to Modern Economics*. New York: Academic Press, 1978: 75

• • •

Walking against the wind
No scarf, no document (...)
I go
Why not? Why not?

CAETANO VELOSO, *"Joy, joy"*, lyrics of his Brazilian song, 1967

Contents

Foreword

The book you are about to read is a remarkable analysis and discussion of the theory of economic development and the causes of economic stagnation. It is a theoretical book that helps us understand why countries tend to develop and why countries like Brazil, which grew extraordinarily after World War II and were reaching the standard of living of rich countries, entered an endless period of economic stagnation in the 1980s, after which they began to grow slowly and fell behind the rich countries.

This is not a book about the Brazilian economy, nor a book with a single theory of development, but a book in which we see how heterodox, Keynesian-developmental theories have evolved, and how these theories compare with the neoclassical neoliberal theory—the dominant theory taught in universities in core countries, which since the 1980s have adopted them and practically imposed them on countries on the periphery of capitalism.

Rather than complicating economic theory, this book simplifies it. It shows that, fundamentally, there are two strategies, or two forms of economic organisation of capitalism—the developmental form, which assumes moderate state intervention in the economy and economic nationalism, and a liberal form, which limits state action to property and contract guarantees and fiscal balance responsibility, while rejecting economic nationalism when it is practiced by periphery countries.

For both developmental and liberal economists, economic development depends on investment, and investment depends on the expected profit rate. The difference lies in the fact that liberals believe that, with market freedom, the profit rate will be satisfactory, the investment rate will be high, and the allocation of factors will be efficient, so that "we will live in the best of all possible worlds." Developmentalists think differently. They defend market freedom, but they do not expect more from it than it can deliver.

Economic theory is the science that studies the coordination of economies by the market and the state. Therefore, it studies capitalism from an economic point of view. In this form of social organisation, it is important to distinguish the core (or centre) from the periphery of capitalism. In capitalism, it is not only companies, but also the nation states that compete with each other. For this reason, it is necessary that each country, without denying the importance of international cooperation, defends its interests and is an economic nationalist.

Secondly, it is important to understand that, contrary to what liberals think, economic sectors are not equivalent. Economic development is associated with increased productivity which, in turn, tend to increase not only as the productive capacity of each worker increases, but also with the shift of labour from sectors with low value added per person, which are not very sophisticated and pay low wages, to sectors with high value added per person, which are more sophisticated and pay higher wages. Therefore, developmentalists say that economic development is industrialisation, or more broadly, is productive sophistication.

For the core countries, it is not in their interest for the countries on the periphery of capitalism to industrialise. They do not want to have more competition than they already have. As a result, they try to prevent periphery countries' their industrialisation and use economic liberalism as an instrument of domination—more specifically, the law of comparative advantage in international trade. This is an absurd law that ignores the fact that countries can learn and, therefore, their advantages change. In the 19th century, the English told the Germans that their country was "essentially agricultural", but Germany became an industrial power. This law also assumes full employment—which allows liberal economists to claim that, in order to industrialise, periphery countries need to reduce their agricultural or mineral production—even though full employment is the exception, not the rule.

To discuss developmental theories, André Nassif divided his book into two parts. In the first, he discusses structuralist developmental theories; in the second, he deals with neoclassical liberal theory. He dedicated seven chapters to developmental theories, with which he identifies, including a chapter on their conceptual roots and another on their implications for public policy.

Chapter 1 presents the basic ideas about economic development—the ideas of Adam Smith, Karl Marx, Joseph Schumpeter, and, in some passages, John Maynard Keynes. Smith explained the wealth of nations through investment and the division of labour; Marx gave emphasis to the expected profit rate, the interest rate, and capital accumulation. Schumpeter showed that, in the perfect competition assumed by liberals, the profit rate is very low; only innovation can create a competitive advantage that creates demand for the firm, increases its expected profit rate, and leads it to invest; Keynes, finally, criticised the liberal neoclassical theory by showing that supply does not automatically create demand, showed that in capitalist economies capitalists can hoard money instead of investing, and argued that only the management of aggregate demand can ensure that competent firms have low interest rates and satisfactory profit rates that will lead them to invest.

In Chapter 2, Nassif discusses the structuralist developmental school, or classical developmental theory, which emerged together with the first developmental economists. It is a critical theory of neoclassical liberalism, an abstract and ahistorical theory. With classical developmentalists, economic development began to be seen as an historical phenomenon that was identified with industrialisation. And through this, the first critical models of neoclassical liberal theory emerged: the Rosenstein-Rodan big-push model, the centre-periphery model and the external constraint model of Raúl Prebisch, the labour displacement to manufacturing model of Arthur Lewis and the increasing returns model of Nicholas Kaldor. They were all Keynesian economists who emphasised the role of aggregate demand. Nassif points out that in the 1960s, Kaldor formulated the "laws of growth", among which the most important, or original, was the defence of industrialisation, due to the fact that there are increasing returns to scale in the manufacturing sector that spread to the economy.

In Chapter 3, we have the ideas of ECLAC, the Latin American structuralist version of classical developmentalism. Raúl Prebisch was the main economist of this current, which he built within the scope of ECLAC—the United Nations Economic Commission for Latin America and the Caribbean—with the help of many economists, particularly Celso Furtado. Since he was the head of an international agency, Prebisch did not talk about imperialism, but about centre and periphery. He showed that economic development was structural change or industrialisation and criticised the core for defending an unequal exchange—an exchange of sophisticated goods for simple goods. He also showed how developing countries are subject to an external restriction—the permanent "lack" of US dollars: while in rich countries the income elasticity of demand for imports is less than one, in periphery countries the income elasticity of demand for imports of manufactured goods is greater than one. A problem for which there is only one solution: industrialisation.

In Chapter 4, the focus is on the contribution of Celso Furtado, who thought of development and underdevelopment as expressions of the centre and the periphery. Underdevelopment is not a stage prior to industrialisation and development, but is an historical configuration created by the centre when it imposes itself on the periphery; it is a form assumed by the international division of labour, in which the core industrialises while the periphery is responsible for producing agricultural and mineral goods. Furtado always used the historical-structural or historical-deductive method to construct his theory of development and always placed it within the framework of interdependence between nations. In the chapter on Furtado, André Nassif recalls that, back in the 1950s, the great Brazilian economist practically identified the Dutch disease when analysing the economy of Venezuela. It is a pity that he did not pursue this idea later.

Nassif defines Chapter 5 as "a prologue to new developmentalism: notes on the inflation targeting regime and fiscal austerity". In this chapter, he argues that classical developmentalism gave relatively little importance to macroeconomic theory and claims that Bresser-Pereira (myself), with his new developmental theory, sought to fill this gap. Also note that I realised that industrial and technological policies, necessary for development, became ineffective if they were not accompanied by macroeconomic policies, mainly exchange rate policy and monetary policy, which create the environment for those microeconomic policies to have an effect. Nassif then discusses the inflation targeting policy, which central banks adopted when, back in the 1980s, they saw that the monetarist policies proposed by Milton Friedman, which were dominant for a brief time, were not helping them control inflation. Needless to say that the inflation targeting regime, as applied in Brazil, is critically analysed and evaluated by Nassif. And in this chapter, he highlights the importance of the theory of inertial inflation, which Yoshiaki Nakano and I, in São Paulo, and economists from PUC-Rio (Pontifical Catholic University of Rio de Janeiro), in Rio de Janeiro, developed. I find it interesting that Nassif saw the inflation theory as a prologue to new developmentalism, because, for me, this theory, and particularly the paper "*Fatores acceleradores, mantenedores e sancionadores da desigualdade*" (Bresser-Pereira, L.C. and Nakano, Y., Brazilian Journal of Political Economy, vol. 4, no. 1, 1984), played such a role.

After this prologue, Nassif dedicates Chapter 6 to the new developmental theory—which a group of Brazilian economists and myself have been building since the 2000s. Naturally, I felt very flattered and happy to be placed alongside the pioneers of development. Until the late 1990s, I was a post-Keynesian macroeconomist and a classical developmentalist. However, at the end of that decade, after 20 years of near stagnation in Latin American countries, I realised that additional theoretical models were needed to understand the problem of development and stagnation. We began by criticising the high real interest rates and the exchange rate that appreciated the Brazilian currency in real terms in the long run. Although liberal economists in the governments claimed that the prices were determined by the market, we saw that the interest rate was much higher than the international interest rate plus the Brazilian risk, and that the exchange rate tended to appreciate in the long term. Consequently, capable firms became uncompetitive and did not invest, while the purchasing power and consumption of workers and rentiers were artificially high. We also saw that, contrary to conventional theory, the real exchange rate is a determining variable for investment. We could affirm this because we also affirmed that the exchange rate is not merely volatile around the current equilibrium but tends to remain appreciated in the long run. For two reasons: because the growth policy with external debt appreciates the national currency in the long term and because an unneutralised Dutch disease keeps the real exchange rate appreciated for the manufacturing sector, not for commodities. Finally, we affirm that the macroeconomics that matters is a macroeconomic theory and a macroeconomic policy of development in which the state should be responsible for about 20 percent of total investment and the government should guarantee the general conditions for capital accumulation, that is, investing in education, science and technology, investing in infrastructure, maintaining institutions that guarantee the proper functioning of the market, guaranteeing the existence of a local financial system capable of financing investments and keeping the five macroeconomic prices in the right place: the real interest rate should be relatively low; the real exchange rate, competitive; the profit rate, satisfactory for industrial companies to invest; the real wage rate growing with the increase in productivity; and the inflation rate at a low level.

André Nassif discusses new developmentalism with great competence because he is one of the most notable Brazilian developmental economists. When I met him in 2008, however, he had just published an article in the journal I edit, the "Brazilian Journal of Political Economy", an article in which he refuted the thesis that I was then beginning to defend, based on the theory I was developing, that Brazil was undergoing a serious process of deindustrialisation. André, however, is an economist who thinks with autonomy and clarity. Over time, he changed his opinion on deindustrialisation and became one of the economists who has made the greatest contributions to new developmentalism.

Chapter 7 is a conclusion to the analysis carried out. In it, André Nassif emphasises that economic development is only successful when it results from a national project. He also takes the opportunity to discuss recent contributions to development theory. He then cites authors such as Ha-Joon Chang, Erik Reinert and Mariana Mazzucato, who showed that all successful countries in the catching up process were guided by developmental principles, and not by neoclassical precepts (inherited from David Ricardo) of unconditional adherence to laissez-faire and free trade practices; Alice Amsden and Robert Wade, developmentalists focused on East Asian countries; neo-Schumpeterian authors, such as Mario Cimoli, Giovanni Dosi and Gabriel Porcile; and neoclassical but developmentalist authors, such as Dani Rodrik.

The second part of the book is devoted to neoclassical liberal development theory. In Chapter 8, Nassif discusses liberal theories of international trade; in Chapter 9, neoclassical growth theory; and in Chapter 10, the Washington Consensus and neoliberal ideology. These are very interesting chapters, but I confess that I have no patience with what neoclassical liberals call development theory. As Celso Furtado said, it is nothing more than ideology. An ideology that appears not disguised as theory in Chapter 10. Chapter 11 is André Nassif's critique of these theories and their narrow policy implications.

We thus have a beautiful book. A brilliant analysis of development theories by a developmental economist engaged in the struggle for development—a difficult struggle that will only be won when developmentalism returns to being the form of economic organisation of the capitalism dominant in Brazil and Latin America and when we know how to reject the growth policy with external debt, decide to neutralise the Dutch disease and return to the state the role of investing in strategic sectors of the economy.

Luiz Carlos Bresser-Pereira
Emeritus Professor, São Paulo School of Economics (FGV-EESP)
São Paulo, January 2025

Preface

The theoretical discussion on the main factors and economic policy strategies that lead underdeveloped or developing countries to become developed has always been a field of dispute between liberal and developmental economists. This divergence became explicit in the theory and practice of economic policies between the end of the 18th century and the beginning of the 19th century, when Alexander Hamilton, the first United States Secretary of the Treasury after independence, and Friedrich List, the German nationalist economist, rejected the liberal recommendations of classical political economists, who pointed to free trade as the best strategy for countries to achieve a high level of material and social wealth. The subject continues to be one of the bones of contention between neoclassical liberals and developmentalists: while the former are defenders of laissez faire and international free trade strategies, or at best a minimum degree of state intervention, developmentalists advocate active state intervention in support of economic development.

In Brazil, this discussion frequently arises in traditional media (press, television and radio) and digital media (social networks such as Facebook, Instagram, among others) in a fragmented, passionate and strongly ideological fashion. But the strongly ideological bias embedded in this debate is not exclusive to Brazil. It occurs in most countries. Not that economic theories are free from ideology either. As I argue in one of the chapters of the book, not even theories that are "sold" as "pure" are free from the ideologies inherent in social class conflicts, political positions, economic interests, cultural influences, and so on.

However, I believe that when formulating and analysing theories or proposing solutions to economic issues, economists should strive to separate appearances and easy (or ideologically biased) discourse from the essence ("theory"). They should prioritise the regularity of observed facts (the so-called empirical regularities), as well, and take into account the historical, political and social context. It is also essential to respect the empirical evidence and historical experiences of countries in the capitalist world.

My main objective in this book is to present the theoretical debate on development and stagnation in the most organised and clear way possible, and in a language that is not restricted to economists and economics students but is also accessible to anyone interested in the subject. From early on, we economists learn that economic theory is extremely abstract because it is developed in a very complex real world, through interactions with a great diversity of agents (firms, households, government, banks, etc.), who operate in different markets and with often conflicting interests. However, I believe that, with some didactic effort, theories, including the most complex economic theories, can be made accessible to non-specialist audiences. I have, therefore, tried to write in clear language, but without neglecting academic rigour in explaining the theories. I have maintained the technical terms familiar to economists but have added the respective concepts in footnotes (some relatively long) to facilitate understanding by non-economists. The unification, into a single volume, of the main theoretical foundations of economic development, including the contribution of theories formulated in Latin America, makes the material also useful as a study guide for undergraduate and graduate students and other professionals.

While the discussion presented in the book is eminently theoretical, this does not prevent me from alluding, in an illustrative manner, to specific cases of countries, successful or not in the development process. Brazil is the example that appears most frequently because it is where, in the periphery world, two distinct phases are quite clearly recorded: the first, between 1950 and 1980, in which economic policies were strongly influenced by developmentalists. The second, from 1990 to the present, in which economic policies are marked by neoclassical liberal ideas, notably neoliberals. It is no coincidence that in the period 1950–1980, Brazil followed a relatively sustained trajectory of economic growth, and that since 1980—a decade marked by the foreign debt crisis, high inflation and the transition to the adoption of neoliberal strategies—until the present, the country still has not managed to free itself from stagnation.

I would like to express my gratitude for the attentive reading of friends from the academic world, who made comments and suggestions to the original text. My thanks to Alfredo Saad Filho, André Lara Resende, Carlos Aguiar de Medeiros, Carmem Feijó, Cyro Andrade, Eliane Araújo, Fábio Terra, Gabriel Porcile, José Márcio Rego, Luiz Carlos Bresser-Pereira, Luiz Gonzaga Belluzzo and Patrícia Cunha. Cyro Andrade and Fábio Terra deserve a special and double thank you, who, in addition to their technical comments, also made suggestions for improving the style and language. Any remaining imperfections are, of course, my responsibility.

I wish you a good read!

André Nassif
Department of Economics, Fluminense Federal University (UFF)
Rio de Janeiro, January 2025

Figures and Tables

Figures

Tables

Introduction

Economic Development and Stagnation: the Different Theoretical Views

Economic development is one of the most important themes in economic science because it determines, although not exclusively, the material progress and level of well-being of societies. With this book I intend to present and analyse the phenomenon of development by comparing the different theoretical views, as well as the respective economic policy recommendations of the two main *lato sensu* schools of thought responsible for the development of economics as an integral discipline of the social sciences: the structuralist-developmentalist, hereinafter referred to as developmental or developmentalist; and neoclassical liberal.

While the focus of the book is on development, in several passages I will deal with the phenomenon that is antagonistic to development: stagnation. The theoretical and empirical literature offers enormous bibliographical material on the multiple factors that lead to the economic development of a nation, but it comprises relatively scarcer references on the causes of prolonged stagnation. There is at least one reason that justifies this imbalance: one of the most important objectives of economics is to understand, through the development of theories and the search for empirical evidence, how economic development takes place and what guides a poor (or developing) nation to becoming rich (or developed). Therefore, most economists are more interested in identifying the driving forces of development than in seeking explanations for economic stagnation, even though it is intuitive to deduce that this paralysis occurs when those driving forces are blocked.

Since Adam Smith, there has been a relative consensus that development occurs through a sustained increase in labour productivity (measured by the value added per worker in the production of goods and services) over time.[1]

1 Labour productivity in a given productive activity is measured by the ratio between the value added and the total number of workers employed (or, alternatively, the total number of hours worked) in that same activity. Value added is understood as the increase in new value (measured in monetary units) generated by each worker in the production of a good or service. For example, the value added generated in the production of an automobile is measured by the difference between the unit value of the automobile (expressed in monetary units) and the value of all the inputs (parts, pieces and other components) needed for its production. In other words, value added is the new value added by workers to the value of the inputs used

 | DOI:10.1163/9789004734296_002

Since the average level of productivity of the economy as a whole is low in poor countries compared to that of rich countries, development is considered successful when the average levels of productivity and per capita GDP (gross domestic product divided by the total population) of those countries reach levels similar to the average achieved by developed countries (catch up).

First of all, it is important to distinguish between two important indicators: the **levels** of average productivity and per capita income, on the one hand, and the **rates of change** of these same levels over time, on the other. If economic development occurs when these levels are caught up with those of developed countries, it is easy to deduce that the necessary condition for this to occur is that the rates of change of productivity over time are positive, sustainable and higher than the rates of change of this same indicator in rich countries. If in a poor country, with a still low per capita income, or in a developing country, whose per capita income has reached the average level observed in the world economy, the productivity growth rates are extremely low and much lower than the averages observed in the world economy over a long period of time, a process of economic stagnation will be observed in that country. If this process continues for decades, it may lead to economic regression (falling behind). In other words, the process of stagnation can be understood as the antithesis to the process of economic development.

At the theoretical level, since the classical political economy, economists have sought to analyse and identify the main driving forces that sustain the significant rates of change in productivity and the process of economic development in a given country, allowing it to catch up in the long run. Practically all theoretical schools identify capital accumulation and technological progress—both induced by physical investments (machinery, equipment and infrastructure) and innovations—as the fundamental driving forces. However, as the popular saying goes, the devil is in the details. Broadly speaking, while the theoretical frameworks of Smith, Marx, Schumpeter and the entire classical-structuralist-developmentalist (or simply developmental) tradition that followed them between the 1940s and 1960s identify the sustained increase in productivity as the **channel** through which economic development takes place, the Ricardian-neoclassical liberal (or simply neoclassical liberal) tradition attributes that very indicator as the **main cause** of this same process.

Indeed, in the neoclassical liberal framework, economic progress fundamentally depends on the efficiency with which productive resources (capital,

in the production of a good or service. For the economy as a whole, gross domestic product (GDP) is calculated by adding together all sectoral value added, while average aggregate labour productivity results from GDP per worker.

labour, natural resources and others) are mobilised, combined and allocated in the production of goods and services. It is not by chance that this concept reached its peak of prestige in the mid-1950s, when the standard neoclassical model[2] demonstrated that economic growth can only be sustained if technological progress continues to operate in the long term (Solow, 1956). However, in the neoclassical growth model, technological progress reflects the most efficient possible combination with which productive resources are incorporated, intra-sectorally and inter-sectorally, in the production of goods and services. Since in the neoclassical liberal conception this combination defines technological progress—or, to use the expression consecrated by this current, total factor productivity (TFP)—it follows that economic growth depends fundamentally on productivity performance over time. In other words, for this line of thought, the change in productivity is the **cause** of economic development.

In the developmental tradition, the process of economic development occurs through the advancement of labour productivity over time, but this, in turn, depends on other driving forces, whose deeper roots had been clearly exposed by Adam Smith (1776) in "The Wealth of Nations". Although this author agreed that the economic development of nations was embodied in the increase in labour productivity, this depended predominantly on the advance of the social division of labour and the size of the market. In short, Smith defended the hypothesis that the greater the social division of labour, the greater the increase in productivity. However, since the social division of labour is limited by the size of the market, the increase in productivity ultimately depends on the size of the market. The entire developmental tradition that flourished from 1940 onwards took up and developed, with different nuances, that Smithian hypothesis. In a simplified way, the fundamental role of the size and expansion of demand in the long run is underscored as the source from which the advancement in labour productivity and, therefore, economic development emanates.

When comparing the two theoretical approaches, it is worth highlighting that since in the neoclassical liberal view economic development depends on the relative efficiency with which available productive resources are combined, it is irrelevant whether social wealth is driven by agriculture, industry or services. An increase of $1.00 from the primary sector is equivalent to an equal increase of $1.00 from the secondary or tertiary sectors. In the language

2 Economic theories are usually presented as "models", which consist of representing reality in a simplified way, choosing the most relevant variables for understanding the economic problems that emerge in a much more complex real world. A model generally contains assumptions, hypotheses and conclusions related to the problems in question.

of economists, the neoclassical liberal conception assumes that all productive sectors are subject to constant returns to scale. This means that if a company, a productive sector or even the economy as a whole doubles all the resources needed to generate a particular product or aggregate product, the resulting production will vary in the same proportion (that is, it will simply double). Therefore, average productivity will remain constant. Translating this same hypothesis into monetary terms, if we assume that the prices of productive resources remain constant, the unit costs of the product will also remain constant in the long run.

The developmental tradition rejects the idea that all sectors of the economy operate with constant returns to scale. Although traditional agricultural production technologies, because they do not rely on modern machinery and equipment, are subject to constant or even decreasing returns to scale,[3] this condition does not prevail in the manufacturing industry. The common point highlighted by economists of this school is that most of the manufacturing industry has three characteristics that make it special: (i) it is the main source for the generation and diffusion of technical progress for all sectors of the economy; (ii) it operates under **static** increasing returns to scale, given that the cumulative effects of technological revolutions and technical progress over time mean that production, in most of its segments, is predominantly intensive in fixed capital and characterised by technological indivisibilities.[4] Consequently, if entrepreneurs make new investments that result in doubling the production factors used in these segments, the resulting production will more than double, causing average productivity to increase and unit costs to fall, if the prices of these factors remain unchanged; and (iii) it operates under conditions of **dynamic** increasing returns to scale, since the cumulative effects of technical-scientific progress, by expanding innovative capacity, the stock of knowledge and the experience accumulated in the learning process (the so-called learning by doing), cause the unit costs of companies or even of entire segments to decline as total accumulated production increases over time. Owing to these collective characteristics, the developmental tradition attributes to the manufacturing industry the potential to operate as the engine of economic growth in the long term.

---

3 Following the same reasoning as before, under decreasing returns to scale, if all the inputs needed to produce a given agricultural product are doubled, the resulting production will vary by less than double and, therefore, the average productivity of that activity will be reduced.

4 In this case, the system of machinery and equipment that make up a steel, automotive, or pulp and paper plant cannot be fragmented when sales fall and entrepreneurs are forced to reduce production.

For the developmental school, as well, in contrast to the neoclassical liberal school, development is not restricted to sustaining economic growth in the long term. Additionally, development is also conceived as a process that involves profound structural changes, especially in the increase in the share (measured in added value) of the gross domestic product (GDP) of the most technologically sophisticated segments, as we will see later. Not only that, it also encompasses the improvement of physical infrastructure (railways, highways, ports, sanitation, etc.) and human infrastructure (education, health, culture and leisure), the reduction of social inequality and the guarantee of citizenship rights. As Amartya Sen (2000: 18) emphatically argues, development involves rights that transcend the field of economics, such as the full exercise of freedom. To achieve this, it is necessary to remove "poverty, tyranny, lack of economic opportunities, systematic social destitution, neglect of public services and intolerance or excessive interference by repressive states".

Based on historical experiences after the Industrial Revolution (1750–1850),[5] the developmental school highlights that the process of economic development replicates the following stylised facts, or empirical regularities:[6]

i. in the transition from an underdeveloped to a developed economy, productive resources, notably labour, are gradually reallocated from the traditional agricultural sector, with low productivity, to the industrial sector which, due to its high capital-labour intensity and greater power to generate and disseminate technical progress, is considered the most productive in the economy. This implies that economic development is embodied in a process of continuous diversification and structural change directed towards industrial segments with greater productivity and technological sophistication.[7] It is no coincidence that the developmental school prefers the term "economic development" to "economic growth", because the former implies growth with structural change;

5 Throughout this text, the reader will notice the use of the term "industrial revolution" with capital or lower-case letters. We are following the convincing argument of David Landes (1969) according to which capital letters should be used only for the British Industrial Revolution, which signified not only the outbreak of radical technological changes, with significant impacts on society and culture—like the other industrial revolutions that followed—but also the consolidation of capitalism as the hegemonic mode of production in the world economy. The other industrial revolutions were caused only by radical technological changes and caused changes in social and cultural habits but were introduced in the context of the capitalist system already widespread in the global economy.

6 See McCombie and Thirlwall (1994) and Ros (2013).

7 See Lewis (1954).

ii. since the manufacturing industry as a whole is subject to static and dynamic economies of scale, as it grows and diversifies, absorbing resources from the low-productivity sector, it tends to command and sustain the increase in average productivity rates of the economy as a whole as long as significant inter-sectoral productivity differentials (gaps) persist;[8]

iii. even when a country has already managed to reach a level of per capita income close to the world average, thereby achieving the status of a middle-income or "emerging" economy, productivity gaps between agriculture, industry and services persist. Therefore, Kaldor (1966) conceptualises economic development as a process through which an economy transitions from a stage of "immaturity" to that of industrial "maturity";[9]

iv. only when a country reaches the stage of industrial maturity would the tendency to reallocate resources from the agricultural and manufacturing sectors to the services sector reflect a process of deindustrialisation that could be understood as beneficial and natural. By this time, with the agricultural sector already mechanised and with productivity levels significantly higher than in the traditional or intermediate phase, intersectoral productivity gaps will have been substantially reduced;[10]

v. if the development process is interrupted by premature deindustrialisation, before the stage of industrial maturity has been reached, the economy loses structural traction to continue growing with positive and sustainable advances in productivity in the long term;[11]

vi. the asymmetric diffusion of technical progress in the global geoeconomic space is one of the factors explaining the persistence of significant technological gaps between developing and emerging ("periphery") and developed ("centre or core") countries.[12]

---

8 This is the so-called Kaldor-Verdoorn law, according to which the higher the growth rate of industrial output (in terms of value added), the higher the growth rate of industrial productivity. Since the increase in productivity in other sectors depends on the growth in productivity of the manufacturing sector, this is, in the end, the main determinant of the rate of change in the average productivity of an economy. See Kaldor (1966) and McCombie and Thirlwall (1994, Ch. 2).

9 In this book, I use the term "industrial maturity" in a slightly different way than Kaldor (1967). Although Kaldor argues that even developed countries may not necessarily have reached this stage if significant intersectoral gaps persist, I identify maturity as the stage at which a given country is fully industrialised.

10 See Kaldor (1966).

11 See Palma (2005).

12 See Dosi, Pavitt and Soete (1990).

And what about the service sector? This, like the traditional primary sector, was historically assessed as having a low level of technological sophistication and low productivity. However, since the so-called third industrial revolution—which began slowly after World War II and was accelerated by the spread of microelectronics and the information and communication technology (ICT) industries from the 1980s onwards—several new segments of the service sector, namely banking automation, digital software and applications, the internet and other information networks, among others, have stood out for their greater technological intensity and unique capacity to operate under static and dynamic increasing returns to scale. More recently, with the advent of the fourth industrial revolution, led by robotics, artificial intelligence (or AI), big data, the Internet of Things (or IoT), and various advanced digital technologies, new segments have emerged in the services sector characterised by those distinctive features that only the manufacturing industry had in the past.

For economic development theorists and policymakers, the important question is: will these rapid technological changes lead to a reduction or elimination of the role of manufacturing as an engine of growth in developing economies? The answer is no, but with one condition: judging by the changes underway, the manufacturing sector is becoming increasingly intertwined with various service activities that are intensive in digital technology.

According to Zysman et al. (2013: 100), the technological revolution led by new service segments has been so overwhelming that "the distinction between industrialised products and services is blurred, as the former increasingly incorporate services into their production value". The examples are numerous: from automobiles that incorporate various onboard electronics and digital controls, to Apple products such as the iPad, iPhone and iPod, whose competitive success depends on the additional offering of advanced services, such as the Apple Store and iTunes, to industrialised consumer goods operated by fully automated and digital controls (IoT). Furthermore, with regard to the services sector itself, the digital revolution will delimit, in a much more pronounced way, the distinction between knowledge-intensive segments, characterised by high productivity, and traditional services (commerce, retail, low-skilled personal services, etc.), with low productivity.

Recent and ongoing technological revolutions have led to several trends in the organisation of global production, namely: (i) the enormous fragmentation of production on a global scale—and the consequent transformation into so-called "global value chains"—concomitantly induced by increased competition and greater requirements for economies of scale as one of the necessary conditions for sustaining the competitiveness of the main players;[13] (ii) the greater creation and appropriation of value in the initial stages (research and development, R&D) and final stages of the production and commercialisation cycle of products (logistics, marketing and additional services); (iii) the dramatic drop in direct labour inputs and, consequently, in average production costs, induced by the increasing incorporation of robots in the production process; and (iv) the radical transformation of the manufacturing process ("Industry 4.0"), driven by the joint incorporation of the radical innovations mentioned above (robotics, AI, IoT, etc.). With respect to this last trend, Bianchi and Labory (2018: 51) observe that "the ongoing fourth industrial revolution will represent a real integration between science and the productive system, and not just a mere interaction, as occurred in previous industrial revolutions".

Overall, current trends reinforce the developmental argument that the manufacturing industry will continue to act as an engine of growth in developing countries that aim to approach the international technological frontier and catch up. However, economic development strategies, including in the poorest countries, cannot do without the radical technologies of Industry 4.0 or the services provided by ICTs. These countries will, otherwise, be left out of the international competitive game. Furthermore, the manufacturing industry, increasingly intertwined with digital services, must act as an integral part of the ecosystem of complex technologies that radiate to the entire economic system.

Theoretical differences are also reflected, but more intensely, at the normative level. Broadly speaking, the neoclassical liberal school advocates domestic and international laissez-faire policies (i.e., free trade). As I will discuss in Chapter 11, within the neoclassical liberal framework, the economic policies suggested are strictly derived from theoretical models, whose distinctive features are a high level of abstraction and the frequent (although not generalised) use of unrealistic assumptions and hypotheses. For example, the defence of laissez-faire and free trade is based on the hypothesis that capitalist economies operate under ideal conditions of perfect competition in all markets

13 Between the mid-1990s and the end of 2010, this trend led to a change in strategy among large multinational companies. In order to reduce manufacturing costs, particularly labour costs, they moved industrial plants to Asian countries (especially China), often delegating the production of durable consumer goods designed in R&D laboratories in their home countries to other companies, through manufacturing contracts (outsourcing). It is not yet clear whether this trend will be reversed in the coming decades, given the increasing incorporation of robotics into large-scale production processes and the redefinition of industrial policies in developed countries in response to the long-term impacts of the Covid-19 crisis in 2020.

(goods, production factors and capital).[14] If these conditions are met, those theoretical models guarantee that the modification in relative prices will be able to eliminate any excess supply or demand in the different markets, providing an optimal allocation of productive resources and a socially optimal distribution of economic production.

Therefore, in the normative sphere of the neoclassical framework, there would be no theoretical justification for government intervention. Since the free functioning of markets ensures the achievement of the so-called "Pareto optimal" (social optimum), any government intervention would be ineffective in improving general welfare conditions, unless it worsens the situation of at least one individual. In the sophisticated language of economists, laissez-faire and free trade would appear as economic policy regimes that maximise social welfare (first best), either because they would ensure maximum relative efficiency in the allocation of resources and the distribution of the social product, or because they would make economic development viable.

Despite this, the neoclassical liberal view is not naive enough to rule out the possibility that markets may, in practice, deviate from the ideal conditions of perfect competition. If this were to occur, evidence of "market failures" would

14 The microeconomic theory of different market structures and competition patterns contrasts two patterns of competition: perfect competition and monopoly. In addition to these, there is also a third intermediate pattern: oligopoly. Perfect competition is an abstract and idealised structure characterised by highly unrealistic assumptions, such as the atomisation of microentrepreneurs and many consumers in the market (such that none of them individually has the power to determine the price); perfect substitution between the goods produced (considered completely homogeneous); the inability to operate with technologies subject to economies of scale; and the total absence of barriers to the entry of competing producers, among others. With these hypotheses, the main result is that competing firms have to accept prices determined by the market, can only sell at prices equal to marginal costs, and due to the total absence of barriers to entry, they only obtain normal economic profits in the long run, that is, profits that reflect only the opportunity cost of capital. In a monopoly, however, since the hypotheses are practically the antithesis of perfect competition, the monopolistic firm can determine its mark-up (that is, profit margins on direct production costs), has power over the prices charged in the market and, due to the total barrier to entry for potential competitors, is able to obtain positive economic profits (or extraordinary profits, also called "monopoly profits"). In oligopoly, the results are more diverse, being close to the results of a monopoly if the level of barriers to entry is very high, or to perfect competition if the level of barriers to entry is very low or non-existent (the case of "monopolistic competition"). Thus, monopolistic competition is a *sui generis* case of oligopoly in which, despite the presence of economies of scale and product differentiation, the absence of barriers to entry (at least as a theoretical hypothesis) means that strong competition between large-, small- and medium-sized firms only allows them to obtain normal economic profits in the long term. For details, see Pindyck and Rubinfeld (2014).

justify government intervention. Incidentally, the neoclassical liberal acceptance of government interventions to correct market failures stems precisely from the recognition that, in the real world, the existence of various imperfections in the functioning of markets (imperfect competition, price rigidity, externalities, etc.) causes there to be a divergence between marginal private and social benefits, preventing the achievement of the maximum welfare situation consistent with Pareto's optimal.

In this context, government intervention is only accepted on the grounds that, although laissez-faire at the domestic level and free trade at the international level continue to be the recommended optimal policies ("first best"), government interference through the use of domestic economic policy instruments (production subsidies, R&D incentives, etc.) or international trade policy instruments (import tariffs, anti-dumping duties, etc.) are justified and accepted only to fulfil the objective of correcting market failures, compensating for any losses in well-being of society as a whole. However, even if the intervention instrument serves the purpose of remedying such failures, it will always be assessed as a second-best mechanism, compared to the first-best inherent in the free functioning of markets.[15] Moreover, as I will show in Chapter 11, the neoclassical liberal perspective restricts the defence of intervention mechanisms as much as possible, under the argument that "government failures" may be greater than market failures.

The developmental school, on the other hand, presents theoretical and empirical arguments to support the defence of state intervention through the adoption of policies oriented towards economic development. In addition to the theoretical and empirical arguments, which will be analysed in Chapter 7, the indisputable historical evidence also advocates in favour of this school of thought: according to the classic book by Amsden (2001), except for Hong Kong and Switzerland, cases that are, in fact, highly debatable, as they had specific peculiarities associated with scientific and technological development, there is no other historical experience of a nation, including England throughout its Industrial Revolution, that has achieved the status of a developed economy without the adoption of industrial policies and other mechanisms of state protection.

In other words, the catching up process depends on the adoption of industrial policy, which, in the developmental view, should not be reduced to the mere correction of market failures, whether they be market failures themselves, coordination failures or information failures. As Nassif, Bresser-Pereira

15 See Corden (1974).

and Feijó (2018: 364) point out, the developmental approach sees industrial policy as "the combination of government incentives at the sectoral level (import tariffs, subsidies permitted by multilateral agreements guided by the World Trade Organization (WTO), long-term government credits for strategic investment projects, among others) with horizontal policies (notably, infrastructure, education and government incentives for R&D)". They (op. cit.: 364) also emphasise that, "when industrial policy focuses on specific segments of the economy, incentives should primarily fall on those with the greatest capacity to generate and disseminate productivity gains to the economy as a whole." In short, more than static efficiency, industrial policy should seek dynamic efficiency, translated into significant rates of change in productivity and sustainable economic growth in the long run.

It must be acknowledged that, although it is relatively easy to design ingenious industrial policies, the hardest part is implementing them consistently. As the saying goes, talk is cheap, action is what matters! Although there is no rule of thumb, the experiences of successful countries in East Asia, especially South Korea and Taiwan,[16] teach us that the success of industrial policy depends simultaneously on the combination of several factors, specifically:[17] (i) selectivity of priority activities, segments and sectors, while respecting the main lesson of the Ricardian principle of comparative advantage that no country is capable of being efficient in all activities; (ii) focusing on activities, segments and sectors with the potential to trigger and disseminate technological innovations; (iii) creation of mechanisms that enable enterprises in the manufacturing and service sectors subject to economies of scale to become competitive in order to reach the global market; (iv) constant collection of results from companies that have tariff protection or receive government benefits; (v) limitation of the deadlines for granting customs protection and other forms of incentive to local production to the minimum necessary to obtain adequate conditions of competitiveness; (vi) **permanent** prioritisation of government investments in physical infrastructure (diversified transport modes, urban planning and mobility, sanitation, etc.) and human infrastructure (adequate health system, education, science, technology and technical and digital training at all levels, from early childhood to higher education); (vii) policies to attract foreign direct investment (FDI) that incorporate incentives for multinational companies to transfer or spillover technology to local firms; and (viii) perhaps most importantly, the continuous coordination and harmonisation between the country's industrial policy and macroeconomic policy, which requires policymakers to

16 See Wade (1990).

17 See, in this respect, Nassif (2019).

make efforts so that the mechanisms of macroeconomic policy, normally managed with the objective of ensuring growth and monetary stability, also serve to anchor the expected objectives of industrial policy, especially the increase in productivity and the pursuit of catching up. As I will show in Chapter 7, no industrial policy program, no matter how well designed, will be able to yield promising results in an almost permanent environment of high inflation, high real interest rates, and an overvalued national currency in relation to a basket of currencies of the main international partners.

An Illustrative Case: Brazil from Economic Development to Stagnation

Although this book does not analyse the Brazilian economy, it is worth summarising Brazil's experience as an illustrative case of a country in which the development process was interrupted in the early 1980s and, since then, has accumulated, as of 2020, four decades of economic stagnation, as shown in Figure 1. The significant reduction in the GDP trend after 1981 (the least steep dotted line), compared to that prevailing in the period 1950–1980, marks an extended period of economic stagnation that, in the long-term perspective, was never reversed in the following decades.

The stagnation observed in the post-1980 period can be confirmed by comparing the average annual growth rates of real GDP and labour productivity. The significant economic growth observed between 1950 and 1980, in which average annual growth rates of real GDP of 7.4% were recorded, was accompanied by an increase in labour productivity, which grew at an average annual rate of 4.5%, as illustrated in Figure 2. Between 1981 and 2020, Brazil recorded average annual growth rates of just 2.0%, well below the average global growth of 2.7% per year observed in the same period.[18] Figure 2 shows that the average annual productivity growth rate was negative in the 1980s (the "lost decade"), but even in the following three decades, the poor performance of this indicator of economic efficiency meant that the average annual growth rate was close to zero over the period 1980–2020.

18 Calculated by the author based on Ipeadata (Brazil's Institute for Applied Economic Research), for Brazil, and the World Bank, World Development Indicators, for the world. The change in world real GDP in 2020 is included in the International Monetary Fund document, "World Economic Outlook: Managing Divergent Recoveries", April 2021, p. 9.

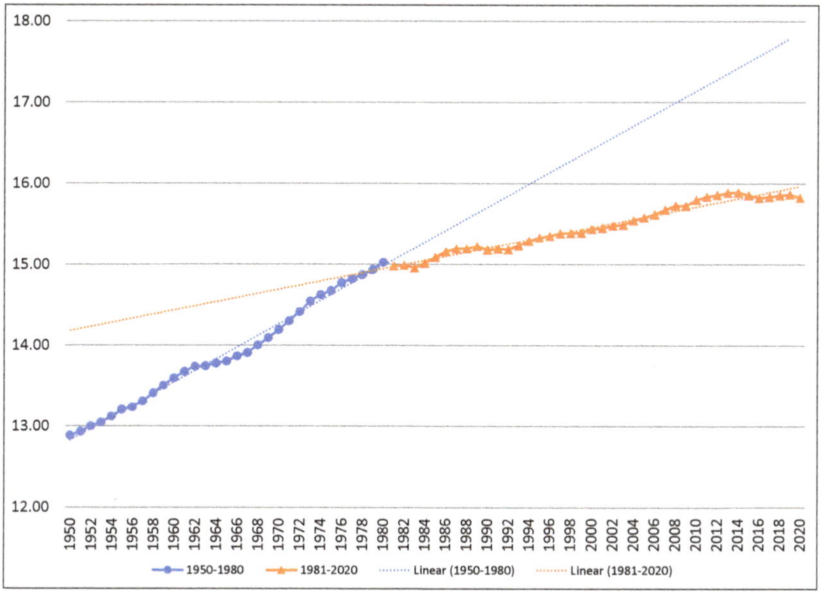

FIGURE 1 Evolution of real GDP in Brazil (1950–2020) (real GDP in logarithms)
SOURCE: BRAZILIAN INSTITUTE OF GEOGRAPHY AND STATISTICS—IBGE

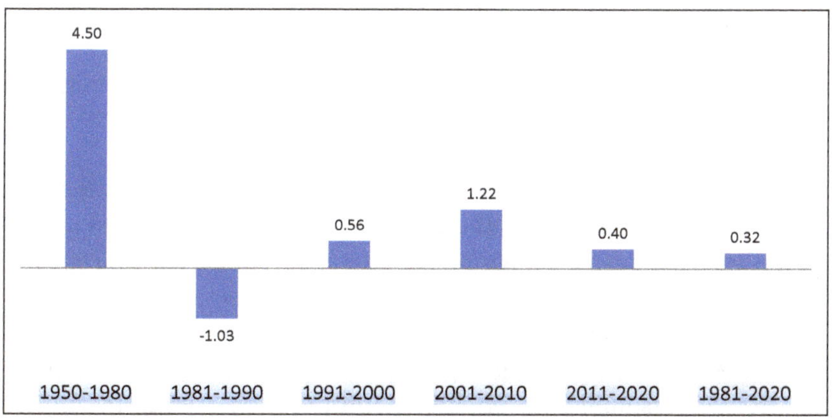

FIGURE 2 Aggregate labour productivity growth rates in Brazil (1950–2020) (annual averages in %). *Note*: Productivity calculated as the ratio between the total added value of the economy and the number of persons employed; added values transformed into constant values by the respective sources.
SOURCES: GRONINGEN GROWTH AND DEVELOPMENT CENTRE, HTTPS://WWW.RUG.NL/GGDC/PRODUCTIVITY/, FOR THE PERIOD 1950–1980; AND FGV-IBRE, FOR THE PERIOD 1981–2020, HTTPS://IBRE.FGV.BR/OBSERVATORIO-PRODUTIVIDADE/ARTIGOS/NOTA-METODOLOGICA-DOS-INDICADORES-ANUAIS-DE-PRODUTIVIDADE-DO-0. ACCESSED ON 29/03/2021

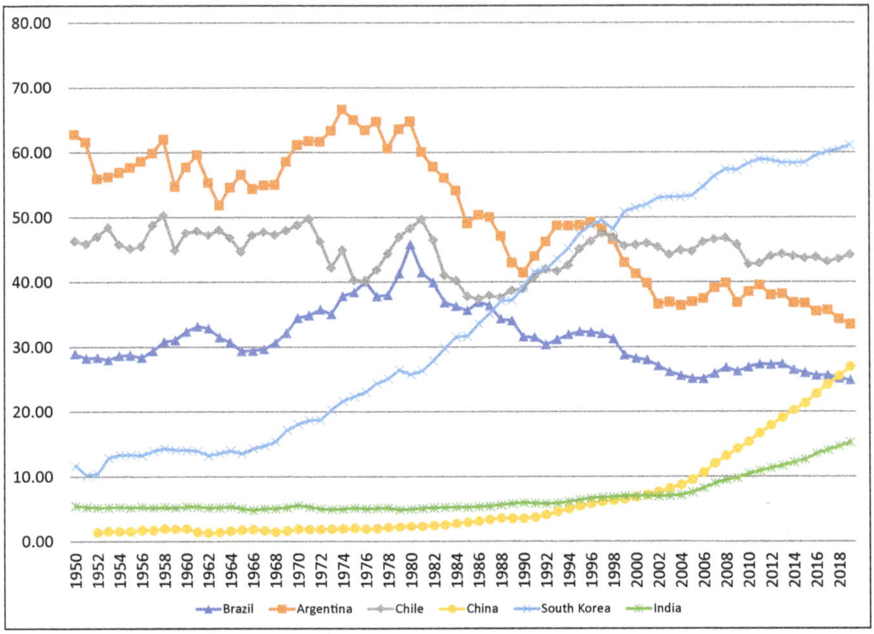

FIGURE 3 Aggregate labour productivity in Brazil and selected countries relative to the United States (1950–2019) (in index numbers; labour productivity in the United States = 100). *Note*: Productivity calculated as the ratio of real GDP (supply side) to total employment. Real GDP calculated in purchasing power parity, in 2018 US$ millions; for China, data available from 1952 onwards.
SOURCE: THE CONFERENCE BOARD TOTAL ECONOMY DATABASE (ADJUSTED VERSION, APRIL 2019), ACCESSED ON 15/07/2020

The stagnation of labour productivity in Brazil, observed after the 1980s, could not help but be reflected in the country's relative backwardness in relation to the rest of the world. Figure 3 illustrates the evolution of aggregate labour productivity in Brazil and in some selected countries in relation to that of the United States. Roughly speaking, this indicator offers an approximate measure of the relative technological gap of economies compared to the international frontier, assuming, in simplified terms, that on average the United States still commands the global technological vanguard.

The comparison between Brazil and South Korea makes the most sense. Both countries began their industrial policy strategies geared toward economic development and the promotion of catching up in relatively similar periods: Brazil, at the beginning of the 1950s, and South Korea, from the following decade onwards. It should be noted that South Korea was significantly behind Brazil until just past the mid-1960s, when both countries were already undergoing a process of accelerated economic growth and reducing their relative technological gap with the United States.

However, while South Korea has maintained a virtually uninterrupted trend of reducing the technological gap to this day, Brazil only managed to sustain this trend until the end of the 1970s. Since the early 1980s, Brazil's decline has been so significant that in 2019 its productivity gap in relation to the US economy, being 75%, was already higher than the 71% in 1950. To use the economic term, Brazil has entered a period of falling-behind. The Argentine and Chilean economies already had relatively more efficient economic structures than Brazil in the early 1950s, and only maintained this superiority for the rest of the period due to the significant decline in Brazilian relative productivity from 1980 onwards. China and India have been able to sustain the process of catching up with the United States since the early 2000s. However, given the gigantic size of their populations, the relative gaps between both economies are still significant. In any case, it is worth noting that by the end of the 2010s, China had already managed to achieve a relative productivity gap with the United States that was lower than that of Brazil.

The growth (1950–1980) and stagnation (1981–2020) trajectories of the Brazilian economy involve nuances that, even at the risk of oversimplification, can be summarised as follows: the period 1950–1980 was marked by import substitution strategies in which the government, through distinct industrial policy programs ("National Development Plans"), granted customs protection and various government benefits to national and foreign companies, with the aim of promoting economic development through industrialisation. There was also a huge effort to diversify Brazilian exports, by increasing the share of manufactured goods in total exports.

There were many problems, though, with this development strategy. For example, the lack of selectivity in defining priority segments, the high relative costs resulting from protection schemes, the limited efforts to promote improvements in the country's educational standards, the low performance in indigenous technological innovations and the significant increase in the concentration of national income precisely during the greatest economic growth (between 1970 and 1973, the years of the false economic "miracle"). And these were not the only factors: at the macroeconomic level, since the mid-1950s, there has been undeniable complacency with high inflation rates and rising foreign debt. However, it is fair to say that the significant static inefficiency in the allocation of productive resources has been largely offset by significant dynamic efficiency, reflected in the high average annual growth rates of real GDP and labour productivity mentioned above.

The period 1981–2020, with the exception of the "lost decade" of the 1980s—plagued by the external debt and high inflation crises—corresponded to liberalising economic reforms in the domestic, foreign trade and external financial spheres, as well as Brazil's adherence to economic policy regimes aligned with the so-called Washington Consensus. This Consensus, which represented the milestone in the alignment of the Latin American periphery with neoliberalism, will be analysed in detail in Chapter 10. Unlike the period 1950–1980, the improvement in static efficiency in the allocation of resources, embodied in greater access by Brazilian consumers to relatively cheaper imported products after trade liberalisation (1990–1994), was not accompanied, however, by the dynamic efficiency of the Brazilian economy, given the meagre growth of real GDP and the practically zero rates of change in labour productivity, not to mention the accelerated process of premature deindustrialisation that has been observed since the 1980s.[19]

What to Expect from This Book

The objective of this book is to present and analyse, in reasonable detail, development theories, comparing the different theoretical approaches and economic policy recommendations of developmentalists and neoclassical liberals.

My intention is to offer the reader three original contributions in this book: the first is the inclusion, in the section concerning developmental economic thought, of theories developed in Latin America, with emphasis on Prebisch's centre-periphery model, Celso Furtado's theories of underdevelopment and development, and the new developmental theories developed by Luiz Carlos Bresser-Pereira and other authors; the second is the incorporation, in the part related to the neoclassical liberal view, of the emergence and spread of neoliberalism, a subject that is rarely discussed in textbooks dedicated to the study of theories of development and stagnation; the third is the attempt to make the entire content of the book not restricted to those specialised in economics, but accessible to readers from other branches of knowledge interested in the topics covered here. To this end, I have made every effort to ensure that the content is understandable and useful, avoiding the use of mathematics whenever possible. In the few cases where it was necessary to use simple equations, I tried to interpret them as clearly as possible to facilitate their understanding.

19 According to calculations by Morceiro and Guilhoto (2019), between 1980 and 2018, the share of added value from the manufacturing industry in Brazilian GDP fell from 19.7% to 11.3%, at constant 2018 prices.

By the end, it will be possible to see that the theoretical approaches and normative implications of both schools of thought are almost completely irreconcilable. Among the various reasons that explain the impossibility of conciliation, only one will not be explored throughout the various chapters of the book: the methods used by the two views. In the developmental method, the approach to economic phenomena is strongly based on historical and social particularities, and the hypotheses are predominantly founded on empirical regularities; in the neoclassical liberal method, the approach is hypothetical-deductive, which is more typical of the hard sciences, whereby, regardless of the realism of the hypotheses and the historical and social contextualisation, priority is given to the logical connection between assumptions, hypotheses and conclusions, as well as mathematical and formal rigour.[20]

Four caveats are in order. The first is that the theoretical discussion does not intend to exhaust the vast literature on the subject, being restricted, especially in the neoclassical liberal case, to authors who have approached it from the perspective of economies open to trade in goods and services (and, when applicable, to the capital flows) with the rest of the world; in the developmental case, the analysis will focus on the authors who conceived development as a process of structural changes towards sectors subject to static and dynamic increasing returns to scale.

The second is that, unlike most books dealing with the problem of economic development, I opted to present the developmental theoretical view before the neoclassical liberal one. The reason for this choice is due to the interruption in what was a long period of economic development between 1950 and 1980 in periphery countries in Latin America (Brazil, in particular). Notably, this break coincided with the abandonment of most of the economic policy recommendations stemming from the developmental theory. From the mid-1980s onwards, precisely when public policies began to be strongly influenced by neoclassical liberal precepts, these countries entered a prolonged period of stagnation, from which they have not managed to escape from until today (2024, at the time of finishing this book). Thus, the ordering preference I give to developmental theory is a way of highlighting the importance of considering alternatives that have sufficient theoretical and empirical foundations, given the ineffectiveness demonstrated by neoclassical options.

The third is that, although the discussion in the book is predominantly theoretical, I will refer to specific cases whenever necessary. However, the reader will notice that, in several passages, Brazil is the most frequent illustrative reference. This is because Brazil is, in the periphery world, one of the countries

20 For the reader interested in this issue, it is worth reading the article by Bresser-Pereira (2009).

in which neoclassical liberal (especially neoliberal) policy recommendations have most influenced policymakers in the last three decades.

The fourth is that, as the reader will also notice, I explicitly align myself with the developmental view, according to which laissez-faire and unconditional free trade policies, as well as government intervention mechanisms predominantly oriented towards correcting market failures, are incapable of overcoming stagnation and restoring economic development on a sustainable basis. This implies that, although markets (of goods and services, production factors and capital) are important agents in the process of economic development, government intervention is essential to induce the allocation of resources towards the productive sectors responsible for the efficiency of the economy in dynamic terms.

Organisation of the Book

In addition to this Introduction, the book divides the theoretical debate on development and stagnation into two parts: the first covers the developmental school; and the second, the neoclassical liberal school.

I begin with the organisation of Part 1 (Chapters 1 to 7), dedicated to the developmental school. Chapter 1 presents the conceptual roots that influenced the developmental view. In this chapter, I review the theoretical propositions of Smith (1776), Marx (1867; 1894) and Schumpeter (1911; 1942), according to which economic development depends on the expansion of demand in the long run ("the social division of labour is limited by the size of the market"), capital accumulation and the incorporation of activities, segments, and sectors subject to increasing returns to scale and disseminators of technical progress.

Chapters 2 to 7 analyse, respectively, the theoretical and normative propositions of the main groups that form the developmental school, namely: the so-called classical developmentalism of the 1940s, 1950s and 1960s, as well as its recent theoretical unfoldings (Chapter 2); the ECLAC branch, responsible for formulating the centre-periphery model, which constitutes the theoretical basis of the theses of ECLAC (Economic Commission for Latin America and the Caribbean) on development in Latin America and the national-developmental policies adopted on the continent between 1950 and 1980 (Chapter 3);[21] Furtado's contribution, who, by incorporating in an original way the economic, historical and social specificities of Latin American countries (especially Brazil)

21 ECLAC is a United Nations institution, created in 1948, headquartered in Santiago, Chile, of which Raúl Prebisch was the second executive secretary (1950–1963).

in the theoretical analysis of underdevelopment, development and stagnation, created, in practice, a school of thought unto itself, bestowing, like the ECLAC branch, greater emphasis on the role of public policies in overcoming underdevelopment (Chapter 4); and the new developmental theory, resulting from the efforts of the Brazilian Luiz Carlos Bresser-Pereira, who, by bringing the macroeconomic regime to the centre of theoretical analysis on development and stagnation, updates and complements the contributions of classical developmentalism and the national-developmentalism in ECLAC (Chapters 5 and 6). Acting as a conclusion to Part 1, Chapter 7 analyses the normative implications of developmental theories, defends the return of national development plans in the Latin American periphery and other developing countries that suffer from economic stagnation, and examines the theoretical arguments in favour of public policies aimed at resuming development and overcoming the long period of stagnation in Latin American economies over the last four decades.

Part 2 (Chapters 8 to 11) discusses the theoretical and normative propositions of the neoclassical liberal school. Chapter 8 focuses on the propositions made in the context of economies open to trade in goods, services and knowledge, unraveling the arguments in favour of the practice of laissez-faire and international free trade. Chapter 9 looks at the neoclassical macroeconomics of economic growth and ends with the heterodox (neo-Schumpeterian) critique of neoclassical growth models in the context of economies "open" to free international trade in goods, services and knowledge. Overall, the neoclassical theories presented in Chapters 8 and 9 have some affinity with the Ricardian proposition that economic development is a phenomenon that unfolds from the free and more efficient allocation of resources in capitalist economies. Chapter 10 critically discusses the propositions of the Washington Consensus, which led to the radicalisation of laissez-faire practices, free trade and liberalisation of capital flows in the global economy, that is, to "neoliberalism". Chapter 11, acting as a conclusion to Part 2, analyses the normative implications of neoclassical liberal theses on development, arguing why government intervention policies, based on the neoclassical concept of market failures, are not sufficient either to overcome stagnation or to put periphery countries back on the path of sustainable economic development.

The Conclusion at the end of the book highlights the main aspects of developmental and neoclassical liberal schools. It also outlines the fundamental reasons why both schools are guided by theoretical and normative approaches that are almost completely irreconcilable.

PART 1

The Developmental School

Prologue to Part 1

In this Part 1, I will analyse the main factors underlying what triggers and sustains successful economic development processes, according to the developmental approach. This school is guided by two main theoretical objectives: to understand the mechanisms through which backward ("underdeveloped") economies manage to achieve per capita income levels and standards of living similar to those of advanced ("developed") economies; and to elucidate the factors that cause several countries to fall into chronic economic stagnation and regression (falling-behind), especially after having exhibited, for some decades, significant rates of labour productivity growth and having followed relatively successful trajectories of economic growth and catching up.

Developmental theories are based on the factors of the economic-productive structure responsible for the transition from an underdeveloped to a developed economy—because of this, these theories are called "structuralist". They are also concerned about the possible problems that can lead a developing economy to fall into the trap of stagnation.

Initially, I show how the conceptual roots of developmentalism are present in the theories of Smith, Marx and Schumpeter, authors who, not by mere coincidence, had as a common focus the analysis of the driving forces of economic development. Next, I analyse developmental theories, from the "classical" to the most recent, also highlighting the contribution of theories developed in Latin America, notably Prebisch's centre-periphery model, Furtado's theories of development, underdevelopment and stagnation and the new developmental theories, developed by Luiz Carlos Bresser-Pereira and other Brazilian authors. Since developmental theories present solid arguments in favour of state intervention to support development, Part 1 concludes with a chapter in which I present theoretical justifications, as well as empirical and historical evidence, in favour of designing and adopting national development plans by national governments.

 | DOI:10.1163/9789004734296_003

CHAPTER 1

The Conceptual Roots of Developmentalism

1 Introduction

Development theories do not hold the day-to-day behaviour of the economy in the short or even medium term as their focal point. Their main objective is the dynamics of the economy in the long run. Thus, instead of being concerned about fluctuations in GDP, income, and employment in short and medium intervals, say, over a period of one to five years, development theorists focus on the tendential behaviour of these variables over the long term. This has been the case ever since economics acquired the status of a science with Adam Smith's Wealth of Nations in 1776.

For the structuralist-developmentalist authors, in particular, the central concern is to devise laws that steer a poor country toward overcoming underdevelopment and reaching the status of developed—a situation in which per capita income is equal to that of richest countries.[1] To this end, this school of thought seeks to understand the complexity inherent to the productive and social structures of underdeveloped countries (hence the term structuralism), as well as analysing the conditions for these countries to satisfactorily follow the trajectory of catching up in the long run. This perspective also investigates why middle-income countries, such as Brazil, remain stagnate for decades after having followed a catching up trend of sustained growth over a long period.

The developmental group's obsession with overcoming underdevelopment was such that, from the 1940s on, a specific field of theoretical analysis began to form, which later became known as "development economics". This is not to say that the laws governing long-term trends of capitalist economies had not been on the radar of economic science since the time of classical political economists. Quite the contrary, those economists, and later Marx and

1 In practice, post-war multilateral institutions maintained for some time the tradition of classifying countries as underdeveloped (low per capita income), developing (medium per capita income), and developed (high per capita income). In recent decades, however, the United Nations and the World Bank have reduced these to just two groups: developing countries, which include the poorest, and developed countries. To make the classification even less precise, the International Monetary Fund (IMF) currently categorises countries as advanced (high per capita income), developing (low per capita income), and emerging (medium to medium-high per capita income).

 | DOI:10.1163/9789004734296_004

Schumpeter, did focus fundamentally on the problems of economic development. But if a reader examines the theoretical works of Smith, Marx and Schumpeter more closely, they will conclude that the main concern of these authors was in establishing general laws that explain long-term trends, either in an economy with productive structures technologically close to that of a mature economy, or in an already developed capitalist economy. Smith and Marx did allude, with some frequency, to very poor countries on the periphery of capitalism. However, the scenario that formed the basis of their theoretical investigations was the British economy, post-Industrial Revolution, and as such, an economy which already had a technical-productive structure almost (in Smith's case) or fully (in Marx's case) mature.

Despite the analytical fulcrum of developmentalists having shifted to the investigation of the underdevelopment versus development dichotomy, three characteristic forces of economies already in obvious development were, implicitly or explicitly, incorporated into their approaches, those being: (i) static and dynamic increasing returns to scale,[2] typical of manufacturing production technologies, and which guided Smith's vision (1776); (ii) capital accumulation, pioneeringly conceived by Marx (1867) as the main pillar of capitalist development; and (iii) technological progress that, although subtly present in Smith's ideas and explicitly in Marx's approach, would be deepened by Schumpeter (1911; 1942) as the main engine of economic change. Given the enormous influence of these authors in the formulation of the developmental theoretical models, this chapter synthesises their ideas regarding these three main forces.

This chapter is, thus, divided into three sections: the first presents the pioneering ideas of Smith concerning the role of increasing returns to scale and of the expansion of domestic and foreign demand (i.e., exports) as driving forces of economic development in capitalist countries. The second section analyses Marx's theory, which highlights capital accumulation and changes in the technological base as the main elements of capitalist development. The third section discusses the foundations of Schumpeter's theory, which underscores the role of technological innovations in their various dimensions (processes, products, and others) as the central explanatory factor of economic development.

2 The reader will do well to remember these concepts, already presented in the Introduction, as they will be useful to better understand the content of this book.

2 Smith and Increasing Returns

Smith (1776) was one of the first to suggest that capitalism, as an evolutionary system, does not necessarily move towards positions of "general equilibrium".[3] He did postulate, though, that the free fluctuation of relative prices—the famous "invisible hand"—contributed to an economy functioning harmoniously. In his formulation, economic development is understood as a process that is sustained by positive rates of change in labour productivity. Using the British economy, which was fully immersed in the Industrial Revolution, he recorded a notably growth in productivity, resulting not only from the upsurge in radical innovations, such as the incorporation of machinery in the productive process and the spread of the factory system, but also from the rapid increase in the social division of labour.[4] By branching out economic activities into distinct productive processes, the social division of labour was also extended to the production of goods. This revolutionised the internal organisation of factory activities.

Ergo, what Henry Ford would do almost a century and a half later, in the 1910s and 1920s, that being introducing a strict division of tasks and serial production in the American automobile industry, had already been observed by Smith (1776: 41–42) when describing the internal division of labour in a "very small manufacture", the pin factory. In the words of Smith:

> One man draws out the wire, another straights it, a third cuts it, a fourth points it, a fifth grinds it at the top for receiving the head; to make the head requires two or three distinct operations; to put it on, is a peculiar

3 The general equilibrium theory was devised by economist Léon Walras (1874). Considering an economy in which supply and demand in all markets operate interdependently and under strict conditions of perfect competition, the "invisible hand" (i.e., the mechanism of relative prices in a laissez-faire regime), according to his formulation, will cause each market to reach a single position of equilibrium between supply, demand, and prices, ultimately resulting in the general equilibrium of the economic system. For an instructional presentation of this theory, see Pindyck and Rubinfeld (2014, Ch. 16).

4 Radical innovations are those that cause major disruptions to prevailing technologies, whereas incremental innovations are those that cause continuous changes in existing production processes and products. Examples of the former are the steam engine and the power loom in the 18th century; electricity, chemistry, and the automobile industry between the late 19th and early 20th centuries; the computer and the internet at the end of the 20th century; and digital technologies (artificial intelligence, the internet of things, etc.) in the 21st century. An incremental innovation, for example, is the evolution of cellular devices from analogue devices to smartphones.

> business, to whiten the pins is another; it is even a trade by itself to put them into the paper.

The perception that the infant industries during the Industrial Revolution relied on technologies subject to increasing returns to scale was implicit in Smith's argument on the social division of labour being limited by the extent of the market. Hence, Smith views economic development as the result of a sequence of causal factors, which must be understood as a reflection of increased productivity. This, in turn, is dependent on the advancement of specialisation provided by the greater social division of labour. At the end of the day, though, it is the size of the market (or, as commonly referred to now, aggregate demand) that factors most in boosting labour productivity and, therefore, development. In the words of the author himself (Smith, op. cit.: 53):

> As it is the power of exchanging that gives occasion to the division of labour, so the extent of this division must always be limited by extent of that power, or, in other words, by the extent of the market. When the market is very small, no person can have any encouragement to dedicate himself entirely to one employment, for want of the power to exchange all that surplus part of the produce of his own labour, which is over and above his own consumption, for such parts of the produce of other men's labour as he has occasion for.

Notice how Smith argues for the advantages of specialisation, not because they provide greater relative efficiency in resource allocation—as postulated by Ricardo (1817), which will be discussed in Chapter 3—but because, by **diversifying** the productive structure of the manufacturing sector activities and **increasing** the scales of production by making them compatible with the dimensions of demand, countries can reduce the absolute unit costs of production through the increase in productivity. For Smith, the competition between independent producers within each productive segment causes the prices of the produced goods to fall to levels close to the unit costs. Furthermore, by assuming reduced barriers to entry in the various sectors, Smith concluded—along with classical and even Marxian political economy—that the profit rate tends to converge, in the long run, to an average level observed in the economy as a whole.

It should be made clear that in Smith's theoretical framework, and also in classical political economy, there was the assumption of strong intra- and intersectoral competition, but not the neoclassical concept of "perfect competition".[5]

5 For the reader interested in the model of perfect competition, see Pindyck and Rubinfeld (2014, Ch. 8 and 9) and Koutsoyannis (1979, Ch. 5).

If the several unrealistic assumptions of perfect competition prevailed in the real world (an infinite number of producers and buyers, homogeneous products, total absence of any kind of barriers to entry, inclusive technologies, etc.), prices would equal unit economic costs in the long run. This would provide capitalists with only "normal" profits, compatible with the opportunity cost of invested capital. In the classical and Marxian concepts of competition, however, there would not be, in the current historical context, extraordinarily high monopoly profits, but only profits compatible with the average of the different markets, determined by intercapitalist competition.

Smith is considered the father of economic liberalism because of his arguments in defence of laissez-faire practices domestically and of international free trade, not to mention his radically contrary position to the mercantilist practices that prevailed in absolutist European states between the 15th and 18th centuries. On this, Smith (1776: 381) argued that:

> Whether the advantages which one country has over another be natural or acquired, it is in this respect of no consequence. As long as the one country has those advantages [that is, being able to produce at lower prices than its counterparts], and the other wants them, it will always be more advantageous for this latter rather to buy of the former than to make.

This position is particularly interesting because, as will be shown in Chapter 7, it is difficult for a country to gain competitiveness in the production and selling of manufactured goods in domestic and world markets without some temporary protection scheme being granted, with due discretion, to local entrepreneurs. This may include, for example, production subsidies or customs duties on imports. The obstacles to obtaining competitive conditions in the industrial sector are even greater when there are already other countries at a higher competitiveness ranking, having previously achieved greater technological advancement.

This was precisely the case in England in the last quarter of the 18th century. During this period, the monopoly of mechanisation enjoyed by English capitalists in the manufacturing industry granted them the privilege of operating with economies of scale sufficient to produce industrialised goods that met, under competitive conditions, domestic demand and also generated exportable surpluses for nearly the entire world. Because of that, the defence of liberalism was ideologically comfortable for Smith and other renowned economists of classical political economy, such as Ricardo and Mill.

It is true, particularly for Smith, that the general argument is that foreign trade has the dual benefit of enlarging additional markets for a country's exportable products under competitive conditions (i.e., cheaper than its foreign trade partners) and of enabling imports of other goods whose domestic prices are greater than on the international market. However, Smith is adamant in attributing the expansion of exports to the rest of the world as the most important dynamic source for widening the social (including international) division of labour, which promotes increased productivity and, consequently, accelerates the country's economic development. Most of all, to dispose of the surplus product over and above domestic consumption, Smith says (1776: 372) that,

> By means of it, the narrowness of the home market does not hinder the division of labour in any particular branch of art or manufacture from being carried to the highest perfection. By opening a more extensive market for whatever part of the produce of their labour may exceed the home consumption, it encourages them to improve its productive power, and to augment its annual produce to the utmost, and thereby to increase the real revenue and wealth of the society.

In fact, it is worth noting that the unified voices of classical political economists in favour of laissez-faire regimes and international free trade had greater resonance on a theoretical level than in the practice of British trade policy. List (1841: 111), a German economist who was a great critic of the liberal recommendations disseminated by classical political economists, recalled that in the period immediately before the Industrial Revolution, British monarchs

> realised that their infant manufacturing system would never be able to face, under free competition, the "old", but traditionally consolidated, foreign Italian, Belgian and Dutch industries. Consequently, through a system of external restrictions, privileges and domestic incentives, they sought to transplant the talents, wealth and entrepreneurial spirit of those foreigners into the interior of the national territory.

Furthermore, protection mechanisms were strengthened and lasted for a relatively long period into the initial phase of the Industrial Revolution. Chang (2003: 17) documents that, in 1820, the average import tariffs of the British manufacturing industry were still among the highest in the world (between 45% and 55%), even though the UK industry already had, for the most part, state-of-the-art technologies. These customs tariffs only converged to zero in 1875, when the British manufacturing industry had already consolidated its technological, competitive and economic hegemony in the international arena.

3 Marx and Capital Accumulation

Marx is the first author to view capitalism as a dynamic system ("mode of production"), governed by laws inherent to its own logic of operation, but particularly subject to a general law of capital accumulation. Although Marx's main treatise, "The Capital", whose first German edition dates to 1867, contains philosophy, history, sociology and economics, and is based on the methodology of historical and dialectical materialism, I limit myself to the synthesis of the author's theories most directly associated with economic development.

Marx understood capitalist economic development as the result of capital accumulation. However, since capital is the result of social labour in a system in which apparent wealth is expressed as an "immense collection of commodities",[6] the genesis of development is the production of value, measured in social labour ("abstract labour"). This, in turn, is broken down into paid work—which is, in Marx's terminology, the real wage or variable capital and corresponds to the reproduction cost of the labour force—plus unpaid work—which is equivalent to the portion of the value generated by labour that is appropriated by the capitalist class, that is, the surplus-value.[7]

Considering the production of any particular commodity (say, yarn), the surplus-value is the difference between the total labour value of the commodity (expressed as social labour) and the labour value expressed in the two forms of capital that comprise said product: (i) constant capital, understood by Marx as past labour or dead labour and associated with the costs (always measured in labour) of all means of production involved in the production of that yarn (the value of wear and tear on machinery and equipment, of all raw materials consumed, of auxiliary inputs, etc.), and (ii) variable capital, corresponding to the real wage paid as the reproduction value of the labour force, framed by Marx as paid labour or living labour. Marx (1867a: 286) argues that "that part of capital, represented by labour-power, does, in the process of production, undergo an alteration of value. It both reproduces the equivalent of its own value, and also produces an excess, a surplus-value, which may itself vary, may be more or less according to circumstances."[8]

The concept of surplus-value is important in the Marxian concept of capitalist development because it is the source from which profits and capital accumulation emanate. In the words of Marx (1867a: 655), "the employment of surplus-value as capital or the conversion of surplus-value is called capital accumulation". It is important to remember that, since the author assumes

6 Marx (1867a, Volume 1, Chapter 1).

7 Marx (1867a, Volume 1, Chapter 6).

8 For details, see Marx (1867a, Volume 1, Chapters 6 and 7).

that the capitalist class acts simultaneously as owner of private means of production and manager of its own businesses, part of the income arising from surplus-vale is used for its own consumption, while the other part is transformed into investments to increase productive capacity, aimed at accumulating future capital.[9] So, in Marx's view, what drives the capitalist to invest in order to accumulate capital is the search for future profits, as similarly understood by authors from distinct schools of thought, including Smith, Keynes and Schumpeter.

In the case of Marx, however, the profit flows generated and appropriated by the capitalist class correspond precisely to the surplus created in the social production process, the surplus-value, and make up the basis for financing the process of capital reproduction on a large scale, that is to say, investments in additional productive capacity. Furthermore, because profits are also a constitutive part of the key variable in the decision-making process of capitalists' investments—in other words, the long-term profit rate corresponding to the ratio mass of profits/total capital employed—they act as indirect determinants of capital accumulation, according to Marx's theoretical formulation.

Thus, if in the Marxian understanding profits form the basis for financing economic development and capital accumulation, they can be considered equivalent to social savings. This is because they represent the surplus of the social output (equivalent to the aggregate social labour-value, or in easier terms, GDP) over total expenditures expressed by the sum of the past labour-value, incorporated into the means of production, and the labour-value of the reproduction of the labour force itself. However, unlike the neoclassical liberal conceptualisation, which would identify social savings with the idea of abstinence or renunciation of social consumption, in Marx it is understood as the result of the appropriation of social surplus by the capitalist class. This distinction is essential, because in the neoclassical approach, future investments depend on greater restrictions on aggregate consumption in society, in other words, on previous savings. In the Marxian framework, though profits (coming from surplus-value) form the basis for financing capital accumulation, they should not be confused with previous savings or something equivalent. The reason is that, as Marx always stresses, while the location where profits are generated (in the capital production process) differs from where profits are realised (in the markets), such a discrepancy operates as a potential focal point for provoking economic crises of overproduction and nonfulfillment of surplus-value.

9 Still, it is important to stress that the function of surplus-value is to finance capital accumulation, and not the consumption of capitalists.

Different from the classics (Smith, Ricardo and Mill), for Marx, capitalist dynamics do not proceed harmoniously. His analytical reasoning can be summarised as follows:[10] In the short term, production capacity and adopted technologies are considered as given. Capitalists, then, make productive investments, in search of profitable opportunities, through the mobilisation of constant capital (purchase of machinery and equipment, raw materials and other productive inputs) and variable capital (purchase of additional labour force). As all costs are expressed in labour-value, Marx conjectures that this movement could lead, in principle, to an increase in real wages and, as a consequence, to a reduction in the share appropriated as profits (surplus-value). Ultimately, this movement could result in the depletion of the available labour force. The general law of capital accumulation, though, tends to prevent this trend because upon realising that profits are being squeezed out by the increase in the wage share in the income generated, capitalists introduce new production techniques by replacing labour with more efficient machinery and equipment.

In other words, in the long run, the pace of capital accumulation tends to be fed by technological progress, whose tendential effect is not only to increase labour productivity, but also to change the technical composition of total capital. This is done through an increase in constant capital in relation to variable capital—or using the author's expression, on the distribution of capital between its constant and variable natures, increasing the organic composition of capital. In Marx's view, technological progress accelerates economic development for two main reasons: the first is that, when embodied in incremental investments in machinery and equipment that incorporate more efficient techniques, it leads to an increase in labour productivity, consequently, allowing the flow of goods produced per employed worker to be increased and unit costs to be reduced. The second is that any eventual adverse impacts on the profit share of capitalists in income, resulting from increases in real wages, would only have an effect in the short term, since they tend to disappear completely in the long term through the positive effects of technological progress on profits. In fact, technological progress leads to a reduction in variable capital (expressed by the relative decrease in total number of workers employed and, therefore, of the mass of labour incorporated) with respect to constant capital (represented by the addition of more productive machinery and equipment, as well as raw materials and other necessary additional inputs). This causes capitalists' profit share to be increased by the impacts stemming from

10 See Marx (1867a, Volume 1, Chapter 22 and 23).

the mechanisation of the production process. To use Marx's terminology, this increases the relative surplus-value, that is, the result of the reduction in paid labour relative to the production of unpaid labour (surplus-value) through greater productivity.[11]

Furthermore, this last effect of technological progress also causes transformations in the appropriation of social capital, since as the organic composition of capital expands, that is, the constant capital/variable capital ratio, the intensification of capitalist competition, intra- and intersectorally, intensifies the trends of concentration and centralisation of capital. While the former involves the elimination of companies and capital of smaller sizes by larger ones, the latter implies the capture and centralisation by the financial system of all surpluses scattered about and originating from capital of all sizes—micro, small, medium and large.[12]

Marx was a pioneer in pointing out, with relative precision, the role of industrialisation (which he called mechanised industry or factory system) in the development of capitalist countries, as well as the impact of technological progress on the tendency towards industrial concentration. For this reason, he exerted enormous influence on non-Marxist thinkers who would later present new theories of development, such as Schumpeter and several structuralist-developmental economists, points that will be discussed in Chapters 2 and 3. Regarding the interrelationship between industrialisation, diversification of the productive structure, technological progress, economic development and structural unemployment, it is worth reproducing this long and, in certain aspects, almost prophetic excerpt from Marx (1867: 295; 317):

> In proportion as machinery, with the aid of a relatively small number of workpeople, increases the mass of raw materials, intermediate products, instruments of labour, etc., the working-up of these raw materials and intermediate products becomes split up into numberless branches; social production increases in diversity. The factory system carries the social division of labour immeasurably further than does manufacture [understood, by the author, as manual production], for it increases the productiveness [i.e., the interaction between means of production and technical progress] of the industries it seizes upon, in a far higher degree. (…). Modern industry never looks upon and treats the existing form of a process as final. The technical basis of that industry is therefore revolutionary, while all earlier modes of production were essentially

11 Marx (1867a, Volume 1, Chapter 10).

12 Do pay attention to the fact that, since bank interest, such as that conceived by Marx, is a category of income originating from the social surplus (i.e., from capitalist profits), the author, therefore, considers it a completely unproductive income.

conservative. By means of machinery, chemical processes and other methods, it is continually causing changes not only in the technical basis of production, but also in the functions of the labourer, and in the social combinations of the labour-process. At the same time, it thereby also revolutionises the division of labour within the society, and incessantly launches masses of capital and of workpeople from one branch of production to another. But if modern industry, by its very nature, therefore necessitates variation of labour, fluency of function, universal mobility of the labourer, on the other hand, in its capitalistic form, it reproduces the old division of labour with its ossified particularisations. We have seen how this absolute contradiction between the technical necessities of modern industry, and the social character inherent in its capitalistic form, dispels all fixity and security in the situation of the labourer; how it constantly threatens, by taking away the instruments of labour, to snatch from his hands his means of subsistence, and, by suppressing his detail-function, to make him superfluous.

3.1 *Capitalist Dynamics and Structural Unemployment*

Marx's controversial thesis that capitalist dynamics would tend to generate structural unemployment, providing capitalists with an industrial reserve army that would guarantee them an almost infinitely elastic labour supply in the long run, must be interpreted in a less dogmatic way, isolating the real trends from Marx's fatalistic perspectives on the development of capitalism. In effect, this thesis means that, in the long run, if there are supply-side factors that impede the normal course of economic development, they may be related to any number of other factors (for example, the weakness of physical infrastructure, the health conditions of the population, among others), but not the unavailability of the supply of labour. This occurs because of the long-term effects of technological progress, which, although implying an absolute increase in constant capital (machinery, equipment, robots, raw materials, and other productive inputs) and in variable capital (the labour force), the latter tends to fall relatively as a proportion of total capital employed. In short, Marx correctly suggests that, *in the long run*, it is impossible to achieve full employment,[13] given the impacts from the mechanisation of production.[14]

13 Full employment occurs when all working-age workers find employment opportunities at the prevailing market wage. According to Keynes (1936), in this situation, which is rare in capitalism, there would only be voluntary unemployment, corresponding to the share of workers who prefer idleness and leisure to work.

14 It is worth remembering that Marx's analysis is related to the tendential problems of capitalism over the long term, and not, as in Keynes (1936), to capitalism's short-term cyclical fluctuations.

In fact, Marx was aware that the great technological revolutions, by modifying the technical-scientific basis of the economic system, bring with them the opening of new productive branches, especially in the manufacturing industry, as well as increasing employment opportunities for the working class. However, by noticing as well that the cumulative impacts of technological progress in the long run made productive activities more capital-intensive, Marx (1867a: 705; 710) was led to conclude—correctly, in my view—that

> it is capitalistic accumulation itself that constantly produces, and produces in the direct ratio of its own energy and extent, a relatively redundant population of labourers, i.e., a population of greater extent than suffices for the average needs of the self-expansion of capital, and therefore a surplus population. [and that] Capitalist production can by no means content itself with the quantity of disposable labour power which the natural increase of population yields. It requires for its free play an industrial reserve army independent of these natural limits.

It should be stated that both conclusions are only acceptable if they are considered in the context of long-term development trends. Indeed, contrary to Marx's argument, in cycles of accelerated expansion it is possible for growth in average real wages to eventually be above the growth rate in the economy's average productivity. Nevertheless, this movement is not sustainable because inter-capitalist competition pressures entrepreneurs to adopt technological process innovations, allowing them to increase capital intensity and free up labour. As a result, unit costs are reduced, either because they can operate with greater economies of scale, or because they reduce relative costs associated with the labour force.[15]

Supposedly, it was his deterministic vision on the interrelationship between technological progress and movements in the labour market that led Marx to the mistaken thesis of the pauperisation of labour. That is to say that, according Marx's expectations, average real wages would tend to remain permanently at the minimum level necessary for the subsistence of the working class.[16] Although empirical evidence actually confirms that, under laissez-faire,

15 This same argument is used by Kaldor (1966) to justify why capitalist development does not face restrictions related to the inelasticity of labour supply in the long run.

16 The subsistence wage corresponds to the quantity of goods and services necessary to support the working class and their families throughout their lives. This real remuneration varies with changing historical, social and cultural conditions. Thus, the subsistence wage of the English worker today is, evidently, higher than that observed at the end of the 19th century.

capitalist development tends to increase the concentration of national income in the upper strata of the social pyramid, Marx's thesis that "the absolute general law of capitalist accumulation" is to make the industrial reserve army produce official pauperism has historically proven to be incorrect.

3.2 *Downward Trend of the Profit Rate*

Even more controversial is Marx's hypothesis that average profit rates tend to fall continuously in the long run, on account of the increasing organic composition of capital. This hypothesis is important because, as will be seen later, it led the author to suggest, albeit not emphatically, that capitalism could be suppressed by its own contradictions. Marx reasoned as follows: putting aside the complications inherent in the problem of transforming values into production prices, which are understood as the magnitude of effective values recovered by capitalists in the circulation of capital, Marx considers the masses of surplus-value as equal to the masses of profit.[17]

Surplus-value rates (also called exploitation rates by Marx and expressed by the ratio of mass of surplus-value to variable capital) are not necessarily equal to profit rates because these are calculated by the ratio of mass of profits to total capital, or the ratio of mass of profits to constant capital plus variable capital.[18] Thus, assuming, for mere simplification, equal rates of surplus-value in all branches (say 100%), Marx conjectured that capitalist economic development, by leading to a progressive increase in the organic composition of capital (that is, the ratio of constant capital to variable capital), causes rates of return to decline, tendentially, in the long run. As Marx clarifies, (1894a, Volume 3: 255), "the fall in the profit rate does not derive from an absolute decrease, but only from a relative decrease in relation to the variable component of total capital, from its decrease compared with that of constant capital". Although it is the observed movements in profit rates that guide the decisions of capitalists regarding additional investment choices, the downward trend in

17 For Marx, the economy's total profit is intimately associated with surplus-value, independently of the fact that it is spread across the different categories of industrial profit, commercial profit, interest and land rent. Hence, his affirmation that "the fall in the profit rate expresses, therefore, the decreasing proportion between the surplus-value itself and the total capital advanced, which is why it is independent of any and all distribution of this surplus-value between different categories". See Marx (1894a, Volume 3: 252).

18 In the numerical examples presented by Marx, he provides different profit rates in hypothetical productive branches, but since active competition forces the migration of capital from the least profitable branches to the most profitable ones, the "general rate of profit (or "average rate of profit") of the economy results from the actual average profit rates in each of those branches. See Marx (op. cit., Chapter 10).

the profit rate appears as a result of the process of capital accumulation itself. Marx (1894, Volume 3: 157) argues that:

> As the process of production and accumulation advances therefore, the mass of available and appropriated surplus-labour, and hence the absolute mass of profit appropriated by the social capital, must grow. Along with the volume, however, the same laws of production and accumulation increase also the value of the constant capital in a mounting progression more rapidly than that of the variable part of capital, invested as it is in living labour. Hence, the same laws produce for the social capital a growing absolute mass of profit, and a falling rate of profit.

The previous excerpt suggests that the forces the drive the capitalist system are the same ones responsible for its contraction in the long run. This occurs because technological progress and capital accumulation, by mobilising an increasing amount of constant capital (machinery, equipment, raw materials and inputs) in relation to variable capital (the living labour force), provoke an increase in average productivity and, consequently, a fall in economy prices. These prices fall because of a supply-side adjustment in the long run: on account of rising productivity, the total quantity of goods produced increases per unit of time, but the costs per unit produced fall. This is because each individual good embeds not only a smaller amount of dead labour, arising either from the wear and tear on machinery and equipment or from the smaller relative flow of incorporated raw materials, but also a smaller relative quantity of living labour.

The mass of absolute profits increases because gigantic production scales, provided by the increase in productivity, more than compensate for the fall in prices. However, if the profit rate is expressed by the mass of profits relatively to total mobilised capital rate, the more than proportional increase in the denominator in relation to the numerator leads to a decline in that rate in the long run.[19] In addition, Marx (1894a, Volume 3: 303) argues that, in the long run, the owners of the means of production that operate with obsolete productive methods and with higher prices are pressured, through competition

19 The denominator increases more than proportionally because, as Marx reminds us (1894a, Volume 3: 266–267), the profit rate must be calculated by dividing the mass of profits realized (i.e., after the goods are sold) by the total capital employed in production (i.e., by the capital consumed in each good, plus the capital not consumed). This is because the cost price of the total capital mobilised does not recover in a single period of productive rotation.

with innovators, to replicate new production techniques. This means that the tendency for the profit rate to fall does not depend "absolutely on the will of the capitalists", given that it is a "general law" related to competitive dynamics and inherent to the development of the system.

Despite granting the downward trend of the profit rate with an irrevocable general law, intrinsically inherent to the process of capitalist development, Marx (1984a, Volume 3, Ch. 14) also points out several factors that could neutralise it, the so-called countertrend laws. Examples include the increase in the exploitation rate through lengthening the working hours in order to extract a greater mass of absolute surplus-value; a drop in the prices of capital goods which contributes to the formation of the constant capital value; the liberalisation of imports which lowers the domestic prices of production goods and essential goods that make up the workers' consumption basket, among others. Therefore, the presence of these "factors contrary to the law" caused Marx (1894a, Volume 3: 271) to qualify the profit rate drop as only a "law of tendency" which, despite being inherent to the capitalist mode of production, could be recurrently nullified with escape valves created by the dynamics of that same system.

In any case, a theoretical problem in formulating the laws of tendency for the downward trend of the profit rate is the lack of greater attention to the dynamics of long-term demand. Even though the demand side was present in Chapter 21 of Volume 3 of "The Capital", which is dedicated to the expanded reproduction scheme wherein Marx[20] demonstrates that capitalism is subject to overproduction crises owing to the problem of realising demand, this aspect is practically non-existent when Marx analyses the tendency for the profit rate to fall.[21]

Even though, at the time of Marx, the Marshallian analytical foundations on the behaviour of market demand were not known, suppose that most of the goods produced in the economy have high price-elasticity of demand. In other words, suppose that the quantities of the goods demanded by consumers

20 Marx (1885, Volume 2, Chapter 21).

21 Marx (1894a, Volume 3, Chapter 13). Possas's (1989: 48, italics in the original) incisive criticism of the law of tendency for the profit rate to fall is also of a theoretical nature. But to highlight the inconsistencies in Marx's arguments, Possas maintains focus on the supply side. For him, "Marx's law of tendency for the profit rate to decline, likewise the 'law of limit' of capitalist economic movement, *has no basis*." Among other reasons, this is because, according to Possas (op. cit.: 46–47), "since labour productivity is generally increasing in capitalism, and not the other way around, the profit rate will only tend to fall if diminishing returns occur in the utilisation of the means of production in a significant and systematic way".

grow in greater proportion than the decline in prices. While this is a realistic hypothesis, far from the analytically abstract categories conjectured by Marx, it is also quite plausible: In countries that experienced a rapid process of capital accumulation, a significant share of the aggregate output is composed of manufactured goods of medium and high technological sophistication, produced using mechanised or automated methods, whose demand is, in general, quite elastic to market prices.

Therefore, if on the supply side the driving forces of productivity provoke an increase in the organic composition and a fall in prices, as Marx thought, aggregate demand can expand and remain hot for a reasonably considerable period of time, to the point of maintaining sufficiently high levels of utilised productive capacity and making the realised profit flows more than offset the increase in the mobilised capital stock, avoiding thus a fall in the economy's average profit rates. It is true that the hypothesis raised here, inherent to the dynamics of long-term demand, could also be interpreted as a law of countertrend. Yet, all the countertrend factors suggested by Marx are associated with the dynamics of supply, without any relationship to the behaviour of long-term demand.[22]

It is possible that the author's emphasis on the supply side has a relationship to the actual historical context, wherein the existence of a significant mass of unemployed workers in the English industrial centres and the absence of trade unions limited real wages to the minimum subsistence level, restricting, thus, the dynamism of domestic demand for goods and services. There are those who interpret this law of tendency as the Marxian formulation of business cycles, in which short or long periods of expansion and contraction alternate, followed by eventual periods of stagnation, but mediated by cyclical ruptures of crisis and recovery, and to which the process of capital accumulation is subject.[23]

In fact, although Marx (1894a) had made it clear in several passages in Volume 3 of "The Capital" that the downward trend in the profit rate is essentially a long-term tendential problem, it is nevertheless necessary to recognise that he was aware that the process of capital reproduction is frequently

---

22 In addition to the factors already mentioned, Marx (1894a, Volume 3, Ch. 14: 271–279) points out the following "countertrend" causes: "compression of wages below their value; relative overpopulation, which concerns the large number of available or released workers and is more evident in countries where the capitalist mode of production is more developed; and the expansion of share capital, whose dividends, by not entering into the equalisation of the profit rate, generate a profit rate lower than the average rate."

23 This is the interpretation of Marcelo Dias Carcanholo, in his presentation of the most recent Brazilian edition of Volume 3 of "The Capital" (1894a:17).

accompanied by "sudden stoppages and crises in the production process" (op. cit.: 289) and that the "fall [in the profit rate] promotes overproduction, speculation, crises and superfluous capital, in addition to superfluous population [i.e., unemployed workers]" (op. cit.: 282). Thus, notwithstanding Possas' (1989: 29–30) warning that "the law of tendency for the profit rate to fall (...) constitutes for Marx the maximum expression of capitalism's subjection to internal economic laws of movement", it can, indeed, be associated with the development process and cyclical crises of capitalism.

It is not clear whether from this general law of tendency for the profit rate to fall, Marx also deduces that capitalism is doomed to be suppressed by its own internal contradictions. In Chapter 15 as well, he comments that the fall in profit rate "slows down the formation of new independent capital and, thus, appears as a threat to the development of the capitalist production process". Yet, threat implies a possibility, not a tendency to extinction. In that same chapter (op. cit.: 301–302), there is notably the affirmation that

> the historical mission of the capitalist mode of production is the relentless development, in geometric progression, of the productivity of human labour. But it betrays this historical mission when, as in this case [being due to the effects of the downward trend of the profit rate], it opposes the development of productivity, slowing it down. This only demonstrates that this mode of production is decrepit and increasingly close to disappearing.

This passage must, however, be read with caution as it was taken and adapted from Marx's manuscripts by Friedrich Engels, the editor of Volume 3 of "The Capital". In fact, Engels warns, in a footnote, that the quoted excerpt, although written "on the basis of the author's manuscript, extends in some points beyond the original".[24] Either way, as Schumpeter (1942: 87) points out, with respect to the interesting question of whether capitalism will survive, the "yes" or "no" opinion of any economist regarding the "summary of facts and arguments" related to attempts to develop social prognoses is what matters the least. For Schumpeter, "what counts are the facts and arguments themselves.

24 As is commonly known, Volumes 2 and 3 of "The Capital" were edited by Engels after Marx's death, based on the manuscripts left by him. Engels states in the preface to Volume 3 (op. cit.: 33) that he had to "rework the factual material provided by Marx, in order to draw his own conclusions from it, yet still, as much as possible, within the Marxian spirit, the entire passage was placed between brackets and marked with my initials [i.e., F.E.]". The excerpt cited is one of those that appears in Volume 3, edited between brackets.

These contain everything that is scientific in the final result. Everything else is not science, but prophecy."

If this is the case, we can conclude that Marx was not peremptorily deducing from his laws of tendency for the downward trend of the profit rate that capitalism would be subject to an end. He was simply analysing what could happen if new factors did not oppose that trend. The new factors do, in fact, appear principally as radical technological revolutions at the end of the 19th century (after Marx's death) and have continued through to our current century. These include mechanics, electricity, chemistry, and automotive revolutions between the end of the 19th and beginning of the 20th centuries; microelectronics, computing and the Internet at the end of the 20th century; and the so-called Industry 4.0 (robotics, artificial intelligence, the Internet of things and big data) in the current century.

These technological revolutions did not corroborate the Marxian general law of tendency for profit rates to fall and did much less to the standardisation of profit rates between different productive branches into a general profit rate. If capitalism is doomed in the long run, it will be for reasons other than those related to the tendency for the profit rate to fall.

Even so, it is worth recognising that the author's importance to the understanding of the dynamics of the capitalist system in general is indisputable. Possas (1989: 53) is right in stating that "Marx's other economic laws of tendency and movement remain solid and must be seriously considered in any theory of capitalist dynamics". One does not need to be a Marxist to recognise not only the soundness of his arguments concerning the importance of capital accumulation and technological progress—which Marx referred to as "changing the technical basis"—for capitalist economic development, but also for the validity of his general laws of tendency towards industrial concentration and persistence of structural unemployment in the long run.

4 Schumpeter and Technological Progress as a Process of "Creative Destruction"

Marx's understanding of capitalism as an evolutionary system that continuously, but not linearly, revolutionises the technical-productive base exerted enormous influence on Schumpeter, an avowedly non-Marxist author. His main contribution consisted in elaborating a theoretical framework in which innovation and technological progress feature as the most important explanatory factors in capitalist economic development. His vision on the subject, originally presented in the book, "Theory of Economic Development", published in German in 1911, was refined in "Capitalism, Socialism and Democracy", in 1942.

In the "Theory of Economic Development", Schumpeter presents a development model with a high degree of abstraction. The author's main objective is to demonstrate theoretically that the functioning of capitalist economies is not compatible with the system idealised by the standard neoclassical theory, according to which all markets (goods, labour and capital), operating under ideal conditions of perfect competition, are brought to a permanent state of general equilibrium. In such a case, one cannot speak of economic development, but of, at best, a system whose growth pattern is compatible with stationary equilibrium. In his model, Schumpeter devises the general operating conditions of this system in equilibrium to subsequently demarcate the essential characteristics that differentiate it from a fully capitalist economy.

The Schumpeterian model starts from the conception of an economic system that, although containing some generic elements of a market economy, such as private property, free enterprise and free competition, is not yet confronted with fundamental factors that could lead it to operate, in practice, as a capitalist economy. Thus, in this initially idealised system, the existence of productive units is assumed, though not yet capitalist companies, and through a combination of only two factors, labour and land, but not capital, these productive units generate production flows in each period intended to continually satisfy consumer needs. Note that, in this economy, as there are no capitalists, we can neither speak of the existence of capital.

Since the productive units use only labour and land, national income is broken down into wages and land income. In this Schumpeterian framework, the owners of production units are considered neither capitalists nor even entrepreneurs. They are remunerated with managerial wages and possible windfall gains. Strictly speaking, as there is no productive surplus, there is also no appropriation of direct and indirect income arising from the ownership of capital, such as profits, interest, etc. In the words of Schumpeter (op. cit.: 26), in this idealised system,

> total prices must also equal the total production costs of goods and services [including the personal efforts of the production unit owner], and these, the revenues obtained by the products. To this extent, production must flow essentially without profit. It is a paradox that the economic system, in its most perfect situation, should operate without profit.

Furthermore, with the future being completely predictable, decisions are made without any type of uncertainty. As a result, currency functions only as a unit of account and means of exchange for goods and services produced. There is also no place for the credit system. Production units are limited to replicating existing production methods for traditionally sought-after goods, so that in this idealised system, according to the author (op. cit.: 16), "the economic logic [simply focused on human needs] prevails over the technological one". The objective of production is consumption and there is no possibility of overproduction, meaning the totality of the flows produced always finds buyers in the market. On this imaginary system, which routinely reproduces itself in time, and which he calls circular flow, Schumpeter (op. cit., 1911: 12) states that:

> everywhere in the economic system, a demand is, so to speak, anxiously awaiting each offer (…). From the fact that all goods find a market, it again follows that the circular flow of economic life is closed; in other words, the sellers of all commodities appear as buyers in sufficient measure to acquire the goods that will maintain their consumption and productive equipment in the following economic period and at the level obtained until then, and vice versa.

Despite the high degree of theoretical abstraction, Schumpeter's intention is to suggest that this is the system conceived and idealised by standard neoclassical theory, that is, general equilibrium, to devise and analyse the behaviour of capitalist economies. However, these two economic systems, the imaginary one of circular flow and the real capitalist one, are essentially incompatible with each other. So, what routine and self-reproductive factors, when inserted into the former system, would rupture that system and trigger a development process as typically observed in capitalist economies? Schumpeter offers three central and simultaneous elements to be introduced into the circular flow economy: technological innovations, entrepreneurs and credit.

These three factors are enough to break the doldrums of the circular flow and initiate a development process compatible with the real functioning of capitalist economies. However, unlike the analysis of Smith and Marx, the Schumpeterian model is completely abstract and ahistorical. Schumpeter (op. cit.: 47) resorts to this methodological strategy using the justification that "every process of development ultimately rests on the preceding development. But to see the essence of the thing clearly, we will abstract from this and admit that development arises from a situation without development."

Although appearing at first glance to be exogenous factors, the addition of technological innovations, entrepreneurs and credit cause an endogenous rupture in the circular flow process. This occurs because, from a microeconomic perspective, the process of capitalist development is, by its very nature, fed by competition, the search for profits and the efforts of companies to obtain privileged positions, preferably a monopoly, in the markets in which they operate.[25] This is why economic development is understood by Schumpeter (1911: 47, emphasis added) as

> only the changes in economic life that are not imposed on you from outside, but arise from within, from your own initiative (...). Development, in the sense that we take it, is a distinct phenomenon, entirely foreign to what can be observed in the circular flow or in the tendency toward equilibrium. It is a spontaneous and discontinuous change in the flow channels, a disturbance in equilibrium, which alters and **forever** displaces the previously existing state of equilibrium.

That said, the technological innovations conceptualised by him, which appear as the "fundamental phenomenon of development" according to the author (op. cit., Ch. 2), have become, in practice, definitive and widely accepted. They are (1911: 48–49): (i) a new productive process, being, for example, the mechanisation and automation of automotive production or the robotisation of cell phone manufacturing; (ii) the launch and dissemination of a new product, such as a car or a smartphone device; (iii) new forms of internal organisation of production systems, for example, serial production under Fordism, or just-in-time production with inventory savings under Toyotism; (iv) the acquisition of new sources of raw materials, such as low-carbon steel for the manufacture of automobiles or silicon wafers for the fabrication of cell phone chips; and (v) the opening of a new market, such as the globalisation of production by multinational companies. In addition to this, Schumpeter distinguishes innovation, which involves the launch and diffusion of new processes and new products in markets, from invention, which results from basic and applied research by public and private institutions.

25 Traditional neoclassical theory always incorporates the hypothesis that the objective of capitalist companies is to maximise profits. However, in practice, as other microeconomic theories of the firm emphasise, this objective can be abandoned in favour of other objectives, such as increasing market share through economies of scale, which allow the firm to charge lower prices than its competitors, increase its presence, achieve monopoly positions, etc. Penrose (1959), implicitly following the Marxist tradition, shows that the main objective of the capitalist firm is to grow, an objective that can be reached without necessarily achieving maximum profit in the short term.

The predominant role of the Schumpeterian entrepreneur is to introduce innovations and be willing to face the uncertainty and risk of success or failure that comes with it. Therefore, what drives the entrepreneur toward innovative efforts is the search for profits and monopoly positions, definitive or transitory. As Possas (1987: 175) reminds us, the Schumpeterian entrepreneur, who "is not to be confused with the capitalist class, although that class is nourished by successful entrepreneurs, is defined by his/her function—that of putting innovations into practice, being able to accumulate other economic functions as an individual".

The role of credit, in turn, is to advance resources to the entrepreneur to finance the investments required for the innovations. This can range from research and development (R&D) efforts for projects and prototypes to the necessary investments for launching the innovations themselves. By including the banking and credit system as an additional factor in his analytical scheme, Schumpeter aims to show that the financing of economic development in capitalist economies does not depend on previous savings, which is, in fact, non-existent in the circular flow. Thus, the role of banks is to advance capital to finance investments in innovations.

As the fruits of successful innovations are reaped in the form of profits, the debts incurred by entrepreneurs can be paid off in the form of interest. In other words, albeit for completely different reasons, Schumpeter, like Marx, views bank interest as derived from business profits. But, in complete reverse of the Marxian perspective—and it could not be otherwise since Schumpeter was notoriously non-Marxist—capital, for Schumpeter, is reduced to the flow of loanable funds from banks to innovating entrepreneurs. Yet, it disappears as soon as the latter transform it into payment flows for the acquisition of all means necessary for the innovative flow: purchase of capital goods and production inputs, remuneration, among others. As Possas (1987: 177) stresses, from the Schumpeterian perspective, "the capitalist, in turn, is defined by the function of capital, and his only role is to run the risk associated with loaning the funds necessary for the investment that contains the innovation". In short, while the capitalist takes on the credit risk associated with financing innovations, the Schumpeterian entrepreneur takes on the risk of success or failure of the latter.

4.1 *The Creative Destruction Process*

Schumpeter's notion of the role of technological innovations as a fundamental explanatory source of development is so unusual that, like classical, neoclassical and Marxist economists, he is the master of his own school, neo-Schumpeterian. His main contribution was recorded in the famous passage of his work, "Capitalism, Socialism and Democracy" (1942: 112–113), in which capitalist economic development is conceived as a process of "creative destruction", through which the creation, launch and diffusion of radical and incremental innovations lead to the disappearance of technologies and companies that, under the pressure of competition, become obsolete:

> Capitalism, then, is by nature a form or method of economic change and not only never is but never can be stationary. (…) The fundamental impulse that sets and keeps the capitalist engine in motion comes from the new consumers' goods, the new methods of production or transportation, the new markets, the new forms of industrial organisation that capitalist enterprise creates. (…) [The technological changes] illustrate the same process of industrial mutation—if I may use that biological term—that incessantly revolutionises the economic structure from within, incessantly destroying the old one, incessantly creating a new one. This process of Creative Destruction is the essential fact about capitalism.

The modus operandi of this process is mediated by the potential and effective competition that takes place inside and outside a given productive segment, in the national and global geo-economic space. The competitive clash that Schumpeter refers to, though, is not the price competition typical of perfect competition models. In that type of competition, an infinite number of micro-firms producing homogeneous goods that are perfect substitutes for each other, operating in segments devoid of any barriers to the entry of potential competitors, are forced to sell at prices that provide them with practically zero profit margins.[26] For Schumpeter (op. cit.: 114), however,

26 The theory of perfect competition assumes that, in the long run, firms actually operate with zero **economic** profit margins. This means that although their **accounting** profit margins are positive (as a result of the difference between unit revenues and explicit unit costs), by discounting the implicit cost of alternative uses (i.e., the opportunity cost) of the financial resources associated with capital investments, economic profits per unit produced are zeroed. In practical terms, if it were assumed that all productive sectors operated under conditions of perfect competition, firms would not see any more profitable opportunities outside the sector in which they operate. As Koutsoyiannis (1979: 154) defines, perfect competition is a market structure characterised by the complete absence of rivalry [therefore, paradoxically, the non-existence of competition] between companies that operate there. For details, see also Pindyck and Rubinfeld (2014, Ch. 8).

> in capitalist reality, as distinguished from its textbook picture, it is not that kind of competition [i.e., through prices] which counts but the competition from the new commodity, the new technology, the new source of supply, the new type of organisation (the largest-scale unit of control for instance)—competition which commands a decisive cost or quality advantage and which strikes not at the margins of the profits and the outputs of the existing firms but at their foundations and their very lives.

4.2 *Development and Business Cycles*

For Schumpeter, technological innovations act not only as the dominant driving force of capitalist economic development, but also as the main explanatory factor of business cycles. His theory on the interaction between development and cycles can be summarised as follows: by introducing a set of technological innovations, embodied in new products and new productive processes in one or more industrial branches, and by making additional investments in productive capital required to achieve it, innovative companies, by breaking the circular flow, trigger a cycle of prosperity. According to Schumpeter, for the innovative process to trigger a boom cycle, innovations must occur in several productive sectors. In the boom phase, successful innovative companies extract extraordinarily higher profits than their competitors, either because they increase the market share as a result of the diffusion of new products, even with temporarily fixing monopoly prices, or because they reduce unit costs as a result of the incorporation of new productive processes. Thus, the prosperity phase or economic boom phase is characterised by the increase in investments in physical capital necessary for the introduction of innovations, by the decline in unemployment, and by the rise in wages and prices.

For Schumpeter, as the first innovative wave emerges from within the circular flow that, by hypothesis, operates under full employment, temporary inflation follows because of both the displacement of factors to innovative sectors and the expansion of credit that finances the new investments. However, this temporary inflation tends to dissipate as soon as an expansion in the supply of new products and a reduction in prices brought about by more efficient production techniques is observed in the boom phase. This means that inflation and deflation are both long-term structural phenomena inherent to the development process itself.

During the boom phase as well, non-innovative companies, faced with competitive pressure, are compelled to react, generally engaging in imitation strategies through reverse engineering of products launched on the market and/or by replicating new production methods. The diffusion of innovations occurs as imitating companies succeed in this strategy, and this movement, or secondary wave, to use the author's expression, is accompanied by the expansion of aggregate supply and the tendency for prices to fall. However, as consumer demand shifts towards products resulting from innovation, many companies unable to keep up with the pace of technological progress are eliminated by the process of creative destruction.

The reversal of the boom phase begins when the innovative impulses that could still be registered in the secondary wave run out. The competitive clash triggers a downward movement in prices, which Schumpeter considers the main explanatory reason for the outbreak of the recessive phase of the cycle. More than that, the recession is understood as a competitive struggle through which the economic system seeks a new position of equilibrium. In the author's words, "the economic nature of the recession lies in the diffusion of the achievements of the boom throughout the economic system, through the mechanism of the struggle for balance".

Some conclusions can be drawn about Schumpeter's theory of development. The first is that cycles are an inseparable part of the long-term trends of capitalist economic development. Thus, unlike Keynes's theory, for which economic fluctuations are explained by the volatile behaviour of effective demand over time, for Schumpeter business cycles are more associated with the great waves of prosperity and contraction that accompany the introduction, diffusion, and maturation of technological innovations. From this perspective, Schumpeterian cycles are more similar to long-term trends than to cycles themselves.

The second conclusion is that prosperity and recession are understood, respectively, as the departure from and return to the equilibrium position of the circular flow. Although Schumpeter seeks to show that capitalist development is incompatible with the system remaining in equilibrium positions, he is unable to free his theory from the influence of the neoclassical conception of general equilibrium. This is so much the case that the recession is only considered over when a new equilibrium position is reached. Furthermore, if the contraction were to exceed the original equilibrium position, the economy would fall into a depressive process. In this regard, as Possas (1987: 188, italics in the original) summarises, "there is then a *complete cycle* of four phases: prosperity, recession, depression and recovery, where each one has its own logic".

The last conclusion is that, in Schumpeter's understanding, technological innovations are almost exclusively the factor responsible for the dynamism of capitalist economies. Though recognising that the proliferation of new technologies requires additional investments in physical capital, the main flaw in Schumpeter's theory, unlike Marx's, consists in giving little importance to the process of capital accumulation. This is why Celso Furtado (1952: 13) is correct to complain that the main weakness of the Schumpeterian model comes from its extremely abstract and ahistorical characteristics. He is also correct to emphasise that "the problem of economic development is an aspect of the general problem of social change in our society, and it cannot be fully understood without restoring its historical content".

Even so, Furtado (op. cit.: 13) exaggerates when he states that "Schumpeterian simplification, on the one hand, takes us away from the true economic problem of development, and, on the other hand, it serves us very little as a general explanation of the phenomenon". After all, the theory of economic development enriches and increases the explanatory potential of real-world phenomena precisely when its crucial, abstract and historical elements are combined in a creative way, allowing us to understand the dynamics of capitalist economies, whether developed or developing.

5 Conclusion

The theories of Smith, Marx and Schumpeter demonstrate that the process of capitalist development arises from three main driving forces: the expansion of domestic and international demand (that is, exports, net of imports), in such a way as to facilitate the flow of production from sectors subject to increasing returns to scale, notably the manufacturing industry; capital accumulation, induced by the support of the economy's investment rate; and technological progress, which helps sustain development, even if in the creative destruction form.

Although the three authors offer powerful tools for understanding the development process, their theories do not contemplate the factors that lead a given country to overcome its condition as an underdeveloped economy, nor achieve per capita income levels and standards of material well-being compatible with the average level of developed economies. Despite this, increasing returns to scale, capital accumulation and technological progress as creative destruction, respectively elaborated by Smith, Marx and Schumpeter, appear as the fundamental ingredients in the formulation of development theories. As will be seen in the next chapter, the main task of this line of thought consisted in theoretically analysing not only the factors that allow the transition from underdevelopment to development, but also possible obstacles along the way that could interrupt the catching up trajectory, causing developing countries to face long periods of stagnation.

CHAPTER 2

Classical Developmentalism and Its Recent Unfoldings

1 Introduction

This chapter is dedicated to the analysis of classical developmentalism. The development theories that proliferated between the 1940s and 1970s received the moniker "classical developmentalism" because, influenced by the theoretical framework of classical political economy rather than neoclassical theory, they brought the discussion on the factors that inhibit poor countries from overcoming underdevelopment into a central focus of economic analysis. This school of thought's main objectives are, therefore, to explain why many countries tend to perpetuate conditions of economic backwardness and to prescribe the mechanisms through which such countries could follow successful paths of catching up with developed countries, as well as analysing the possible problems that can steer developing countries into a stagnation trap. The fundamental factors, as discussed in Chapter 1, that trigger and sustain economic development, including increasing returns, market dimensions, capital accumulation by means of industrialisation, and technological progress, were accepted and incorporated by classical developmentalism. They were, however, adapted to the particularities of the productive structure and general conditions at that time in underdeveloped economies.

Although classical developmentalism focuses predominantly on the long term, some authors (namely Hirschman and Kaldor) were famously influenced by Keynes's (1936) principle of effective demand, according to which growth and economic fluctuations (i.e., alternating cycles of expansion, slowdown, recession and recovery) are fundamentally determined by the behaviour of aggregate demand. This means that the Keynesian principle attributes the main cause of capitalist economic crises to insufficient effective demand, whether that be consumption, investment or exports. In these cases, increasing government demand is essential for inducing the resumption of private demand and economic recovery in the short term.

The originality of the ideas of classical developmentalism was such that Paul Krugman (1993: 16), when considering the theories being proposed to understand the underdevelopment-development dichotomy, regards those theories as having reached a high level of sophistication in the period ("high

 | DOI:10.1163/9789004734296_005

development theory", as expressed by the author). Though this line of thought has hosted a diversity of authors, such as Paul Rosenstein-Rodan, Arthur Lewis, Albert Hirschman, Ragnar Nurkse, Tibor Scitovsky, Gunnar Myrdal, Nicholas Kaldor, Raúl Prebisch,[1] among others, I will limit myself to the theoretical models I consider most relevant to understanding the complexity of overcoming conditions of underdevelopment. And only when convenient, I will add in the recent theoretical discussion on the factors that can lead a developing economy into a chronic process of stagnation.

2 Economic Development as Structural Change: the Lewis Model with Unlimited Labour Supply

Lewis's (1954) development model has become a classic because its basic assumptions characterise the structural conditions of an economy that is still in an underdeveloped stage: a very low per capita income level, with the majority of the economically active population unemployed or underemployed and with opportunities of being employed only in agriculture, a sector which is considered "backward" since it has the lowest productivity in the economy, at least in the initial stages of development. Given that the population growth rate of this hypothetical country is generally high due to the underdevelopment[2] conditions themselves, it is easy to deduce that the agrarian sector is incapable of absorbing the labour surplus of the active working-age population. If this state is maintained, the fate of this economy would be to perpetuate conditions of poverty and stagnation.

Despite the high degree of theoretical abstraction, many development experiences, successful or not, can be analysed, at least partially, utilising the Lewis model. This includes the impressive catching up trajectory—but not yet

1 Bresser-Pereira (2020) reminds us that Prebisch, the theorist responsible for the original formulation of the centre-periphery model, is considered a classical developmentalist. Yet, as that model focuses on the historical specificities and structural heterogeneity of underdeveloped countries (the "periphery"), notably those in Latin America, when placed in the context of the international division of labour, this model will be discussed in the next chapter, which is dedicated to Latin American structural-developmentalism.

2 After the Industrial Revolution, despite the drop in mortality rates, poor countries tended to record birth rates much higher than those in developed countries, due to the lack of family planning and limited access to contraceptive methods. According to the economist and demographer Iraci Del Nero da Costa (1977: 201), many poor countries maintained "an agricultural birth rate and an industrial mortality rate", which meant that the demographic explosion in these countries tended to reach alarming levels.

completed—followed by China since the early 1980s. The model is based on three basic assumptions: (i) underdeveloped economies, especially overpopulated ones such as Egypt, China and India in the 1940s, have a huge contingent of unemployed labour (hence the term "unlimited supply") in traditional agriculture or underemployed in the main urban centres; (ii) there is a structural duality, whereby traditional agriculture (the "subsistence sector"), by adopting rudimentary production techniques in the initial stages of development, operates at very low productivity levels, while the manufacturing industry (the "capitalist sector"), by using "reproducible capital" and more sophisticated techniques, exhibits greater productivity differentials; and (iii) real wages[3] reflect the marginal productivity of labour in each sector, so that rural workers are paid the minimum necessary for their subsistence.[4] Yet, because of the unlimited supply of labour, real wages in the manufacturing sector, as well as average real wages in the economy, are also determined by the subsistence sector. In practice, the capitalist sector also pays a low real wage, although marginally higher than in the subsistence sector as a way of attracting workers to urban centres. Thus, Lewis considers the relatively low initial costs to be acting as a stimulus for investments in the manufacturing sector.

According to the Lewis model, the process of economic development follows a logical path. Before analysing this long-term process, it is worth emphasising that the author—like most economists who formulate economic theories—is concerned with speculating, strictly, the mechanics of economic development in the theoretical field. Therefore, the various obstacles that could interfere with the logical predictions of the model are ignored, such as political conflicts,

3 Variables in economics are expressed in nominal terms (i.e., at current prices) when they incorporate the prices observed over a given period, or in real terms (i.e., at constant prices) when the inflation of the period is removed from the nominal prices (thus, prices are said to have been deflated). Therefore, real wages, when disregarding the price variations that occur in a given period, express the real purchasing power of wages (hence the reason for the term "real") in terms of the goods and services purchased in the market.

4 It is interesting to note that, although Lewis's model is implicitly influenced by Smith and Marx, this does not happen with respect to the behaviour of real wages, which is determined by the Neo-Ricardian theory of marginal productivity. In this viewpoint, if certain factors of production, such as land and capital equipment, are kept fixed, as additional workers are incorporated to increase total production, the increase in output provided by each (i.e., their marginal productivity) increases, but at decreasing rates. As a consequence of this "law of diminishing returns", originally developed by Ricardo (1815) and accepted as a mantra by neoclassicals, the real wages paid in each sector depend on the respective marginal productivity. In Lewis's (1954: 416) model, however, as long as the total supply of labour at the subsistence wage level exceeds its demand, average real wages in the economy will be determined by the reduced marginal productivity of the traditional sector.

clashes between social classes, the power of economic lobbies, pressure from the media, etc.

With the stimulus to the manufacturing sector, the investments made there trigger an expansion process in which workers in the subsistence sector gradually migrate to the capitalist sector, as capital accumulation and economic development advance. Despite the increase in labour demand by the manufacturing sector, average real wages in the economy will remain depressed until all surplus labour from the backward sector is exhausted. In the meantime, Lewis argues that the additional investments driving capital accumulation and sustaining economic development are financed by the increasing profits in the manufacturing sector. Following the tradition of classical economists, Lewis (1954: 430) asserts that "the main source of savings is profits and if we find that savings are increasing in proportion to national income, we can be certain that this is because the share of profits in national income is increasing".

Lewis (op. cit.: 438) does not rule out the possibility that, similar to Schumpeter's model, initial investments are financed by credit. This scenario could result in a transitory period of inflation since credit can create purchasing power at a faster rate than an expansion in supply. Nevertheless, with the economic expansion in the following periods, the incurred debt and inflation would be eliminated. From then on, economic growth would be predominantly financed by increasing the profit share in national income. As long as there is an unlimited supply of labour, profits will remain the main source of financing investments. Therefore, it is possible and desirable that most of the financial resources needed to finance development come from domestic savings, rather than external savings, whose profits (and other forms of income) may not remain in the country. But even beyond that, as Lewis (op. cit.: 431) states, poor countries do not save so little "because they are very poor, but because their capitalist sector [i.e., the manufacturing sector which controls capital accumulation] is very small".

Furthermore, as the productivity level of the subsistence sector is much lower than that of the manufacturing sector, when development results in the displacement of productive resources (notably labour) from the former to the latter sector, the average productivity of the economy begins to exhibit positive and sustainable rates of change. This means that economic development is a process that involves structural change, whereby the factors of production (mainly labour) move from the low productivity sector (agriculture in the underdevelopment phase) to the high productivity sector (manufacturing). Influenced by Smith and Marx, Lewis identifies the manufacturing sector as the engine of capital accumulation and the main source for generating and disseminating technological progress. He is, therefore, one of the pioneers in highlighting the role of industrialisation as the dynamic channel for overcoming underdevelopment.

The reader must have noticed that the average real wages in the economy, by being dictated by the subsistence sector, remain at low levels throughout the period in which countries transition from underdeveloped economies, with low per capita income, to developing ones, with per capita income levels close to the world average. At this stage, the Lewis model predicts a strong concentration of national income in favour of profits. It is therefore worth asking: could the stagnation of real wages be a permanent price at the workers expense?

The answer is "no". In the long run, the exhaustion of surplus labour from the backward sector causes two immediate effects: (i) the real wages paid in the manufacturing sector increase and their variations from then on follow the productivity gains in this sector, thus definitively detaching themselves from the real wages paid in the subsistence sector. When this occurs, the economy reaches the so-called "Lewis turning point", the moment from which the economy's average real wages start to follow the variation in average aggregate productivity, and in so doing reduce the profit share in national income; and (ii) the subsequent economic development will have to deal with the problems arising from the shortage of labour and the pressure of real wage increases on capitalist profits, which, according to Marx, should continue to act as the main financing source for capital accumulation.

The main contribution of the Lewis model consisted of the theoretical demonstration that one of the principal sources of productivity expansion and sustainability throughout the initial catching up period—that is, until previously underdeveloped economies reach average levels of per capita income—emanates from the forces associated with **structural change**. Having reached the Lewis turning point, it is necessary for capitalists to look for alternatives to overcome the surplus labour exhaustion problem and to sustain profits and capital accumulation. Lewis identifies two possibilities for achieving this objective in the long run: opening the country to immigration and/or searching for new profit opportunities by exporting capital through multinational companies, created from the largest domestic companies, which would be located, preferably, in developing countries that have a labour surplus and relatively lower real wages.

These two possibilities, though, are limited, in my judgment, since they would only provide conditions to temporarily, but not definitively, reverse the tendency for the profit share to fall in national income when the labour surplus is exhausted. A third, more effective alternative to resuming the trend of expanding capitalist profits would be the introduction of innovations that accelerate labour-saving technological progress. This fact is, however, completely neglected in Lewis's model, as I will discuss later.

There is no doubt that Lewis was able to demonstrate theoretically that the increase in the economy's average productivity results from a transformation process within the productive structure (i.e., structural change). Specifically, resources (especially labour) migrate from the traditional agricultural sector, which is subject to constant (if not decreasing) returns to scale, to the manufacturing sector, which is subject to increasing returns to scale.

Despite this, Lewis's model contains at least two flaws. The first is to consider that, in the absence of government intervention and stimuli, the small size of the market in a poor country has sufficient traction to induce and sustain investments and capital accumulation in the initial phase of overcoming underdevelopment. While the labour surplus in the traditional sector and the potential for expanding profits in the manufacturing sector are necessary conditions, they are not, however, sufficient for industrial entrepreneurs to make investments and, consequently, sustain capital accumulation without the prospect of an expanding potential demand in the market. The greatest initial obstacle for economies to break free from underdevelopment is the small size of the internal market. Therefore, it is unconvincing that industrial capitalists are inclined to make investments induced only by supply-side stimuli, such as initially low labour costs, without any driving forces emanating from the prospect of expanding demand in the long term.

That flaw would have been ruled out if Lewis had explicitly considered a policy of customs protection for domestic industry.[5] With ad valorem customs tariffs and other protectionist measures for the infant industrial sector, the relative prices (expressed in domestic currency) of manufactured products from abroad would rise. This would result in the replacement of imported goods by goods produced in the country. There would be an effective stimulus to the demand for manufactured goods and investments in the industrial sector. As this stimulus does not appear explicitly in the model, it is concluded that Lewis incorporates Say's law,[6] which is accepted by Ricardo, Mill and neoclassical liberals but rejected by Keynes (1936). According to Say's law, it is supply that

5 Interestingly, Lewis (op. cit.: 462) concludes his essay in a laconic way, stating that the Ricardian law of comparative costs, which theoretically underlies the defence of free trade, represents, however, "an equally valid foundation for the protectionists arguments in countries with a labour surplus", that is, in poor countries. Yet, the protectionist instrument had not previously appeared in any passage of Lewis's model.

6 Say's law refers to the French economist Jean Baptiste Say, who originally formulated the law in his *Traité d'Économie Politique*, published in 1803.

generates its own demand, and not the other way around.[7] In effect, although the hypothesis that **financing** investments depends on capitalist's profits is acceptable, as postulated by the classicals and Marx, the investment **decision** itself does not depend on savings, as Lewis mistakenly assumes, but on the expected increase in potential demand.

The second flaw in the Lewis model is that technological progress does not receive the importance it should as a complementary explanatory factor in development—neither immediately after the initial impulse, triggered by industrial diversification via the absorption of labour from the traditional sector, nor when the manufacturing sector faces an absolute shortage of labour, which is surprising! The role of technological progress, it must be noted, is not completely neglected but appears in the model embedded in the formation of physical capital, in other words, in the greater productive potential of industrial machinery and equipment. The problem is that the way capital formation is treated in the model leaves the impression that the catching up trajectory observed in the phase in which economies overcome underdevelopment is permanently realised by the diversification of the industrial structure into the low or medium skilled labour-intensive segments. When, in fact, already at this initial stage, the acceleration and sustainability of economic development depend on the internalisation of capital-intensive segments, such as the machinery and equipment industry itself and various segments that produce industrialised durable consumer goods. Thus, Lewis does not attach much importance to the fact that, as the development process is fed through the reallocation of surplus workers from the agricultural to industrial sector, capital accumulation and technological progress tend to act as endogenous drivers for the pace of growth in average productivity and employment in the economy.

It is not by chance that when the surplus labour is exhausted, Lewis highlights the opening to immigration and the decision to make direct investments abroad, and not the introduction of labour-saving technological innovations, as factors that make it possible to circumvent the tendency to compress profits by increasing real wages. These are the determinants that, according to the neo-Schumpeterian theoretical tradition and empirical evidence, allow capitalists to anticipate the labour-force shortage. As Dosi and Orsenigo (1988: 30), authors influenced by Schumpeter, point out when evaluating the dynamic impacts of technological progress in the long run, it appears that "its dual nature tends to produce greater savings in productive inputs, including labour,

---

7 In fact, the implicit incorporation of the assumption of Say's law is not restricted only to Lewis's model, but also to the theoretical models of other classical developmentalists, such as Rosenstein-Rodan (1943) and Nurkse (1951).

than the generation of additional net demand for these same resources." In other words, as I argued in the previous chapter, capitalist competition forces entrepreneurs to introduce new labour-saving technologies before the economic system faces the absolute scarcity of labour.

3 The Big Push Model and Development as a Balanced Process

Although written ten years before Lewis's essay, Rosenstein-Rodan's (1943) big push model highlights that the main factor inhibiting economic development from taking off in backward economies with a large surplus of unemployed or underemployed labour force in the rural sector is the reduced initial size of their internal markets. Even though industrialisation is initially driven by light, labour-intensive industries, companies rely on a potentially high demand for their products, so that they can achieve sufficient production scales to minimize their unit production costs and stay profitable compared to potential competitors. Through this model, the author recovers the main classical and Marxian theses: if development depends on industrialisation, capital accumulation and technological progress, then overcoming the problem of a reduced market size is a sine qua non condition for a poor country to move away from a stagnation state and sustain a catching up trajectory.

Since it does not rely on significant demand, the big push model includes the argument that the development process in an underdeveloped economy does not progress if industrial investments are introduced in stages and in small amounts ("bit by bit").[8] On the contrary, promoting industrialisation through the step-by-step installation of industrial sectors could lead to a huge waste of resources, as investment opportunities would be frustrated by insufficient demand. The result would be economic losses and bankruptcies for companies that ventured into such an endeavour.

In his classic model, Rosenstein-Rodan (1943) proposes an ingenious solution to overcome the reduced market size: that investments be made on a large scale, in a block of complementary industries. As soon as they begin to operate, generating production, employment and income, these industries will begin to reciprocally support each other's demand, feeding the process of economic growth over time.

Since the objective is to promote and sustain development and absorb the maximum possible of unemployed or underemployed labour, generally

8 See Rosenstein-Rodan (1961).

low-skilled, investments must happen primarily in a set of labour-intensive industries and in activities aimed at forming social capital (education, health and infrastructure). Particularly in the case of labour force education and training, the author is emphatic in the defence that investments should be the responsibility of the government, since "laissez-faire has never worked properly in this field" (op. cit.: 268). This occurs because it is not in the interest of the private sector to incur investments whose costs are largely irrecoverable, given the possibility of losing the human capital formed through the transfer of trained workers to competing companies.

The justification for investments in industrial blocks to form a big push is illustrated by the famous shoe factory example.

> Let's say that 20 thousand unemployed workers from Eastern Europe are taken from the countryside and transferred to work in a large shoe factory. They receive salaries considerably higher than in the meagre in-kind income they previously had (…). If these workers spent their entire salary on shoes, a market would emerge for their company's products and thus 90% of the problem (assuming 10% in profits) would be solved. The difficulty is that workers are not going to spend their entire salary on buying shoes. If, on the contrary, one million unemployed workers were removed from the countryside and placed not in one industry, but in a whole series of industries that would produce the bulk of the products on which they would spend their wages, which would not be true for a shoe factory but would be true in the case of a system of industries: its own additional market would be created, with an expansion in world production with minimal international disturbance. (op. cit.: 269)

It is clear that the main challenge to overcoming underdevelopment is to create demand large enough to enable efficient and profitable production scales, reducing the risk of failure of the initial impulse triggered by industrialisation. The crucial question is how a poor country, with an insufficient financial system and insufficient industrial technologies and capital to activate demand in complementary industrial blocks, can attract investors with a risk appetite for such an endeavour. Rosenstein-Rodan's answer comes without subterfuge: the bulk of the investments would be financed directly by external capital, under the coordination of the government, who would be responsible for providing mechanisms to encourage the entry of foreign companies.

In fact, in the model proposed by the author, the role of the State goes beyond mere coordination since it will only be possible to substantially reduce the risk of insufficient demand if there is planning, designed and implemented by the government, "comprising the simultaneous planning of several complementary industries" (op. cit.: 267). Moreover, "State supervision and assurance can, therefore, substantially reduce risks and, for this reason, represent a condition sine qua non for international investment on the broad scale necessary" (Ibidem: 267).

The big push model also contains the premise that there is an unlimited supply of labour, but with an advantage over the Lewis model: the recognition that economic development can be leveraged by external economies' power to induce; that is to say, by maximising the mutual benefits provided by the expansion of reciprocal demand for equipment, inputs and final goods when investments are made simultaneously in a group of complementary industries, instead of just in one or another industrial segment. In addition to this advantage, the model suggests, correctly in my opinion, that development policy should be guided by two central lines: (i) priority must be given, at least at the outset of development, to labour-intensive industries, being the safest way to eliminate structural unemployment; and (ii) economic development must be planned as an integrated process, in which capital accumulation, driven by the manufacturing industry, is simultaneously accompanied by massive investments in education and technical training, health, transportation infrastructure, energy and logistics.

Despite this, and although of great practical utility, the big push model contains theoretical and normative implications that are exaggeratedly unrealistic. The first is related to what the government can do in a capitalist economy. There is no doubt that development is unlikely to take off and be sustained under laissez-faire regimes, given that state intervention is essential in the design and coordination of mechanisms to stimulate industrialisation, including through direct participation via the creation of state-owned enterprises in basic industries (e.g., transportation and energy) where investments are not attractive to the private sector. However, the State idealised by Rosenstein-Rodan, whose role is to plan and manage the industrial group that triggers the big push as a "big company or trust", seems more similar to previous socialist experiences that to those of developing capitalist countries. Even in South Korea's development experiences between 1960 and 1990,[9] and China's since the 1980s,[10] the "visible and heavy hand" of the State governing and coordinating decisions in strategic sectors for development does not resemble the State advocated by Rosenstein-Rodan.[11]

9 See Amsden (1989).

10 See inter-American Development Bank (2004) and Cesarin (2005).

11 In my opinion, the expression "state capitalism" is prejudiced against capitalist countries that base their development policy on strong state intervention. In practice, state

The second unrealistic implication is theoretical. Despite accurately identifying that the main obstacle to overcome in order to reach cruising speed on the development path is the scarcity of demand for industrialised goods, the model has contradictory logical conclusions. In essence, when designing a strategy of simultaneous investments in several industrial sectors, development is viewed as a process that, by creating demand, tends to engender and intermittently fulfil supply, which in turn mechanically shapes the forces responsible for feeding demand in the long run. The fruits of progress support an increase in output, employment and income, but there is no place for the impacts of technological changes on productivity.

Furthermore, by treating development as a process of general equilibrium, the Rosenstein-Rodan model, like Lewis's, cannot free itself from the classic Ricardian vice of perceiving the functioning of capitalist economies as subordinate to the logic of Say's law, that supply creates its own demand. As a result, the model arrives at the conclusion that the general balance between supply and demand remains eternally guaranteed. The problem is that Say's law is incompatible with capitalist economic formation, in which decisions are driven by profit expectations and future uncertainty. Because of all these implications, the big push model was sharply criticised by Hirschman, as will be seen below.

4 Production Linkages and Development as an Unbalanced Process

In his classic book "The Strategy of Economic Development", 1958, Hirschman formulates a theory to guide policymakers in countries that are in the initial stages of development. The author follows the main assumption of classical developmentalism, according to which the major obstacle to overcoming underdevelopment is the reduced size of the domestic markets of backward countries. Even recognising the scarcity of capital, technology and savings in these countries, none of these factors would constitute obstacles to the establishment of a sustainable development process in the long term. Particularly in relation to savings, the author, following Keynes (1936), maintains that whatever their initial availability, investments are not effective if opportunities are not opened to entrepreneurs to take risks (animal spirits).[12]

intervention mechanisms are active in all capitalist countries, differing in each only by the degree of intervention, from lowest to highest.

12 The role of savings continues to be one of the most controversial subjects in economics. In Wicksell's (1898) neoclassical view, although it is generated in the real sector of the economy and understood as the portion of income not consumed in goods and services

Where would the initial impulse for development come from in these countries? For Hirschman, despite the small size of their effective markets, many countries count on a potentially broad market to attract sufficiently significant private investments, capable of boosting development through industrialisation. For the author, the fact that significant portions of the income flows of pre-industrialised countries are spent on imported consumer goods is the main sign that these economies have a strong demand capable of attracting domestic and/or foreign investors willing to give the initial stimulus to industrialisation.

Thus, for Hirschman, the principal scarce factor that should be dealt with to trigger the initial impulse for economic development is the political will to remove the obstacles that prevent the activation of private investments and the exploitation of existing economic opportunities. The institution legitimately capable of coordinating this process is the State, which must guide its policy focusing on three main fronts: (i) prioritise public investments in the formation of social overhead capital, i.e., in essential services, such as education, public healthcare, transportation, sanitation, energy, communications, and logistics, without which investments in the activities in the primary, secondary, and tertiary sectors are unfeasible; (ii) stimulate institutional modernisation, notably in the taxation structure and the financial system, allowing, on the one hand, that part of the surplus appropriated by the wealthy classes, traditionally spent on imported luxury products, to be retained by the State in the form of taxes and, on the other hand, that credit be allocated preferentially to finance investments and the consumption of durable consumer goods; and (iii) establish the necessary incentives so that the potentially existing domestic demand, though inactive in an underdeveloped and stagnant economy, boosts private investments in strategic sectors for development.

(real savings), savings flow to the financial market (financial savings) to then be channelled back to the real sector in the form of "loanable funds" required by entrepreneurs for investments. In this conception, real interest rates result from the balance between savings (loanable funds) and investment (demand for loanable funds). Since real interest rates influence (though not exclusively) current investment decisions, this theory concludes that they depend on savings. In other words, when defending the thesis that to encourage investment, society must make sacrifices by giving up part of its current consumption, neoclassicals neglect that credit can be created endogenously by banks as a source of financing without the need for prior savings. Keynes (1936: 64) vehemently rejects neoclassical theory, arguing that investment decisions depend not only on real interest rates, but mainly on entrepreneurs' uncertain expectations regarding future profitability. His main criticism is that ongoing investment precedes savings, stating that "the act of investment in itself cannot help causing the residual or margin, which we call saving, to increase by a corresponding amount."

Hirschman's main contribution consists in the definition and identification of strategic sectors: being those that, once established, have a greater propensity to stimulate demand and investments in other sectors, non-existent or already in operation, causing an intersectoral increase in the output, employment and income that sustain economic growth in the long run. Thus, it is in the manufacturing industry where, since it operates under increasing returns to scale and therefore dictates the pace of growth in the economy's average productivity, the main strategic segments of economic development are located.

Hirschman agrees, in theory, with Rosenstein-Rodan: investments simultaneously made in several industries capable of propagating external economies would be more effective in moving underdeveloped economies away from a state of stagnation. However, he is right to disagree not only with the economic viability of this strategy, but also with the idea that the development process continuously results in a balance between intra- and inter-sectoral supply and demand. In effect, poor countries do not have the initial availability of technological, financial and institutional resources to cope with the magnitude of investments required by the "doctrine of balanced development", an expression used by Hirschman (op. cit.: 50) in reference to the big push theory.

Because the development process involves continuous ruptures triggered by capital accumulation and technical progress, with it all sorts of imbalances emerge, such as the creative destruction of companies, technologies and cultural habits, bottlenecks in the supply of inputs demanded by newly installed industries, pressure on the balance of payments caused by the acceleration of imports of capital and intermediate goods, etc. In other words, unlike Rosenstein-Rodan, the author (op. cit.: 62–65) views development as an unbalanced process.

According to Hirschman (op. cit.), the economic development strategy can be summarised as follows. The State coordinates the acquisition of investments, aiming to alleviate ongoing pressures, and takes charge of those destined for the creation of social overhead capital (education, healthcare and basic infrastructure). By anticipating investments in that area, the author reasons (op. cit.: 83) that the State simultaneously promotes output and income and, consequently, demand in "direct productive activities", that is, in activities controlled by the private sector, especially in the industrial sector. The creation of state-owned enterprises in some basic input industries is allowed, as necessary.

In this way, the State also contributes to attracting foreign capital to the main infant industries, whose direct investments, either because of greater capital intensity and technological sophistication, or the high production scales initially required to make companies economically profitable, scare away local capital at this initial stage. Thus, in line with classical developmentalism, the author supports a development strategy in peripheral capitalist countries similar to core capitalist countries.

Hirschman warns, however, that foreign capital should not replace, but complement and assist, the efforts of national capital to absorb technologies that enable a country to successfully follow a catching up path. As though anticipating the Chinese strategy of treating foreign direct investment from the 1980s onwards, the author suggests that the State introduce mechanisms through which foreign companies are encouraged to transfer technologies to local companies and disperse their investments in different areas across the national geographic space, with the goal of reducing regional economic concentration.

To avoid imbalances in the balance of payments, imports must concentrate on capital goods and technologically more sophisticated industrial inputs. As soon as investments in social overhead capital boost direct activities in the domestic market, development via industrialisation starts. Hirschman's model is nothing more than the theoretical foundation of economic development through import substitution. The reader should notice that his concept of the import substitution process is predominantly theoretical, which distinguishes it from ECLAC's centre-periphery theories, whose approaches also contain historical constraints, as will be discussed in the next chapter.

Although clearly in favour of protecting national industry in its infant phase, Hirschman rightly warns that customs import tariffs should not be set at very high levels. The percentages must be such that local companies can reach sufficient scales to compete internationally in the long run. The author also appears to share Baumol's (1986) classic argument that low levels of customs protection put pressure on technologically more backward companies in developing countries to pursue innovations, even if through imitation, undertaken by competitors that adopt state-of-the-art technologies in developed countries. Since imports play the dual role of stimulating, yet also inhibiting technical progress,[13] the State's great challenge, as Hirschman reminds us, is to dance and balance on the tightrope between protection and free trade.

The strategy of gradually replacing imported products with domestic ones is justified for two main reasons: firstly, because the supply of the greater part of local consumption through imports is not economically sustainable, given

13 This happens because the competitive pressure from imports induces local entrepreneurs to adopt more efficient production methods and seek product innovation, including via imitation. But if protection against external competition is insufficient, such innovative efforts may be aborted by the excessive entry of substitute imported goods which, at this point, have more competitive prices than those produced domestically.

that a poor country, an exporter of primary products, would have enormous difficulty in generating the necessary foreign exchange to finance it. Most likely, the country would be vulnerable to recurring balance of payments crises. Secondly, because the internalisation of the production of goods with high value added per worker, that is, with a significant degree of industrial processing, gives rise to backward linkage effects through the expansion of the local supply of productive inputs necessary for producing the goods, and forward linkage effects through the spread of new productive activities induced by the increase in aggregate income.

Although the identification of these effects had already been elaborated empirically by Chenery and Watanabe (1958), as well as by Rasmussen (1957), Hirschman's (1958) main contribution consisted in formulating a theoretical model that justifies, with convincing economic arguments, development through import substitution in periphery countries.[14] Essentially, in Hirschman's model, overcoming underdevelopment tends to be successful and sustainable in the long term, the greater the backward and forward effects provided by a set of economic activities. As production in the primary sector leads to reduced value added per worker, it is understood that it is in the manufacturing industry where the activities with the greatest potential to generate demand and additional income inside and outside the correlated production chains are.

To give the reader an intuitive idea of the linkage effects, let us assume that the government of an underdeveloped country, through public incentives, is able to attract companies to make initial investments in setting up production plants in the food processing, textile, clothing, footwear and transportation equipment (cars, lorries and buses) sectors. This block of investments triggers an increase in demand for intermediate goods (inputs, parts, pieces and components) that will be used in the manufacturing of products from those industries. Thus, there are backward linkage effects when the increase in production in a set of sectors increases demand in other sectors that supply them with intermediate goods, boosting output growth, employment and income intersectorally. The increase in income produces forward linkage effects by stimulating demand for goods and services in the primary (e.g., agricultural products), secondary (e.g., consumer goods) and tertiary (various services) sectors.

14 As we will see in the next chapter, in the analysis of Prebisch (1949, 1951) and Singer (1950), import substitution in peripheral Latin American countries is analysed as a theoretical model historically conditioned by the external crises experienced by these countries after the Great Depression in the 1930s.

According to Hirschman, the sectors with the greatest potential for inducing demand forward and backward are considered strategic for development and can be estimated using the statistical techniques of the input-output matrix. The author suggests using the so-called Rasmussen Index (1957), which measures the direct and indirect effects emanating from the expansion of production in a given sector on the production linkage of other sectors impacted by it.

Although the model theoretically supports development through import substitution, the author offers the following caveats: (i) even though the linkages are the cause and effect of the output and income growth process itself, the relevant impacts are associated with the backward linkage effects. This means that economic development must be driven by the expansion of final goods industries with a greater potential for boosting the intermediate goods industries (for example, the automotive industry towards the auto parts industries, and not the other way around). Only when a country is close to the international technological frontier does it become irrelevant to respect this order (for example, it would not matter whether mobile phone production or chips are prioritised); (ii) although intermediate goods industries are generally subject to significant economies of scale, it is natural for them to produce below the minimum efficient scale soon after their implementation. However, as the demand for their products is positively impacted by forward linkage effects, their production tends to converge towards the optimal scale in the long run; (iii) having high linkage power is a necessary, but not sufficient, condition to prioritise the establishment of a certain industry in a country. The condition that is sufficient is having a high potential to absorb technologies and achieve efficient production scales in the long run, which depends on the growth rate of per capita income and the income distribution pattern; (iv) as the model also suggests, accelerated growth in demand in industrial segments that operate with extremely high technical scales and highly sophisticated technologies (notably, sophisticated machinery, equipment and intermediate goods) must have their production supplied primarily by imports; (v) consequently, export promotion must be permanently stimulated as a strategy to generate the currency necessary to pay for external purchases, in order to mitigate the risks of a balance of payments crisis; and (vi) to prevent developing economies from being shaken by periodic crises or entering a period of stagnation, the government must manage two sources of pressure: structural inflation, resulting from possible delays in acquiring investments for the intermediate goods and basic inputs industries to meet demands in the final goods sectors; and balance of payments imbalances, essentially caused by the acceleration of imports of cutting-edge technology in machinery, equipment and intermediate goods.

Hirschman's model would be practically irreproachable were it not for the near neglect of the role of technical progress as a dynamic driving force of development resulting from structural changes. Since the author attributes the main dynamic impacts to increases in quantities demanded and supplied intra- and intersectorally, the model leaves the impression—in my opinion a mistaken one—that economic development materialises only as a capital accumulation process through the expansion of output, employment and income, when it also involves technological changes that provoke political, cultural and social transformations, which is in line with the analyses of Marx and Schumpeter.

5 Industrialisation, Deindustrialisation and Stagnation

5.1 *Industrialisation and Kaldor's Growth Laws*

Unlike most classical developmentalists, Kaldor does not focus his theoretical work on analysing the underdevelopment versus development dichotomy. Instead, he focuses on the causes of different growth rates between countries, on the forces that guide an economy to a sustained process of development, and on the factors that can lead it to stagnation. Even so, by returning to the central theses of Marx and Schumpeter, he demonstrates that capital accumulation and technical progress constitute the engine of economic development, and industrialisation, the channel through which an underdeveloped economy can catch up in its income levels and standards of wellbeing to those observed in developed countries. But he does not stop there: Kaldor is the classical developmentalist who demonstrates, with greater precision, how the industrial sector acts as an endogenous nucleus of capital accumulation and technical progress in the economy. While in the neoclassical models formulated by Solow (1956), Romer (1986) and Lucas (1988) each value added (say, each US dollar) in the primary, secondary, and tertiary sectors would have the same weight in the GDP growth rate over the long term, in the Kaldorian models the manufacturing sector, in comparison to the others, presents intrinsic characteristics that make it central in determining the pace of economic growth: it commands capital accumulation, generates and propagates technical progress, amplifies static and dynamic economies of scale, determines the advancement of productivity and, ultimately, accelerates the catching up trajectory. Until the end of the 1950s, Kaldor's theory analysed questions of development as "economic growth models", following the tradition of the Keynesian dynamic models started by Harrod and Domar,[15] but with the advantages of

15 Unlike development models, in which hypotheses are based on empirical regularities observed in the functioning of capitalist economies and in which the analysis contains greater contextualisation of the real world, the growth models unfold in a purer and more

renouncing the use of an aggregate production function[16] and rejecting the thesis that long-term economic growth is induced by the supply side, both of which are central elements in neoclassical models. Not by chance, in 1957, Kaldor formulated a theoretical model that would have enormous academic repercussions. In it, technical progress acts as an endogenous driving force of economic growth in the long run, à la Schumpeter, but is induced by additional investment demand flows in relation to the economy's capital stock.

The main justification for this is that, although part of the technical progress results from companies' innovative R&D efforts (the so-called disembodied technology, treated as an autonomous variable in this model), a more significant portion of it is embedded in machines and equipment, where productive investment flows (the so-called embedded technology) are transformed. Thus, without disregarding that some innovations arise from companies' R&D efforts, the fact is that the innovative process translates into the expansion of physical investments, whether they be to introduce new production processes or to launch new products on the market. This is why, in the Kaldorian theoretical model, investments and capital accumulation, both induced by demand, are the leitmotif through which technical progress and economic growth are embodied in the long run.

In a theoretical twist from the 1960s onwards, Kaldor abandoned "growth models" to incorporate but also to improve—in my opinion more completely—the theoretical perspective of classical developmentalists, whereby economic development is realised as a process of profound structural changes. In his seminal articles of 1966, 1967 and 1970, by identifying several empirical regularities observed in the development process, Kaldor formulated a series of propositions that later economic literature came to label as Kaldor's growth laws. In general, these long-term laws corroborate the thesis

formalised analysis, in which the interaction between assumptions, hypotheses and conclusions results from abstractions from the real world.

16 A production function is nothing more than a mathematical expression that relates the amount of output obtainable by a firm when combining factors in a production process (capital, labour and natural resources). The problem with neoclassical growth models lies in extending the concept that, though valid for expressing a firm's individual production, does not make sense for analysing the economy's aggregate output. The main criticism of this methodological procedure is that it is misguided and unreliable for aggregating the economy's capital stock, since, at the level of specific companies and industries, it is expressed in different technological contents, and its value fluctuates continuously according to the technological changes themselves observed over time. For criticisms of this methodology, see Nelson (1981) and Felipe and McCombie (2013). In an article for the Brazilian newspaper "Valor Econômico", Delfim Netto (2016) summarises the central points of the controversy.

the manufacturing industry is the main driver of economic development. They also allow us to isolate the factors that determine productivity behaviour, the results of which can either guide a developing country along the path to the completion of catching up or lead it into a long period of economic stagnation. To keep within what interests us here, I will limit myself to the four fundamental laws.[17]

Kaldor's first law asserts that the growth rates of both the GDP and the manufacturing sector are strongly correlated in the long run. This means that the greater the output growth of the manufacturing industry, the more pronounced and sustainable is economic growth in the long term. The justification is the same as that of classical developmentalism: in the initial and intermediate phases of development, as productive resources are displaced from low productivity sectors and subject to constant or decreasing returns to scale (the traditional agricultural sector) to the manufacturing industry, which has high productivity, increasing returns to scale, and a greater power of forward and backward production linkages, aggregate output tends to increase and be sustained in the long run. In the absence of manufacturing to act as the engine of growth, the economy would be doomed to indefinite stagnation. When the manufacturing sector, however, begins to act as a force that induces growth, the spillovers of its productivity gains to the rest of the economy ensures that the gradual decline in employment in sectors with lower productivity in relation to total employment does not adversely affect output growth in these sectors. In other words, industrial output growth ensures and sustains GDP growth in the long term.

The second law, also known as the Kaldor-Verdoorn law, justifies and complements the previous law.[18] It establishes a strong empirical correlation between growth rates in the manufacturing industry and average labour productivity in this same sector. It should be highlighted that this correlation is of the respective **variation rates**, and not of the **scale** produced or the productivity **value** per worker. The principal reason, strongly emphasised by Kaldor, is that the manufacturing industry, by operating under static and dynamic increasing returns to scale, as it grows, diversifies and expands its share (measured in value added) in GDP, advances economic development.

As the author highlights, static and dynamic increasing returns to scale act as a driving force for economic growth. However, they are not associated with

---

17 The first three laws are taken from Kaldor (1966), and the fourth law is taken from Kaldor (1970). Thirlwall (1983) analyses the Kaldorian laws in greater detail.

18 In the 1966 article, Kaldor recognises that if was Verdoorn (1949), an Italian economist little known in academic circles, who empirically showed the validity of this law.

the action of individual companies, but with the cumulative macroeconomic effects emanating from gross capital formation and technical progress—most of which originate from the manufacturing sector. The main implication of this is the diversification of the productive structure, as well as the emergence, in the form of creative destruction, of new processes and new industrial sectors. This all means that the variation rates in labour productivity in the manufacturing sector respond positively to growth rates of the sector's output, and not the contrary. Note that, in line with the seminal insights of Smith, Young, Marx and Schumpeter, already analysed in the previous chapter, Kaldor does not view the manufacturing industry as a grouping of disintegrated production segments, but as a diversity of interrelated productive chains that, when operating as a "macrosector", produce dynamic feedbacks with each other, in such a way that the technological progress emanating from them radiates, endogenously, to the entire productive system, accelerating and sustaining economic development.

Given the importance of the Kaldor-Verdoorn law for development, McCombie and Thirlwall (1994) detail the results of the various empirical tests that were carried out to corroborate or not its validity. Many confirm the causal relationship proposed by the law. As most of the results depend on the specifications of the variables contained in the econometric tests,[19] the authors (op. cit.: 167) conclude that the debate regarding the law "would make a good textbook exemplifying the problems that affect the reliability of the statistical inference!" They finalise this with: "in spite of the various alternative tests, there is no consensus on the seriousness of the various existing criticisms" of the validity of the Kaldor-Verdoorn law.

Thus, in practical terms, by postulating that the expansion and diversification of the industrial sector tends to radiate its increasing productivity rates to the entire system, thereby sustaining the pace of growth in the long term, the Kaldor-Verdoorn law corroborates the central role of industrialisation in economic development. Based on empirical evidence, Kaldor shows how

19 Although being a theoretically complicated controversy, it is worth informing the reader that it arose after Rowthorn's (1975) critique. For this author, most econometric regressions specify the growth rate of labour productivity as an explanatory variable ("endogenous"), which depends on the growth rate of the manufacturing output (in value added). However, as the first variable is nothing more than the difference between the second and the employment growth rate in the manufacturing sector, a statistical endogeneity problem emerges. According to Rowthorn (1975), the correct option would be to use the growth rate of labour productivity as an endogenous variable, leaving the employment growth rate as the explanatory variable. For details, see McCombie and Thirlwall (1994: 181–184).

sustaining significant investment rates (expressed by the investment/GDP ratio) is a factor that is responsible for more substantial and sustainable rates of GDP growth in the long term. Indeed, as the manufacturing sector is the main locus of capital accumulation and the generation/diffusion of technical progress, the dynamic cumulative effect of these two joint forces is the rise in average aggregate productivity, the reduction in unit costs of production and the maintenance of economic growth.

The two laws of growth mentioned above are intimately interconnected. As stated by Kaldor (1966: 105–106, emphasis between brackets added), relying on authors who have highlighted the role of static and dynamic increasing returns to scale since Adam Smith:

> Adam Smith, like Marshall and Allyn Young after him, emphasised the interconnection between the static [i.e., productivity advances and unit costs fall as the size increase in the scale produced] and dynamic [i.e., productivity advances and unit costs fall as a higher level of output **accumulates** over time with a greater stock of knowledge and technological capability] factors as causes of greater returns, as the scale of industrial activities increases. The greater social division of labour leads to greater productivity, partly because it generates greater skill and technical knowledge (know-how), and also because greater "expertise" tends to generate and disseminate more innovations. Learning is a product of experience (learning-by-doing), which means, as Arrow demonstrated, that productivity tends to grow faster, the higher the GDP growth.

Kaldor's third law, already foretold by Lewis, ensures that the greater the growth rate of industrial output, the greater the transfer pace to the manufacturing sector of unemployed or underemployed workers in sectors that operate under diminishing returns (agriculture and services in the early stages of development). Therefore, the gradual elimination of the surplus of unproductive workers in these sectors induces an increase in the average productivity of those who remained employed there. The simultaneous impacts of this result, combined with those associated with the Kaldor-Verdoorn law, tend to accelerate and sustain significant rates of productivity growth in the economy as a whole.

Throughout the phase of technological "immaturity", significant levels of disparity are observed between the low (agriculture and traditional services) and high (manufacturing industry, including public utility services, heavy construction, and high-tech services) productivity sectors. Upon reaching "maturity" and status as a developed economy, the intersectoral productivity differentials reduce considerably. At this point, the incorporation of technical progress becomes the principal source of productivity gains, including in agriculture, through the absorption of machinery, equipment and other inputs coming from the industrial sector.

Kaldor's fourth law derives from an adaptation of the principle of "cumulative and circular causation". This principle was proposed by another classical developmentalist Gunnar Myrdal (1957), who formulated it to analyse the problem of social and economic disparity between underdeveloped and developed regions. By rejecting the general equilibrium approach to investigate complex phenomena that operate in **long-term** trajectories, such as social and economic development, Myrdal (op. cit.: 29) incorporates the more realistic perspective that, once "the system departs from a position of rest [say, a state of underdevelopment or stagnation], the **changes** that allowed such a shock tend to produce variations that are self-reinforcing in the same direction." He further adds that, "in virtue of circular causation, the economic variables are so interrelated that a change in one of them provokes similar variations in the others, reinforcing, in a cumulative way, the changes that occurred in the original variables and in the others that were affected by them."

So, Kaldor borrows the Myrdalian principle of cumulative and circular causation to formulate his fourth law, which ultimately stems from the interaction of the simultaneous effects of the three laws already mentioned: if a country's productive system starts to benefit from the advances in productivity provided by structural changes that forged and diversified a manufacturing industry, higher rates of output growth in this "macrosector" imply positive and sustained rates of variation in average aggregate productivity and growth. Since this process of structural change in the domestic production system is accompanied by a fall in the relative prices of manufactured goods, there is a simultaneous expansion in the volume and diversification of exports of these goods, whose dynamism in global markets starts to act as an autonomous component of aggregate demand. The result is sustained higher growth rates in GDP and productivity. In the end, we are left with a virtuous cumulative process, through which greater economic growth leads to great productivity, which sustains greater economic growth, and so on.[20]

This cumulative and circular causation should not be interpreted as a linear and always virtuous tendency. Not only are there short-term factors that operate in the contrary direction, such as those that trigger recessive economic cycles, but there also may be forces sufficiently capable of generating

20 For the interested reader, see Dixon and Thirlwall (1975), who mathematically formalised the Kaldorian model of cumulative and circular causality.

vicious circles of cumulative causality, such as states of underdevelopment or long-term economic stagnation. Thus, it can be stated that all types of economies, be they rich, poor, or facing decades of stagnation—like the Brazilian experience since 1980—, tend to self-reinforce such conditions because of the principle of cumulative and circular causality.

Although it has already been brought up in the Introduction, the emergence and diversification of several high-tech segments in the services sector in the 1980s, encompassed in what is conventionally called the information and communications technology industry (ICT), as well as the ongoing explosion of the fourth industrial revolution (or Industry 4.0), captained by automation and digital technologies (robotics, artificial intelligence, IoT, big data, etc.), will be able to modify, but not eliminate, the role of the manufacturing industry as the engine that allows poor economies and those still in the intermediate stages of development to travel the difficult path towards relative technological convergence and development.

There are a few reasons that compel me to nurture such a perspective. The first is that, as Bianchi and Labory (2018) argue, the new technological revolution underway points to a strong integration of the manufacturing industry with the services originating from the digital economy, in such a way that it is more appropriate to envision the diffusion of an ecosystem of complex technologies for the entire economic system. If this is correct, one can expect an enormous expansion of productivity in the productive activities in the three sectors of the economy, resulting not only from the passive absorption of these new technologies radiating from high-tech services, but also from the dynamic feedbacks that will emerge from the integration of productive activities with the aforementioned digital technologies ecosystem. Furthermore, according to Kaldor (1967), since dynamic returns to scale operate predominantly as a "macrophenonmenon", there is no reason to doubt that the "knowledge economy", driven by this integration, tends to potentialize them. Kaldor (1967: 14, emphasis added), based on Young's (1928) classic article, comments that: "Economies of scale do not result only from the expansion of a specific industry, but, above all, from a general industrial expansion [including, I would add, the high-tech segments of the services sector subject to increasing returns] which must be seen, as already proposed by Young, as ***an interrelated whole***."

The second reason that leads me to believe that the manufacturing industry will continue to play a fundamental role in the hard journey from a low- or middle-income country to that of a developed one is that the former cannot simply jump into high-tech segments of the digital economy without having a relatively diversified and thriving manufacturing sector. This means that developing countries that have suffered an intense process of economic regression in recent decades—such as the case of Brazil—will necessarily have to recover their old industry as a complementary condition to advance technologically in the industrial sectors and in the new technologies of the digital economy. Except they must substitute low-cardon technologies for technologies that emit greenhouse gases, to benefit from this opportunity to simultaneously promote innovations in the energy field and contribute to the reduction of global warming.

Back in 1967, Kaldor (p. 54) ruled that poor countries "are left with no other alternative for economic development that involves the mastery of modern technologies and the increase in per capita income over time other than the path of industrialisation." Today, this diagnosis continues to be shared by authors such as Aiginger and Rodrik (2020: 200), according to whom "the manufacturing sector remains crucial for the development and improvement in the well-being of countries of all per income strata, since it constitutes the main source of technological progress."

5.2 *"Natural" Deindustrialisation and Premature Deindustrialisation*

In his theoretical contributions from the 1960s and 1970s, Kaldor reaffirms that, in the long term, economic development depends fundamentally on demand growth for goods and services, as well as the capacity to generate structural changes that lead to the expansion and diversification of productive subsectors with greater potential to achieve dynamic increasing returns to scale. It is these two principal factors that, subjected to the mechanism of cumulative and circular causality, explain the difference between growth rates between countries and geographic regions. Kaldor (1970: 142–144, author's comment between brackets) argues that:

> it makes perfect sense to say that capital accumulation [and, I would add, technical progress] is not only a result (perhaps more), but also a cause of economic development. Either way, the interrelations operate side-by-side. Capital accumulation is predominantly financed by the profits of companies; demand growth, in turn, is responsible for both increasing new capital investments in industry and for creating the means to finance them (...). Furthermore, some regions are highly industrialised, to the detriment of others, because of the principle of cumulative and circular causality, which is nothing more than the existence of increasing returns to scale in industrial process activities. Such benefits relate not only to the dynamic economies inherent in large-scale production, but also to the cumulative advantages provided by industry growth

> itself, such as the improvement in know-how and technical qualifications, the increase in the flow of ideas and learning resulting from the advance in communications, as well as the greater differentiation of productive processes and the specialisation of human activities (...). With all this, if the communication and transport channels between two regions were expanded, the more developed region can obtain greater gains from reciprocal trade opening than the less developed region, whose development can even be inhibited by it.

The warning at the end of the quote above is particularly important because Kaldor (1966; 1967) was the author who pioneeringly identified the tendency for employment in the manufacturing sector to shrink in relation to total employment, a phenomenon known as deindustrialisation. In Kaldor's view, if a country reaches a per capita income level around the world average and continues to pursue its catching up trajectory, surplus employment in agriculture tends to be eliminated, making the absorption of technical progress in this sector become its main source driving productivity. At the same time, the share of relative employment in the manufacturing sector tends to stabilise, while the services sector becomes the main source of employment generation in absolute and relative terms. When a country reaches developed status and a high level of per capita income, the technological changes piloted by the manufacturing industry tend to considerably contract relative to employment in the sector and trigger a process of deindustrialisation which, at this stage, should be viewed as a "natural" phenomenon because it results from the effect of technical progress over the long term.

More recently, based on empirical evidence, Rowthorn and Ramaswamy (1999: 30) suggested that deindustrialisation could be expressed with an inverted U. In their study, the employment share in the manufacturing sector in relation to total employment grows as per capita income advances, reaching a maximum level, and after a certain level of inflection in per capita income, contracts significantly. In the case of developed countries, deindustrialisation has manifested less by the fall in the manufacturing industry's share in GDP (measured as value added at constant prices) and more by the relative contraction in industrial employment. Rowthorn and Ramaswamy's estimations indicate that the income elasticity of demand for manufactured products is significantly greater than 1 when poor countries initiate and sustain the industrialisation process (that is, each 1% increase in per capita income leads to an increase of more than 1% in demand for these products), but it becomes significantly less than one after the turning point in per capita income, when income elasticity of services surpasses that of industrialised products.[21] However, this adverse dynamic effect on the demand for manufactured goods tends to be offset by the fall in their relative prices, as well as by the expansion and diversification of their exports, both reflections of the increase in competitiveness induced by technological progress.

While deindustrialisation in developed countries is usually assessed as a "natural" phenomenon and not necessarily a bad one, the same cannot be said of "premature deindustrialisation", pioneeringly conceived by Palma (2005) to refer to the phenomenon that has afflicted Latin American countries in recent decades. Anchored also in empirical evidence, Palma observed that the average turning point in per capita income from which countries entered the deindustrialisation process drastically decreased from US$20,645 to US$8,691 between 1980 and 1998 (in US$ at 1985 purchasing power parity prices). In other words, according to the author, many developing countries, especially in Latin America, suffer from premature deindustrialisation, not because of technological advances in the last three decades, but because of the adverse impacts of the excessively liberalising reforms on the pace of growth, the productive structure, and the composition of exports. The author adds that such reforms represent the replacement of an agenda in favour of industrialisation for another that is concentrated solely on price stabilisation.

In Brazil, for example—one of the countries most affected by premature deindustrialisation since the mid-1980s—the phenomenon has predominately been embodied in the relative fall in the share of manufacturing value added in GDP and in the dramatic increase in international specialisation in commodities, i.e., in primary and industrialised products intensive in natural resources, whose prices are highly volatile and fluctuate to the whim of mismatches between global supply and demand.[22] Premature deindustrialisation is particularly serious because the relative loss of strength in the manufacturing sector, before the country has managed to reach the average per capita income

21 Generally, the income elasticity of demand measures the proportional effect of the demanded quantity of the good, service, or group of products, resulting from the percentage variation in consumers' income. Although it can only be estimated empirically, it tends to be low (less than unity) for essential products, such as food, and higher (greater than unity) for sophisticated products, including a wide range of consumer durables and services.

22 According to Nassif and Castilho (2020), the share of primary goods and industrialised products intensive in natural resources (commodities) in total Brazilian exports increased, on average, from 49.6% to 66.3% between 1990–1995 and 2011–2016. In the words of the authors (op. cit.: 696), this result revealed an unequivocal reprimarisation of the export basket and "regressive specialisation" of Brazilian foreign trade.

of rich countries, sacrifices the potential for technological development, economic growth and qualified job creation of higher wages in the future.

5.3 *Catching Up and Economic Regression: from Kaldor to Thirlwall's Law*

In the theory formulated by Kaldor (1966: 112), economic development "results from a complexity of interactions and dynamic feedbacks associated with the expansion of supply and demand", but it is the pace of demand growth, whether for consumer goods with high income elasticity, investment goods or exports, which governs the dynamics of long-term growth. Still, Kaldor (1966; 1967) conjectured that bottlenecks on the potential supply side, especially a shortage in the labour force, could reduce economic growth in the long term. Initially, this is what the author thought. His argument was that the absolute shortage of workers could act as a barrier to growth in advanced economies that, in addition to having reached high levels of average aggregate productivity and per capita income, they had also reached the status of "mature" economies.

Once at this level, intersectoral differences in productivity per worker would become virtually insignificant and the entire surplus labour force would have already migrated from agriculture to the manufacturing and services sectors. Under these circumstances, the eventual exhaustion of labour surplus in the agricultural sector, by making the only option for the expansion of productivity in this area be the absorption of technical progress, eliminates the elasticity of structural supply of labour for the manufacturing sector. Hence, economies that had reached such technological maturity would face lower growth rates. The author warned, however, that the majority of the so-called advanced countries, although having managed to reach high levels of per capita income, have not necessarily reached the status of mature economies.

Shortly thereafter, Kaldor (1968) abandons this argument, recognising that the exhaustion of excess workers in agriculture, in line with Lewis's pioneering view, simply means that mature economies can no longer count on growth through the unlimited supply of labour provided by this sector, but also that there are possibilities of overcoming this barrier through other means. One such loophole had already been clearly suggested by Kaldor in his original 1966 article. There he maintained, in the manner of Marx, that the businessman, pressured by intercapitalist competition, could anticipate this shortage by introducing productive techniques for saving scarce resources, especially of labour.

Not by chance, faced with the evidence from the ongoing radical innovations, Kaldor (op. cit.: 121) comments that "a new technological revolution—electronics and automation—will radically reduce the need for work in the industry, so that it will be possible to combine accelerated growth with a **relative** drop in employment." In short, according to Kaldorian theory, supply-side factors may eventually impose conjunctural limitations, but they hardly act as **structural** obstacles to sustaining growth in the long run.

If demand is the dynamic engine of growth, are there limits to its expansion in the long term? For Kaldor, yes, but only when economies reach technological maturity. In poor economies, which have low levels of per capita income, the growth pattern of demand is not very dynamic because a significant part of it is concentrated in essential goods (especially food) with low income elasticity. When development takes off and these economies manage to reach medium levels of per capita income, as in the case of developing countries like Brazil, the increasing pace of demand sharply augments and diversifies towards goods with high income elasticity, notably manufactures. In this phase, enormous opportunities open up to sustain industrialisation and economic growth through a combination of import substitution and export promotion of goods with greater dynamism in global markets.

Historically, successful development processes have shown that, in this phase, profound structural changes occur, in which the relative leading role of agriculture is replaced by the greater relative share of the manufacturing sector, both in the productive structure and in the total export basket. When economies transition to high levels of per capita income, the pace of growth in domestic demand for manufactured goods slows down, reflecting the drop in income elasticity of demand for these products relative to services. This is in line with what Rowthorn and Ramaswamy (1999) would later prove, as illustrated earlier.

Kaldor cautions that, among the domestic (consumption and investment) and external (exports) components of demand, the expansion of exports at a faster pace than imports figures as the most important channel for successful catching up, as well as for avoiding, from that point on, a very sharp slowdown in economic growth in the long run. This happens because the great dynamism in exports performs three simultaneous functions: (i) operates as an autonomous component that influences the growth rate of other components of aggregate demand, including investment; (ii) facilitates technological learning, learning by doing, and gains from scale, reinforcing the competitiveness of the economy; and, perhaps most importantly, (iii) if it maintains a growth rate superior to imports, it allows the generation of currency necessary to pay for the latter, preventing economic growth from being frequently halted due to excessive external debt and balance of payments crises. To avoid confusion, it is worth noting that the Kaldorian perspective highlights the dynamic role of net exports not as the driver of long-term growth per se (export-led growth)—since in countries with continental dimensions such as the United

States and Brazil, the components of the domestic market (investment and consumption) tend to play this role—but as an autonomous driver that can ensure economic growth without the emergence of structural imbalances in the balance of payments.[23]

Based on the Kaldorian premise that the long-term pace of economic growth is dictated by the expansion of net exports, Thirlwall (1979) formulated one of the simplest, best-known, and most robust laws explaining the relative growth differential between countries in the global economy. Named Thirlwall's law, it is expressed by a very simple equation:

$$\frac{\text{GDP}\ \dot{Country}_{BP}}{\text{GDP}\ \dot{World}} = \frac{Income - elasticity\ of\ demand\ for\ exports\ of\ the\ country}{Income - elasticity\ of\ demand\ for\ imports\ of\ the\ country} \tag{2.1}$$

where is the estimated average annual growth rate of a country's GDP compatible with the balance of payments in the long run, and is the average annual growth rate of world GDP.[24] Since the law is treated as a very long-term trend, the interpretation of the equation is as simple as its formula: a country's economic growth rate in relation to the world average depends on the ratio between the income elasticities of demand for exports and imports of

23 The balance of payments computes the foreign exchange flow (normally in dollars) of revenues and expenditures related to trade (exports, imports, tradable services, etc.) and financial operations (direct investment flows, loans and financing, debt repayments, and other modalities of financial capital) realized between a country and the rest of the world. The balance of payments will be in surplus if the total balance has generated greater revenues than the payments in foreign exchange, or in deficit if the opposite occurs. In addition to an errors and omissions account (a residual item, only to ensure the accounting closure of the total amount), the total balance of payments results from the balances of the two principal accounts: the current account (or current transactions) and the capital and financial account. The current account balance includes the balances of trade, services, primary income (arising from receipts and payments relative to services of production factors, such as profits, dividends, etc.), and secondary income (unilateral transfers and donations). The balance of the capital and financial account results from the balances of direct investment, loans and financing, debt repayments, and capital for financial applications in a portfolio of securities and bonds. For a developing country, the most strategic account is the current account, since if it shows a trend of increasing deficits over time, it reveals the country's increasing dependency on foreign capital ("external savings"). In a word, countries that carry their long-term growth strategy on increasing current account deficits tend to raise their external debt level, which ultimately ends up being unsustainable. This puts them in exchange rate crises (balance of payments crises) and severe recessions. For greater detail, I suggest the excellent exposition on the topic done by Simonsen and Cysne (2009, Ch. 2).

24 The details of the theoretical demonstration of the law can be verified in Thirlwall (1979), while the theoretical influences that lead him to formulate it are described in Thirlwall (2011).

that country. Confirmed by several empirical studies,[25] Thirlwall's law offers two important insights into the conditions required for a country's economic development and catching up trajectory to be successful:

i. if a country permanently maintains a growth rate in which the income elasticity of demand for exported products (i.e., the percentage impact on exports resulting from each percentage variation in world income) exceeds the income elasticity of demand for imported products (i.e., the percentage impact on imports resulting from each percentage variation in domestic income), it will be possible to sustain growth compatible with balance of payments equilibrium and a successful catching up trajectory;
ii. the pattern of international specialisation matters. This means that the great challenge for developing countries is to sustain a pace of growth characterised, simultaneously, by structural changes that boost the export volume and share of manufactured goods and services of greater technological sophistication in total exports, as these exports have greater income elasticity of demand in global markets. This is the best alternative for developing countries to escape the trap of excessive dependence on commodity exports. As McCombie and Thirlwall (1994: 244) argue, "for countries that combine low export growth rates with high income elasticity of demand for imports, the message is clear: most of the goods produced will be unattractive, both in domestic and foreign markets", making their respective economic growth rates anaemic and subjecting them to excessive dependence on external financing and frequent structural crises in the balance of payments. Therefore, it matters not only **how much** countries export, but **what** they export as well. It is no coincidence that since Pavitt (1984) proposed a methodology associating each type of technology with the dominant factor that shapes the competitive positioning of companies and sectors in the short and long term, various indicators for the degree of technological sophistication have been elaborated and have become widely utilized in empirical studies. A few of such indicators deserve mentioning: those that measure the degree of technological intensity of each sector, proposed by Lall (2000); those that associate the qualitative structure of the export basket with GDP growth in the long run, elaborated by Hausmann, Hwang and Rodrik (2005); and those of technological complexity (the economic complexity index), which involve measuring the qualitative structure of exports according to the largest number of technological capabilities under the control

25 Thirlwall (2011) himself summarises the main empirical studies that corroborate the abovementioned law.

of companies in a given country, developed by Hausmann and Hidalgo (2010).

Equation (2.1) is called the "strong" version of Thirlwall's law, for it assumes that relative prices (including the real exchange rate) remain constant over time. A "weak" version, which considers the more realistic hypothesis that relative prices undergo intertemporal changes, is expressed by:[26]

$$GDP\ \dot{Country}_{BP} = \frac{\hat{x}}{Income\ elasticity\ of\ demand\ for\ imports\ of\ the\ country} \quad (2.2)$$

where $\hat{x}$ is the (observed) growth rate of exports. While the "strong" version estimates the relative growth rate of a country in relation to the rest of the world, necessary to maintain growth without generating structural imbalances in the balance of payments, the "weak" version estimates the growth rate of that same country in absolute terms, allowing it to be compared with the actual observed growth rate. To provide the reader with an idea of the application of Thirlwall's law in both versions, Table 1 shows the estimations of the parameters of this law for the countries of the BRICS group (Brazil, Russia, India, China and South Africa) in the period 1995–2013.

TABLE 1 Estimated and actual economic growth in the BRICS: Thirlwall's law (1995–2013)

Country	Income elasticity of demand for exports	Income elasticity of demand for imports	Growth rates of observed exports (annual average, in %)	Growth rates of observed GDP (annual average, in %)	Thirlwall's law—"strong" version	Thirlwall's law—"weak" version
	1	2	3	4	1/2	3/2
Brazil	1.74	2.01	6.01	3.17	0.87	2.99
Russia	1.08	2.23	4.17	3.32	0.48	1.86
India	2.66	1.31	9.56	6.95	2.03	7.30
China	5.81	1.56	15.91	9.67	3.72	10.20
South Africa	0.64	1.50	4.23	3.13	0.43	2.82

SOURCE: NASSIF, FEIJO AND ARAÚJO (2016, TABLES 4, 5 AND 6)

26 See Thirlwall (2011).

China and India are the only BRICS countries that, maintaining income elasticity of demand for exported goods (5.81 and 2.66, respectively) superior to that of imported goods (1.56 and 1.31, respectively), managed to follow catching up trajectories in the period 1995–2013. As can be seen in the sixth column (Thirlwall's law, "strong" version), the ratios between the income elasticity of demand for exported and imported goods by China and India (equal to 3.72 and 2.03, respectively) indicate that these countries maintained estimated growth rates, consistent with the balance of payments equilibrium, of 272% and 103% in annual averages, respectively, above the world's average growth. Brazil and South Africa maintained trajectories of economic regression (falling-behind), since their respective average annual growth rates, **estimated** at 87% and 43%, respectively, were lower than the average annual growth rates **observed** in the world economy.

As had occurred in the original article by Thirlwall (1979) for the case of Japan, the econometric tests related to the results in Table 1 did not allow conclusions to be drawn for the case of Russia, who, unlike the other countries in the BRICS group, showed estimated growth rates (Thirlwall's law, "weak" version) that were very different from those observed (annual averages, respectively, of 1.9% and 3.3%). Note also that when comparing the fifth and last columns of Table 1, China and India were the only countries that had actual observed growth rates even lower than what could be achieved without generating structural imbalances in the balance of payments in the long run.

6 Conclusion

The theories presented in this chapter stand out for demonstrating the following stylised facts:

i. development is not limited only to economic growth ("more of the same"), but unfolds in a process in which the latter, to be sustained in the long run, must be accompanied by significant changes in the productive structure. This implies that development is a process through which productive resources (especially the labour force) gradually move from traditional sectors of low productivity (notably, traditional agriculture) to modern sectors of high productivity (the manufacturing industry, accompanied simultaneously or not, by the most productive segments of the services sector);
ii. the cumulative effects of technological progress and capital formation on the ecosystem composed by the manufacturing industry and the digital services associated with information and communications technologies

(ICTS) make the dynamism of these industries determine the economic growth rate and, consequently, the pace of productivity increase in the long term. These tendential benefits occur because the successive impacts of technological progress and capital accumulation cause these industries to obtain both static and dynamic increasing returns to scale. The reader must remember that when investments happen at a certain pace in sectors that operate under such conditions, the growth rate of production in these same sectors varies in greater proportion, making the increase in productivity sustainable in the long run. In the end, when the aggregate dynamic impacts are assessed, the conclusion reached is that the value added of the economy, that is, GDP, also grows at a faster pace and, with it, the evolution of aggregate productivity. Therefore, the rate of productivity growth depends on the rate of economic growth, and not the contrary, as postulated by neoclassical liberals.

iii. laissez-faire policies and adherence to unrestricted practices of international free trade do not ensure the take off and consolidation of the catching up path, as state coordination through planning policies in favour of economic development is indispensable. The rejection of the laissez-faire hypothesis and the recognition of the need for government intervention to coordinate private investments are common aspects of the developmental school as a whole. However, the emphasis regarding the activation of industrial policy instruments (import tariff protection, subsidies, local content etc.), as well as its coordination with the macroeconomic regime, varies between the subgroups. In this respect, the ECLAC school and new developmentalism, which will be discussed in the next chapters, are much more emphatic in defending these mechanisms.

CHAPTER 3

The Centre-Periphery Model and ECLAC's Political Economy: Then and Now

1 Introduction

Underdeveloped countries, notably in Latin America and Asia, did not necessarily reproduce development processes analogous to those of today's advanced capitalist countries, especially those in Continental Europe. In view of this, although structuralist development theses from Latin America have also supported the defence of industrialisation as the only way to overcome underdevelopment—based on arguments identical to those analysed in the previous chapter—,[1] their theories contain two aspects that mark greater advances in comparison to classical developmentalism: on the one hand, the incorporation of historical, social and institutional specificities from each country or region, along with the pattern of insertion of underdeveloped or developing economies ("the periphery") into the global economy; and, on the other hand, the emphasis on economic policy proposals encouraging development ("development policies" and "economic planning policies"), without which it is not possible to promote and sustain successful trajectories of convergence of these economies to high levels of per capita income and well-being. As Celso Furtado (1952) underscores in one of his classic studies, without the interaction of historians, anthropologists, sociologists and other social scientists, economists cannot answer why a society develops nor clearly identify the social agents to whom this process is owed. Yet, Furtado (op. cit.: 14, emphasis added) further adds that "economic analysis can specify the **mechanism** of economic development", but the distinctive historical factors of a country or region must be taken into account.

This chapter and the next lean on the theses of Prebisch-Singer (centre-periphery model) and Furtado (underdevelopment, development

1 It is worth remembering that Latin American structuralist development theses, following the example of classical developmentalism, are based on the hypotheses that the manufacturing sector is the driver of capital accumulation and is the main source for generating and disseminating technical progress, and on the conception that economic development involves structural change, whereby productive resources are reallocated from low productivity sectors to high productivity ones.

 | DOI:10.1163/9789004734296_006

and stagnation), key authors in the formulation of a theory on the development of periphery countries. In this chapter, specifically, the centre-periphery model, which constitutes the ECLAC political economy framework, is analysed in three sections. Section 2 discusses the centre-periphery model on the analytical basis of Latin American structuralist and neostructuralist theories of development. Section 3 analyses the analytical apparatus of ECLAC's political economy as a guiding principle of Latin American national-developmental policies adopted in the period 1950–1980. Section 4 discusses the evolution of the centre-periphery model from the 1980s to the present. I will show how ECLAC's economists, influenced by neo-Schumpeterian evolutionary models and equipped with sophisticated microeconomic instruments, kept Prebisch's original propositions regarding external restrictions on the economic development of periphery countries intact, while also making a critical assessment of the practice of import substitution in Latin America.

2 The Centre-Periphery Model as a Theoretical Basis for Latin American Developmental Structuralism

The centre-periphery model originates from the theses developed by Raúl Prebisch, the second executive secretary of ECLAC, and Hans Singer, an economist at the United Nations Economic Department. Their theses were independently conceived, but at nearly the same time, in 1950.[2] Prebisch (1949), in particular, divides the world economy into two blocks of countries: the "centre" or "core", formed by developed countries, which concentrate innovations and hold the quasi-monopoly position on global technical progress, and the "periphery", formed by underdeveloped or developing countries, which seek to imitate and absorb the technical progress emanating from the core countries.

Based on the dynamics of trade flows of goods and services between centre and periphery countries, Prebisch (1949) and Singer (1950) concluded that the benefits arising from the international division of labour were not transferred to the periphery. This conclusion is contrary to what the comparative advantage theory postulates, a theory which forms the basis of the defence of free trade. Even though this theory will be re-discussed in Chapter 8, which covers the analytical aspects of the neoclassical trade theory, it is appropriate

2 Although Prebisch's seminal article was published in Spanish in 1949, the English edition is from 1950, the same year that Singer's article was published in the *American Economic Review*.

to inform the reader here of its central elements in order to provide greater didactic clarity.

The theory of comparative advantage, conceived by David Ricardo (1817), proposes that under laissez-faire and international free trade, each country tends to specialise in the production of **relatively** cheaper goods and services, in other words, that goods and services are produced with greater relative productivity or "comparative advantage".[3] To illustrate with a hypothetical example, imagine that the global economy, made up of centre and periphery countries, produces two categories of goods: primary, such as soybeans, fruits and coffee; and manufactured, such as clothing, footwear and machinery and equipment. The comparative advantage theory presents a counterintuitive result: even if periphery countries are able to produce some of these manufactured goods (for example, footwear) at cheaper prices, in absolute terms, than the core countries, it is more recommendable that the productive resources be allocated to the production of goods considered **relatively** cheaper.

Therefore, the comparative advantage theory postulates that periphery countries will only be able to maximise efficiency if the economy's resources are used primarily in the production of goods and services with lower comparative costs ("opportunity costs"). This theory is considered, even to this day, the basis for defending free trade and comes with the conclusion that periphery countries should specialise in the production of primary products, and core countries in the production of manufactured ones.

In Ricardo's (1817) original version, the source that determines the comparative advantage of each country is the relative dominance of the technology used in the production process of each good. This, in turn, reflects the greater or lesser relative labour content incorporated into production when compared to other international competitors. However, the theory treats technology as an exogenous factor, that is, a mysteriously inherited gift from laissez-faire and free trade that differentiates periphery and core countries. It, therefore, disregards the fact that technology generation and diffusion result from the simultaneous interaction between the stimuli stemming from government policies and the responses to the innovative efforts presented by the private sectors that command productive activity in a market economy. The theory of comparative

3 Strictly speaking, when considering several productive segments in an economy, comparative advantages are jointly determined by the differences between relative productivity and relative wages of each of them in relation to the corresponding segments of the trade partner. For the reader interested in a detailed analysis of this theory, see Krugman, Obstfeld and Melitz (2015), especially Chapter 3.

advantage neglects the fact that it is this dynamic interaction that results in a greater or lesser rate of capital accumulation and technological development.

Later, the comparative advantage theory gained a theoretical version, distinct but complementary to it, developed by the Swedish neoclassical economists Eli Heckscher (1919) and Bertil Ohlin (1924; 1933). In this version, instead of different relative technologies, the explanation of the different relative costs and prices of goods and services produced in each country became the distinct relative endowment of factors dispersed in the global economy.

Thus, returning to the previous example, periphery countries specialise in primary products, which they produce at relatively lower prices than core countries, because they have a greater relative abundance of factors (natural resources or low-skilled labour) used intensively in the production of these goods. Core countries specialise in manufactured goods, which they produce at relatively lower prices than periphery countries, because they have a greater relative abundance of factors (capital or high-skilled labour) used intensively in the production of these goods. So, this version ensures that, by engaging in reciprocal free-trade practices, each bloc of countries could import goods produced under conditions of comparative disadvantage—the core countries, primary goods, and the periphery countries, manufactured goods—at relatively lower prices than would be possible if they were produced in their domestic market.

Recall from Chapter 1 that Adam Smith's arguments in defence of free trade are highly dynamic and based on the hypothesis that the free exchange of goods in global markets allows each country to expand its exports, consequently supplanting the limitations imposed by the size of the local market. Free trade also allows greater access to imports of other products cheaper than would be possible if they were produced in the local market. Hence, the vision of Smith suggests that the main benefit of international trade comes from the expansion of each country's **net exports**, whose principal impact ultimately translates into greater economic growth in the long run.

The sophistication of the Ricardian principle of comparative advantage allowed traditional neoclassical theory to begin anchoring the defence of free trade in predominantly static arguments. This meant that neoclassical theory was able to build an analytical apparatus that could demonstrate that, under highly restrictive hypotheses (constant returns to scale, perfect competition, laissez-faire, etc.), free trade would provide an optimal allocation of productive resources in the world economy, ignoring, however, the possible beneficial or adverse impacts on the economic growth of each country. Unlike the Smithian view, the neoclassical vision suggests that the main benefit of international trade comes from the expansion of **net imports** from each country, the impact of which ultimately results in greater well-being by increasing total consumption.

The neoclassical version of comparative advantage achieved enormous normative influence through the equalisation theorem of the relative prices of goods and productive factors (the so-called factor price equalisation theorem), demonstrated by Paul Samuelson (1948; 1949). This theorem consolidated the ideological power of convincing periphery country governments of the benefits, including the dynamic ones, arising from unconditional adherence to multilateral free trade. The theorem ensures that if all markets (products and factors of production) function under conditions of laissez-faire and perfect competition, free trade would lead to the equalisation of the relative prices of goods and factors of production in the world economy.[4]

The workings behind how the theorem operates is simple: it is the reciprocal pressure of inter-industrial competition between countries that creates a drop in the relative prices of goods in which each country holds a position of comparative disadvantage.[5] Returning to the previous example, the theorem predicts that free trade leads to both a fall in the relative prices of manufactured goods imported by periphery countries and a fall in the relative prices of primary goods imported by core countries. In parallel, the drop in relative prices of these goods would, in the periphery and centre respectively, result in a drop in the relative prices of the factors intensively used in the production of both: capital and high-skilled labour in periphery countries and natural resources and low-skilled labour in core countries. Furthermore, the theorem guarantees that free trade promotes the contrary movement, being upwards, in the relative prices of goods in which each of these blocs of countries has a comparative advantage, accompanied by an increase in the relative prices of the factors intensively used in their production. In other words, the factor price equalisation theorem ensures that, in a utopian world of perfect competition, real wage and profit rates will be equalised throughout the entire world!

---

4 It is worth highlighting, however, that the theorem is only valid within the framework of the comparative advantage model of the Heckscher-Ohlin-Samuelson version. In the original Ricardian model, since all production costs depend on just one factor (labour), there is not any mechanism that permits wage equalisation through international trade.

5 The neoclassical theories of international trade assume the absence of financial capital flows between countries, restricting international economic transactions to trade flows of tradable goods and services. They also assume that the "physical" factors of production (capital, labour, natural resources, etc.) can move internally (i.e., move from one region to another in a given country), but not internationally. The real exchange rate is thus directly determined by the terms of trade, that is, by the ratio between the price indices of exports and imports. For the reader who is interested in these technical details, see Feenstra (2004).

But what would be the source of economic development in periphery countries if the predictions of the comparative advantage theory and the equalisation theorem of the relative prices of goods and factors of production suggest that these countries will extract perpetual benefits as exporters of primary products and importers of manufactured goods? Although neoclassical theory of international trade does not offer an explicit answer to this question, it does implicitly suggest that the higher pace of capital accumulation and technical progress in the manufacturing sector tends to cause the prices of manufactured products to fall relative to those of primary products in the long run. As a result, periphery countries, by engaging in free trade practices, can accumulate capital and absorb technical progress embedded in the capital goods imported from core countries and incorporate them into local productive activities (including infant industrial segments), thus managing to accelerate their economic development process.

Although there is no historical evidence of a successful nation in which the path to development was at the mercy of extreme dependence on imported manufactured goods,[6] the criticisms of Prebisch (1949) and Singer (1950) are, nevertheless, predominantly theoretical. Their criticisms are based on the thesis that the factor price equalisation theorem does not adjust to the real world and the dynamics observed in international trade.

The reasons for the discrepancy between theory and reality results from the structural heterogeneity inherent in the behaviour of supply and demand for primary products vis-à-vis manufactured. On the supply side, the manufacturing sector has two striking characteristics: it generates, diffuses and exhibits a greater pace of technological innovation; and it operates with technologies subject to static and dynamic economies of scale, thus controlling the dynamics of capital accumulation, technical progress, economic growth and the long-term sustainability of productivity. Consequently, the greater degree of oligopolisation tends to inhibit price competition in this sector, giving enormous power to the leading companies to fix market prices and control desired profit margins.

As Prebisch (1949: 16) observes, if the predictions of the theorem were valid, "given the greater productivity of industry, the terms of trade [that is, the price relationship between the products exported and imported by the periphery] should move in favour of primary products". But this trend does not come about because, on the supply side, the greatest productivity gains, which imply sharp drops in the costs of manufactured products produced in core countries,

6 References for this are found in the books of Amsdem (2001) and Chang (2003).

are not passed on proportionally to prices. On the demand side, the structural heterogeneity observed between exported products by the centre and by the periphery is also notable. In this particular, one of the necessary conditions for the factor price equalisation theorem to be validated in the real world is that the income elasticity of demand for the products the comprise the specialisation pattern of the centre (manufactured) and the periphery (primary) is equal to unity. That is to say, the average percentages of expansion in world demand for primary and manufactured products need to be tendentially equal to the average growth rates in world income.

It turns out that in international trade as well, the so-called Engel's law prevails: the income elasticity of demand for "luxury" goods, which encompass the majority of manufactured goods subject to product differentiation and the manipulation of consumer preferences through marketing, advertising and publicity, is greater than unity; while the income elasticity of demand for "essential" goods, encompassing primary products, which are generally homogeneous and easily replaceable in the market, is less than one.

That said, when observing the historical and economic conditions prevailing from 1870 to 1930, a time when the Latin American periphery countries were guided by a development strategy predominantly "outward" focused, Prebisch (1949) and Singer (1950) concluded that this model tended to replicate perverse and unsustainable growth in the long run. Even in cycles of global economic expansion, the demand for primary goods exported by the periphery tended to grow at a slower pace than for manufactured goods exported by the centre, creating a tendency for the terms of trade to deteriorate. As Prebisch (1951: 23) observes, "imports of primary products by industrial centres tend to grow at a lower intensity than real income. In other words, the income elasticity of demand for imports of primary products effected by the centre tends to be less than unity."

Therefore, the pattern of international integration guided by static comparative advantage makes economic development in the periphery impossible. This is because the secular deterioration of the terms of trade tends to reduce these countries' ability to import. That is, it tends to relatively compress the currency flows necessary to finance the imports of manufactures, notably machinery and equipment intended for capital accumulation. In effect, expressing the value in currency (for example, in dollars) of goods exported by the centre (manufactured) and by the periphery (primary) as resulting from the unit price multiplied by the quantum traded, Prebisch (1949) and Singer (1950) noted that, between 1870 and 1930, the structural heterogeneity meant that, in cycles of global economic expansion, both the price and the quantum of manufactured products exported by the centre grew, in absolute terms, tendentially more than that of primary products exported by the periphery.

In practical terms, assuming that the real exchange rate remains in equilibrium, i.e., that the currency of periphery countries is neither undervalued nor overvalued in relation to the currency basket of core countries, this perverse development process being focused "outward" meant that the value of primary exports tended to fall in relation to the value of manufactured exports. Because of this, periphery countries, when faced with less capacity to import, transferred part of their income to core countries and were subject to recurrent balance of payment crises.

As shown by Furtado (1959), in his classic "The Economic Growth of Brazil: a Survey from Colonial to Modern Times" ("*Formação Econômica do Brasil*"), in the periods that followed frequent exchange rate crises, governments of periphery countries adopted significant devaluations of their currencies, with the aim to reduce prices, in foreign currency, of exported primary goods and, in return, increase the prices of imported manufactured goods. However, since the demand for primary products is inelastic in relation to prices (i.e., not very sensitive) and for manufactured goods, it is elastic (very sensitive), currency devaluations had practically no effect on promoting net exports from periphery countries. This made the adjustment in their balance of payments strongly recessive. In practice, as Singer (1950: 479) diagnosed, between 1870 and the beginning of the 1940s, the global economic scenario opened wide and perpetuated a trend in which

> the industrialised countries [the core] have had the best of both worlds, both as consumers of primary commodities and producers of manufactured articles, whereas the underdeveloped countries [the periphery] had the worst of both worlds, as consumers of manufactures and as producers of raw materials.

How does one evaluate the short or medium periods in which periphery countries benefit from price booms for agricultural products and other commodities on international markets? Would such facts observed, for example, between 1820 and 1830, then between 1840 and 1860,[7] and more recently throughout the 2000s not compromise the Prebisch-Singer theses, whose corroboration crucially depends on the hypotheses of the deterioration of the terms of trade?

7 These data can be found in Coatsworth and Williamson (2002).

The answer is "no". In these transitory periods, the prize obtained by the periphery in the "commodity lottery"—to use the precise expression of Diaz-Alejandro (1984)—does not transform in permanent gains. These are just passing historical circumstances, in which the considerable increase in those products' relative prices results from an exceptional increase in demand by important players on the international scene—such as England at the height of the Industrial Revolution, between 1850 and 1860, and China during its transition to a middle-income economy in the early 2000s. The Prebisch-Singer theses are, thus, based on the hypothesis of **secular** deterioration in the terms of trade, which is repeatedly corroborated by empirical evidence.[8]

Is there, then, an alternative to this international free trade integration that ends up condemning periphery countries to economic stagnation in the long run? As Prebisch (1949: 32) shows, the adoption of exchange controls and the adoption of import substitution as a new development model for Latin American periphery countries from the 1930s onwards "were not the results of a theory, but the imposition of circumstances". This is because the retraction in international demand for primary products during the Great Depression was so severe that when faced with the change in relative prices in favour of local infant industry and the scarcity of foreign exchange to finance manufactured imports, Latin American countries were induced to **spontaneously** orient their development model "inwards", through the so-called process of import substitution.

However, in both his 1949 manifesto article and his 1952 study, with greater theoretical precision, Prebisch voices arguments in favour of the adoption of development policies **deliberately** coordinated by the state. Paraphrasing Marx, for Prebisch and ECLAC's economists, it was not enough to interpret the periphery world, it was also necessary to transform it. Under the influence of ECLAC's political economy, the impulse was given such that, from the 1950s onwards, governments of the Latin American periphery began to anchor their long-term public policies in national development programs.

---

8 Coatsworth and Williamson (2002) confirm that the terms of trade of periphery countries had an almost monotonic deterioration trend between 1870 and the beginning of the 1940s. The International Monetary Fund (IMF, 1994: 92) records "a falling trend in commodity prices throughout the post-war period" and also recalls that "the weakening of these prices is not temporary, but secular". Ocampo and Parra (2003), based on the behaviour of relative prices of a significant sample of commodities and price indices, record a deterioration trend (although not continuous) in the terms of trade between 1900 and 2000. In a recent study, Silva, Prado and Torracca (2016) conclude that in the period 1977–2011 the terms of trade tended to be unfavourable to periphery countries.

3 ECLAC's Political Economy and the Developmental State

No doubt remains that the public policies of a national-developmental nature carried out between 1950 and 1980 in several Latin American countries, including Brazil, were enormously influenced by Prebisch's ideas and the fruitful theoretical debate held at ECLAC. It is interesting that, in the last three decades, the basic theoretical aspects and normative implications concerning national-developmentalism have been critically analysed, including in Brazil, in a biased, disparaging and ideologically prejudiced manner. In fact, the national development plans adopted by the governments of Latin American periphery countries, Brazil included, had problems both in design and implementation. However, these plans, which will be discussed in the next subsection, did not faithfully follow the public policy strategies recommended by ECLAC.[9]

As a matter of fact, almost all countries that developed after the English Industrial Revolution, as well as those still seeking to develop, were not guided by the classical liberal recommendation to let the course of development freely follow ("*laissez faire, laissez passer*") the pattern of specialisation given by their natural comparative advantage.[10] On the contrary, countries like the United States and Germany at the end of the 19th century, as well as Japan, South Korea, Taiwan, China and India after the Second World War,[11] were clearly guided, or are still guided, by national-developmental strategies, anchored in the well-known theoretical argument of protecting the infant industry.

This nationalist argument theoretically supports the adoption of protectionist measures not only in favour of a specific industry, as the expression might suggest, but in favour of industrialisation, which is advocated as a sine

9 There is nothing more incorrect, as I will show later, than the assessment by Sachs and Warner (1995: 4–5, emphasis added) that "the biggest historical error of Prebisch's hypothesis was to **recommend** industrialisation through import substitution, protection with tariffs and import quotas, rather than through export promotion".

10 Interestingly, as shown by the English economic historian Leonard Gomes (1987), unlike Smith and Mill, the greatest defenders of free trade in classical political economy, the liberal activism of Ricardo at the international level was restricted to the fight for the elimination of tariffs on wheat imports into England. Ricardo believed that the trade barriers to this product burdened workers' consumption baskets and, therefore, the real cost of local labour, reducing profit rates in the British manufacturing sector. Thus, for Ricardo the principle of comparative advantage was formulated to demonstrate that some trade is always more beneficial than none, while for Mill and later for neoclassical economists, this same principle would come to be used as the main theoretical basis for the defence of unconditional free trade on a global level.

11 See Johnson (1982), Amsden (1989; 2001), Wade (1990) and Chang (2003) and the Inter-American Development Bank (2004).

qua non condition for catching up. It was pioneeringly declared by Alexander Hamilton (1791), Treasury Secretary of the first post-independence North American government, and elaborated by German economist Friedrich List (1841), when both the United States and Germany remained well behind in relation to England, which held the status of the main technological, economic and financial power in the world economy in the mid-19th century.

The argument is grounded in the intuitive idea that, by engaging in unconditional free trade practices, a poor country lagging in relation to the international technological frontier tends to perpetuate its "natural" position of static comparative advantage, based on primary products or traditional manufactures. Theoretically, the argument is quite solid, as it implicitly captures the hypothesis that the traditional agrarian sector, subject to diminishing returns, is unable to absorb the excess labour created by the population growth rate.

Although Hamilton and List did not have precise mastery of these concepts, they were fully aware that only a development strategy commanded by growth and diversification of the industrial sector would have greater potential to accelerate capital accumulation and technical progress, allowing an underdeveloped country to surpass economic and social backwardness. The protection policies they recommended combined several mechanisms to encourage domestic production and promote national market integration, such as customs import tariffs, production and credit subsidies, public investments in infrastructure, agrarian reform, among others. The argument in favour of infant industry protection is theoretically so powerful that it was not only accepted by the classical liberal economist John Stuart Mill (1848),[12] but also received the endorsement of Article XVIII of the General Agreement on Tariffs and Trade (GATT) and remains preserved by the multilateral rules of the World Trade Organisation (WTO). This clause allows poor countries to impose barriers to imports, aiming to promote the infant industry sector.

The favourable position of ECLAC's economists towards the adoption of protectionist policies encouraging industrialisation in the Latin American

---

12 In general, Mill (1848: 381–382) was enthusiastic about free trade practices supported by the principle of comparative advantage. However, he made an exception for the adoption of protectionist barriers so that a backward country could acquire the technological skills and experience already achieved by a more advanced country, whose "superiority over the first, in a branch of production, often comes only from the fact of having started earlier." Mill, nevertheless, suggests much more rational criteria than many other economists also enthusiastic about protectionism, warning that it is essential to select sectors with a real potential for technological absorption and recommending that the protection period does not exceed what is necessary for protected companies to obtain technological dominance under competitive conditions.

periphery was also backed by the argument for the protection of infant industry, the same one that had justified the protectionist policies of the late industrialising countries in relation to British economic development. In both cases, the argument was founded on the evidence that the engagement of late industrializing economies in free trade practices perpetuated the absolute technological gaps of these countries in relation to countries that had developed earlier. The difference was that ECLAC's argument was reinforced by the evidence that, because of unfavourable trade relations for the periphery, trade liberalism with core countries, which at that time also included the United States and several countries in Continental Europe, hindered the process of economic development in Latin America.

The policies recommended by ECLAC were not restricted to the adoption of "industrial policy" programs, defined as a set of public incentives for activities, segments and production chains with greater potential to accelerate capital accumulation, disseminate technical progress and, consequently, promote economic development in the long term.[13] More broadly, ECLAC proposed—correctly, in my opinion—that the governments of the Latin American periphery be guided by economic planning, through the adoption of national development plans.

ECLAC's economists were aware that the Latin American challenge from the second half of the 20th century onwards was much greater than that faced by the lagging national states at the end of the 19th century, especially the United States and Germany. While in these countries the task consisted of allocating public incentives to the promotion of industries and radical innovations already in development there and created by them (such as machinery and mechanical equipment, electricity, automotive and chemical industries, among others),[14] in the Latin American periphery, government support was oriented to promoting industrialisation through import substitution, commanded by private national, foreign or state investments in sectors whose technology was already nearly mature in core countries. In other words, in the first case, government stimuli were directed at genuine innovations; in the second, at the replication of production, consumption and technology patterns in core countries through imitation.

---

13 Although there are several definitions for the term "industrial policy", this concept, adapted from Chang (1994: 60), seems to me to be more aligned with the strategic objectives of a poor or developing country.

14 With respect to the second industrial revolution, see Landes (1969, especially Chapters 4 and 5).

Prebisch, in particular, was aware of the complexity of such a task, as if foreseeing several microeconomic problems that would arise and that would have to be faced and resolved by policymakers throughout the period of realising development programs in Brazil and Latin America. How can we reconcile, for example, industrial technologies created and existing in the centre, characterised by gigantic technical production scales and high capital-labour intensity, with the smaller size of the markets and the enormous availability of idle labour in the periphery?

Afterall, the engineering projects of industrial plants have technical requirements and incorporate technologically indivisible machinery and equipment,[15] resulting from the faster pace of technical progress and the greater potential demand in the centre. Therefore, it is not always possible to adapt the size of these plants to the relatively smaller market dimensions of periphery countries. As assessed by Prebisch (1951: 39–43): "due to the indivisibilities that characterise most equipment, there is no room for combinations other than those resulting from the large industrial centres (…); save for very few exceptions, underdeveloped countries have no alternative but to use this equipment."

Furthermore, Prebisch already had a clear idea that as the industrialisation process in periphery countries accelerates economic development and reduces the pressure imposed by the balance of payments, the increase in per capita income induces changes in the structure of demand, which, by increasing the demand for goods with high-income elasticity, tends to endogenously accelerate the growth of imports, and thus subjects the periphery to the risks of new external restrictions. Prebisch (1951: 25) diagnoses and suggests mechanisms to overcome the problem:

> It is a well-known fact that through industrialisation Latin American countries tend to grow at a faster pace than their exports. Since the capacity to import depends, fundamentally, on these exports, it is obvious that the real income of these countries, in general, tends to grow with greater intensity than the referred to capacity to import. It follows, evidently, that that considerable volume of imports, which grow with the same or greater intensity than real income, could not become effective

15 In the manufacturing system, it is rare to use equipment in which the capital-labour ratio is one to one, such as domestic sewing machines and agricultural harvesters. In modern industrial plants, continuous and large-scale production systems predominate, using technologically indivisible machinery and equipment, as can be observed in the steel, oil extraction and refining, paper and cellulose, automotive, chips and many other industries. For more details, see Scherer and Ross (1990, Chapters 3 and 4).

unless other imports were compressed to the necessary extent so that the total imported did not persistently exceed the capacity to import; or that this excess be covered by foreign direct investment.

As import substitution is the model that guided development on the Latin American continent, especially in Brazil between the 1930s and 1980s, it is worth detailing its long-term dynamics a little more. Armed with greater theoretical precision, Maria da Conceição Tavares (1962), an ECLAC economist, in her classic work "Rise and decline of the import substitution process in Brazil" (*"Auge e declínio do processo de substituição de importações no Brasil"*), identifies three striking aspects of this dynamics.

The first is that, like analysed by Hirschman, import substitution occurs in sequence, starting in the final consumer goods industries and going towards the intermediate and capital goods industries. However, if in the initial stages the substitution is concentrated only in the ranges of final consumer goods, the internal demand for intermediate goods puts excessive pressure on imports of these inputs, "without leaving room for the capital goods indispensable to the expansion of productive capacity" (Tavares, op. cit.: 45). Hence the recommendation, confirmed by the industrialisation experiences of "big" countries like Brazil, Mexico and Colombia, that policymakers define, in each sequence, the main strategic segments of the consumer, intermediate and capital goods industries in which import substitution would be prioritised, thus avoiding an interruption in the continuity of the process due to balance of payments crises.

The second aspect, inherent to the dynamics of the development model in the Latin American periphery, concerns the barriers that stand in the way of the continuity of the process when it requires import substitution to move to industries with greater technological complexity. At this point, it would be necessary to face several overlapping problems, such as the secrets of technological processing (know-how), the greater difficulty in absorbing technologies, the discrepancy between the high production scales required and the size of the market, massive financing, the risks associated with investment projects, etc.

As a result, at this stage, capital accumulation tends to be faster, while the multiplier effect of intra- and intersectoral investments begins to exert even greater upward pressure on imports. Consequently, so that balance of payments crises do not interrupt the process, the growth rate of exports must exceed that of imports and/or there must be compensatory financing from foreign capital (Tavares, op. cit.: 47). It is no coincidence that in the Brazilian experience, in particular, the relative success obtained from the increase in exports of manufactured goods throughout the 1970s was insufficient to finance the faster growth in imports. This factor, along with the two oil shocks and the spike in international interest rates that occurred during this same period, led to enormous external debt, and the economic crisis and stagnation that started in the 1980s.

The last point, and perhaps the most important, is related to the intrinsically closed nature of the import substitution model. No matter how great the effort was to change the composition and export flows in favour of manufactured goods, whose demand is more dynamic in international markets, the advancement of the substitution process brought with it the tendency to reduce the import coefficient, that is, the ratio between total imports and the domestic availability ("apparent consumption") of goods and services.[16] As Tavares (1963: 39) highlights, "the substitution process does not aim to diminish the quantum of global imports, [but that] this decrease, when it occurs, is imposed by the restrictions in the external sector, and is not desired." Thus, as import substitution advances for a set of industries, new industries appear for substitution. Sooner or later, this process tends to exhaustion.[17]

In the Brazilian case, specifically, Tavares (1963: 115–116), armed with abundant empirical evidence, already called attention to the saturation of the process, as early as the beginning of the 1960s. To circumvent any tendency towards structural stagnation in the long run, she suggested "transitioning to a new model of development, truly autonomous, [that is], in which the development impulse arises within the system itself" and in which the dynamic problems already analysed are considered.

The elaboration of the national development plans in some Latin American countries in the 1950s relied on the assistance of ECLAC—the Brazilian Target

16 Apparent consumption concerns the domestic availability of goods and services, being calculated as the sum of domestic output and imports, minus exports. The import coefficient is thus measured as $\left[\frac{Imports}{GDP + Imports - Exports}\right] x\ 100$. Alternatively, the import coefficient can also be calculated as the ratio of imports to GDP.

17 For the interested reader, it is worth reading Albert Hirschman's (1968) survey on the import substitution process in Latin America. Hirschman comments on the relatively early "disillusionment" with which structuralist economists (among them, Raúl Prebisch and Celso Furtado), in the 1960s as well, assessed the experience of this industrialisation model on the continent. Hirschman recognised that the sequential characteristic of the process brought with it its inherent difficulties, such as "the lack of training in technological innovations, the resistance to accelerating investments in the backward-looking production chains [for example, intermediate goods sectors] and the barriers in accessing international markets via manufactured exports" (op. cit.: 32). Hirschman concluded, however, that the import substitution model was the most appropriate path to accelerate Latin American development.

Plan (*"Plano de Metas"*), by the Juscelino Kubitschek government (1956–1960), was one of them. For the reasons already discussed, it would be obvious that, in the spread of policies to stimulate industrialisation, ECLAC's economists included conventional mechanisms to protect infant industry, such as import tariffs, subsidies for production and investment financing, among others. This does not mean, however, that ECLAC's political economy condoned the perpetuation of draconian protection schemes or the total reorientation of Latin American economies towards the domestic market, isolating them from international trade. In his articles with the greatest academic repercussions and normative influence, Prebisch (1949, 1951, 1959) makes hard-hitting caveats regarding the practical implementation of these stimulus policies, which deserve to be reproduced from their original works. They are the following.

3.1 *Role of the State*

Prebisch (1951: 16) recommends that the State, "when designing a development program, channel efforts to create favourable conditions for private initiative, conferring it with indispensable stimuli to reach the proposed targets." Ergo, "the role of the State as an entrepreneur [i.e., the creation of state-owned enterprises] must be strictly restricted to the strategically necessary cases."

3.2 *Role of Foreign Capital*

Prebisch (1951: 9) suggests that the "process of economic development for the Latin American periphery be commanded by national investments, with foreign investments only playing a complementary role." In fact, this strategy, observed in countries such as China and India in recent decades, has not been found to be effective in Latin America since the post-war period, which has brought problems, to this day, of a diverse nature. I will return to this discussion in the next subsection.

3.3 *Agriculture–Industry Relationship*

The ECLAC analysis highlights the enormous structural heterogeneity not only between the centre and periphery, but also within the periphery itself. It combines a primary export sector, which adopts modern techniques and exhibits high levels of productivity, and an infant industrial sector, which adopts traditional techniques and operates with low productivity. Even within the scope of the primary sector, the productivity differential exhibited between the export-oriented agriculture and the traditional agriculture, which adopts technologies typical of subsistence production, was, and still is, significant.

To reverse the low levels of productivity and the stagnation of real wages in this most backward segment, Prebisch (1951) recommends granting incentives aimed at its capitalisation and technological modernisation. However, he warns (op. cit.: 47) that "if the pace of mechanisation goes beyond the absorption capacity [in industrial and other sectors] of the workers released by it, the problem of technological unemployment is additionally created" and migratory processes that end up causing population swelling and precarious social conditions in urban centres.

The problems inherent to the agriculture–industry duality and within agriculture itself were analysed exhaustively by other Latin American economists, such as Celso Furtado, Ignácio Rangel and Fernando Fajnzylber. In Furtado's (1961) analysis, particularly, but also in Rangel's (1957; 1963), this duality is identified as a hinderance to the formation of domestic markets in Latin American periphery countries, and in the case of Brazil, is aggravated by the presence of latifundia, large estates, inherited after almost four centuries of slavery. This problem will be addressed again in the next chapter.

3.4 *Selectivity and the Protection Level for Local Industry*

Prebisch supports the still valid argument that the protection of the local market should not be indiscriminate, but selective. Additionally, its level must not be insufficient nor exaggerated, but only what is necessary to promote the advancement of productivity.[18] In his own words (Prebisch, 1959: 12–13; 20),

> protection per se does not ensure increased productivity; on the contrary, if excessive, it tends to reduce the incentive to produce. Consequently, so that the periphery can retain the fruits of technical progress in primary activities and, especially, in exports, similar progress must emanate from industrial activities, to sustain the advance in productivity and the increase in real wages, expressed in foreign currency. This will allow, in parallel, an increase in real wages in export activities, therefore preventing real income from being transferred to the rest of the world. (…). Massive or indiscriminate protection, which goes beyond the optimal level, can cause serious damage to the competitiveness of exports and foreign trade (…). The requirement that technical progress emanate from industrial activities has been duly emphasised by the infant industry protection argument. [However], as productivity increases, protection must be gradually reduced, until it is completely eliminated.

18 Under competitive conditions, the appropriate import tariff is the one that equalises the external price to the domestic price, which, by definition, is higher in the phase in which the industry is considered infant and until it acquires sufficient scale and competitiveness.

3.5 *Protection via Import Tariffs (or, Alternatively, Subsidies)*[19] *versus Protection through Exchange Rate Depreciation*

Prebisch (1959: 9) emphasises – correctly, in my view –, that instead of adopting a continuous policy of national currency depreciation, the real exchange rate must be maintained at a competitive **level**, that is, the domestic currency must not be overvalued in relation to that of foreign trade partners. For the author:

> a depreciation or devaluation policy must only be used to correct the overvaluation of the domestic currency, and not as an instrument to promote structural changes in the economy. A selective protection policy, as long as it is not exaggeratedly high—otherwise it generates inefficiency—, is a more appropriate instrument. [This is because] the increase in import customs rates, by making foreign products more expensive, and providing that it affects only a small share of total imports, can be offset by increased productivity, without affecting the general level of prices in the economy.

3.6 *Promotion and Competitiveness of Exports*

The allegation that ECLAC's political economy advocates, for the Latin American periphery, the adoption of a development model predominantly focused on the internal market is false. On the contrary, Prebisch insistently alerts us to the importance of export flows from periphery countries to ensure payments for their imports, thus avoiding growing external debt.

The principal reason is obvious: unlike the neoclassical concept, in which savings ("part of the national income not consumed") is understood as a social sacrifice, obtaining favourable trade balances—mutatis mutandis, an objective rightly defended by mercantilists[20]—allows the generation of domestic savings flows sufficient to alleviate external constraints on economic growth.

---

19 In the short term, direct subsidies on production are less harmful to consumers than import tariffs. While this latter increases the prices paid by consumers, by shifting the demand for imported products to the local market, production subsidies provide an identical stimulus to national entrepreneurs but keep the domestic prices paid unchanged. The onus from the subsidy falls entirely on the government (or rather, on society, who pays the taxes). For more on this subject, see Krugman, Obstfeld and Melitz (2015, Chapter 9).

20 Between the mid-18th century and the first half of the 19th, mercantilists suffered systemic attacks from David Hume, Adam Smith and David Ricardo. However, as Thirlwall (2011) recalls, mercantilist policies, which were far from naïve, were strategically important to the national interests of the main European powers in the period.

This happens because the increase in net exports simultaneously leads to an increase in aggregate income and, all else being equal, an expansion in net flows of foreign exchange into convertible currencies.[21] According to Prebisch (1952: 46; 53), "the greater savings margin resulting from [net] export flows can be used to finance imports of capital goods (...). [For this], efforts are required to increase exports and simultaneously to change the composition of imports through internal production, both in industry and agriculture."

He recognises, nevertheless, that increasing the dynamism of exports and changing their composition in favour of manufactured products is no easy task for periphery economies, whose markets, in the initial phases of industrialisation, are relatively small to achieve competitiveness in industries subject to large economies of scale. Even without having adequate analytical tools at his disposal, Prebisch suggests two strategies for changing the profile of exports, both endorsed, even today, by modern international trade theory.

The first is to ensure that the local industry protection apparatus against imports, as it promotes changes in the productive structure, also functions as a mechanism for creating dynamic comparative advantage and for expanding, in the export basket, the share of more technologically sophisticated manufactured goods with greater income elasticity of demand in global markets. Prebisch (1959: 26) states:

> Industrialisation necessitates a dynamic protection policy, which should be continually reformulated with the objective of introducing new changes in the composition of imports, as economic development progresses and disparities in intersectoral income elasticities of demand are reduced. Trade agreements should not crystallise existing situations but be flexible enough to promote such changes in the structure of imports, in a selective, orderly and rational manner.

This strategy of "local protection as export promotion" was mathematically demonstrated by Krugman (1984). For him, in the presence of oligopolies and high economies of scale, protection instruments (for example, government procurement policy) can shift import demand to domestic companies,

21 Note that this strategy was faithfully followed by the Chinese State in the 1980s and 1990s, which has allowed it to embark on and sustain a process of development ever since. However, until the end of the 1990s, the largest source of net foreign exchange in China came from activities in the Special Economic Zones (SEZs), enclaves in which subsidiaries of multinationals and Chinese companies are permitted to produce exclusively for export. Since activities located outside these SEZs have always been subject to government regulatory mechanisms, their foreign trade policy is guided by a model that Feenstra (1998) calls "one country, two systems". See also Inter-American Development Bank (2004).

reducing their marginal costs, to the detriment of foreign companies.[22,23] Economies of scale are the channel that leads to the expansion in sales of local companies, at the expense of foreign companies. They nourish subsequent reductions in marginal and average costs and change the competitive profile of protected industries, until those industries are able to compete in the international market.

The second strategy suggested by Prebisch (1959) is to favour regional integration agreements with trading partners with similar levels of per capita income. Even if the agreement unites "small" and "large" countries, integration makes the bloc's average level of per capita income become closer to the average per capita income of larger countries. Looking at the example of the European integration strategy towards the formation of a common market from the 1950s onwards, Prebisch strongly recommends that governments make efforts to achieve the formation of a common Latin American market. According to the author (op. cit.: 26),

> with the import substitution process, undesirable fluctuations in exports have been even more damaging to sustaining economic development in the Latin American periphery than in the previous model, in which vulnerability was concentrated in the instability of international demand. The common market, by unifying trade within the area, can gradually correct this situation. This regional integration effort can engender the competitiveness of exports in industrialised goods to countries outside the bloc, as the common market offers enormous potential for reducing the costs of these products.

22 Marginal costs are incremental costs ("at the margin"), related to the use of variable production factors (for example, labour), which enable the production of new product units. According to traditional microeconomics, in the short run, the potential productive capacity is considered given, such that from a certain level of the current production of firms, the increase in additional production ("at the margin") involves increasing additional ("marginal") costs, related to the incorporation of variable production factors (such as labour). This theory maintains that, for production flows below the "optimal" level, the firm is capable of expanding current production with falling marginal costs. For above the "optimal" level, marginal costs are increasing. For this reason, in perfectly competitive markets, the firm is only able to produce beyond the "optimal" level if it manages to increase prices. But this behaviour becomes unviable in the long run, since it would be rejected by the existence of competitors capable of producing at lower prices. For more details, see Pindyck and Rubinfeld (2014, Chapters 7 and 8).

23 Note that Krugman assumes that local firms, before protection and even operating under oligopoly conditions (this is, having market power to set their prices), would be producing below the "optimal" level. Ergo, in the absence of protection (i.e., with import tariffs equal to zero), domestic firms are unable to face competition from imported products.

This new literature on international trade is explicit: the potential to achieve competitive scales in the export of industrialised goods, whose efficiency depends on optimising the required huge economies of scale, is greater, the larger the domestic market. The consolidation of a common market (like the European Union) aspires for no other objective than to maximise gains through economies of scale among member countries, through the expansion of "reciprocal demand" (to use John Stuart Mill's expression) between "large" and "small" economies.

In two seminal articles, which contributed to his winning the Nobel Prize, Krugman (1980, 1981) formally demonstrated that, in the presence of economies of scale, product differentiation and competitive oligopoly ("monopolistic competition"), (i) "the possibility of becoming a large-scale exporter of manufactured goods depends on the size of the domestic market" [Krugman (1980: 36)];[24] (ii) "the majority of global trade is commanded by countries with similar factor endowments" [Krugman (1980: 50)], that is to say, countries rich in physical and human capital command exports of industrialised goods, which intensively incorporate these factors; and (iii) "among countries with similar levels of per capita income and demand patterns [on average], the largest share of trade is of the intra-industrial type, in other words, between similar industrialised goods" [Krugman (1981: 50)], but not identical, because they are subject to product differentiation by model, brand, quality standard, etc.[25]

Hence, the new theory of international trade ("new trade theory") suggests that, to maximise competitiveness in the export of manufactured products, subject to economies of scale and product differentiation, the most strategically convenient model of international insertion for developing countries is, without prejudice to multilateralism, to deepen regional integration[26] with

24 The author recognises that, despite having less formal precision, this conclusion had already been pioneeringly demonstrated by Staffan Linder (1961).

25 Like the intra-industrial trade of French, German, Spanish and Swedish automobiles within the European Union. Examples like this extend to intra-industrial trade of other differentiated manufactured goods, as can be seen in other regional integration experiences (whether via free trade areas or customs unions) such as NAFTA (North American Free Trade Agreement, currently known as USMCA – United States-Mexico-Canada Agreement), ASEAN (Association of Southeast Asian Nations), Mercosur (Southern Common Market), etc.

26 The literature on international trade distinguishes different stages of regional integration, from the simplest to the most ambitious. The simplest is the free trade area, in which trade barriers (tariff and non-tariff) are eliminated between member countries, but each of them continues to apply different import tariffs on other countries outside the bloc; next is the customs union, in which, in addition to eliminating trade barriers, a common external tariff (CET) is imposed on countries not participating in the bloc; then there

countries that have similar levels of per capita income. This theory, thus, corroborates Prebisch's recommendation that the most appropriate strategy of trade insertion for Latin American countries was, and still is, without undermining multilateralism, to favour regional integration agreements between themselves; agreements in place with rich countries must include exception clauses that preserve the possibility to accelerate industrial development.[27]

Strictly speaking, the economic history of Latin America in the post-war era shows that none of the recommendations made by Prebisch were stringently followed by the governments responsible for implementing development programmes on the continent. Even taking into account that monitoring these programmes involves, in practice, much more art than science and that errors can be corrected along the way, the fact is that very little was done to fix them in time.[28]

In the case of Brazil, for example, in contrast to the successful experiences of East Asia, notably South Korea and Taiwan, the main development plans, from the Target Plan (1956–1960) until the end of the 1970s, lacked selectivity, relied on exaggerated mechanisms to protect the domestic market, reinforced dependence on foreign investment, technology and financing, and so on.[29] This shows that, if the theoretical arguments favouring the adoption of development plans coordinated by the State, with the objective of sustaining

---

is the common market, which occurs when, in addition to the elimination of the just stated trade barriers, there is free movement of productive factors (capital and labour) between the bloc's countries. The economic union is reached when, in addition to all the previous eliminated barriers, a single currency begins to circulate among the member countries, monetary policies are adopted and regulated by a unified central bank, and common rules regarding the management of fiscal policy are created. Among the recent experiences with regional integration, the United States, Mexico and Canada Agreement (USMCA) is an example of a free trade area, Mercosur is still, despite its name, an incomplete customs union, the European Union is a common market, and the Euro Zone illustrates an experience, still in consolidation, of an economic union. For more details, see Hoekman and Kostecki (2009, Chapter 10).

27 This means that, even today for Brazil, it is more strategic to deepen regional integration agreements with other Latin American countries than with the United States. In the case of the European Union, the gains from integration could be more auspicious, since there is enormous potential for intraindustrial trade with the richest countries and with other members, whose per capita incomes are closer to Brazilian per capita income.

28 See two excellent books by Fernando Fajnzylber, *"La Industrialización Trunca de América Latina"* (1983) and *"Industrialización en América Latina: de la 'Caja Negra' al 'Casillero Vacío'"* (1990).

29 For a comparative analysis of the development plans in South Korea and Brazil, see Moreira (1995). For the Brazilian case, read Suzigan and Furtado (2006, especially pp. 169–174).

a successful catching-up trajectory, are irrefutable, then the greatest challenge, in practice, is to implement them and achieve good results, since they are subject to the historical, political and cultural idiosyncrasies of each country. The State's biggest challenge, in any capitalist formation, is to circumvent the private lobbies that, while aiming at the unproductive appropriation of income (rent seeking), pressure the State to perpetuate the public benefits granted.[30]

Even so, as already anticipated in the Introduction, in spite of the enormous static inefficiency in the microeconomic allocation of resources, of which resulted in a domestic industrial production system with high prices and quality standards below international standards—save for exceptional cases—, there is no doubt that Brazil managed to maintain a successful catching-up path between 1950 and 1980. This trajectory, though, was interrupted, followed by a long process of stagnation that has lasted since the beginning of the 1980s.

From the 1980s on, with the rise of neoliberalism and the overwhelming criticism of the import substitution model in Latin America, the main ECLAC economists, armed with a neo-Schumpeterian microeconomic theoretical apparatus, began to make a critical assessment of development policies in the region. They compared what was effectively done with what had been proposed, ultimately, suggesting a course correction. In confrontation with the neoliberal view that was becoming hegemonic, ECLAC initiated the formulation of neostructuralist theoretical models. Such a change was not able to restore the normative influence in the conception of public policies in Latin America, but ECLAC managed to keep its academic prestige unscathed.

4 ECLAC's Neostructuralism and the Centre-Periphery Model Today

At the beginning of the 1980s, most Latin American countries were already facing difficulties in accessing international liquidity and in having the availability of currency necessary to pay the external debt services that had accumulated since the previous decade. With the exception of Argentina and Chile, which had adopted radical but unsuccessful liberalising reforms in the 1970s, the other countries on the continent had not yet embarked on this path.

Even before the recommendations for neoliberal reforms—anchored in the precepts of the so-called Washington Consensus, which I will discuss in Chapter 10—had become a widespread pressure mechanism of multilateral institutions, ECLAC's most prominent economists, such as Jorge Katz, Osvaldo Sunkel, Fernando Fajnzylber and Ricardo Ffrench-Davis, equipped with more

30 Similar arguments can be found in the study by Peter Evans (1992), "The State as problem and solution: predation, embedded autonomy, and structural change".

refined microeconomic and macroeconomic instruments, began to undertake a critical assessment of the import substitution model in Latin American, identifying principal errors in the policies adopted and proposing a course correction.[31]

The purpose of this critical rewiew of ECLAC was to face the adverse international context and definitively resolve the problems relating to the external debt crisis and high inflation. They also intended to adjust public policies in order to overcome the stagnation process and resume, as soon as possible, a catching up trajectory on the continent. But let us be clear: policy adjustment did not mean unconditional adherence to neoliberalism; the suggestions were not to throw the sick baby out with the bathwater, but to remove it from the water, medicate it and recreate the conditions for its healthy growth.

Fajnzylber (1983), in his "*La Industrialización Trunca de América Latina*", provides us with one the most comprehensive studies on the policies and results of import substitution in Latin America. It forces us to agree with the author that most of the problems identified there are closely linked to the frailty of the policies adopted since the 1950s. Even though they were able to promote accelerated economic growth until the end of the 1970s, they ended up generating a truncated and incomplete industrial system ("*industrialización trunca*"), most of all in continental-sized countries, such as Brazil, Mexico and Colombia.

Among the main problems analysed by Fajnzylber, all resulting from the chosen policy options, these deserve mention: (i) the perpetuation of indiscriminate and non-selective protectionist practices ("frivolous protectionism"); (ii) the absence of an endogenous core capable of generating and disseminating technical progress in the economic system; (iii) the leadership of subsidiary companies of multinationals in industries with greater potential for technological development, which resulted in a lack of autonomy with respect to investment, innovation and financing decisions and the proliferation of a local business community with a greater aptitude for copying and reproducing than for producing genuine innovations; and (iv) the precarious relationship between agricultural and industry. With the exception of this last problem that has been commented on previously, it is worth analysing briefly the issues associated with the others.

Fajnzylber uses the expression "frivolous protectionism" to demarcate the position that, despite the liberal objection, the consolidation of industrialisation requires classic mechanisms to protect the infant industry. The successful experiences of industrialisation in the so-called "Asian tigers" (notably, South Korea and Taiwan) teaches us that government stimuli, such as discriminatory

31 For the reader interested in the history of Latin American structuralist thought, consult the book by Di Filippo (2021).

import tariffs and other mechanisms to protect local industry, must be applied temporarily and with sufficient intensity to enable technological learning and the achievement of competitive production scales to sell in both the domestic market and the international. This was not what happened in Latin American countries with greater market potential.

In Brazil, in particular, the use and abuse of exaggerated protection and indiscriminate granting of public benefits engendered, in fact, a relatively diversified industrial structure. However, without the pressure for economic performance to be linked to requirements for increasing productivity, reducing unit cost and international quality standards, such an industrial structure, apart from honourable exceptions, proved to be uncompetitive in successfully penetrating global markets.

The combination of high local protection and excessive leniency towards foreign direct investment made it unfeasible to both obtain technological autonomy in the industries responsible for the majority of technical progress and reduce the relative share of manufactured products with high income elasticity of demand in the import basket. Fajnzylber (1983) rightly considers that the dialectical interaction of these two factors impeded the import substitution process, already in the intermediate phase in the 1970s, from transitioning to an industrialisation model commanded by the metal-mechanical (which encompasses the capital goods and automotive industries) and electronics complexes. These complexes, by leading the generation and diffusion of technological innovations, would have been capable of making the pace of investment, capital accumulation and technological progress endogenous to long-term economic growth. In other words, because it was not able to promote an endogenous core that radiated technical progress, industrialisation in Latin America remained truncated and incomplete.

As the author recalls, even in Brazil, the developing country most advanced in industrial growth and diversification between the 1950s and 1970s, this set of key industries was headed by multinational companies.[32] In their countries of origin, the enormous structural barriers to the entry of potential competitors, dictated by the mastery of production techniques and by the significant minimum efficient scales of production required, caused oligopolistic rivalry between established companies to drive and realize technical progress in a Schumpeterian process of creative destruction.

In contrast, in Latin America, the high levels of protection ended up attracting an excess of foreign subsidiaries to those key industries, especially in the

32 Fajnzylber (1983: 151) records that, in the period 1950–1978, the Brazilian industrial sector presented the highest average annual growth rate in Latin America (8.5% against 6.5% for a group of 19 countries on the continent).

sectors that produce durable consumer goods, including automotive and electronics, where companies compete on product differentiation rather than prices. In the Brazilian case, for instance, the exaggerated protection in these sectors ended up housing an excess of many foreign companies and perpetuating very high prices in relation to the international market. As highlighted by Fajnzylber (1983: 192), although operating with high unit costs, due to excessive market fragmentation and reduced production scales, "in the highly protected markets of Latin American, entrepreneurs were free to transfer to the prices, the higher costs associated with the partial use of their production facilities".

Fajnzylber (op. cit.: 176–177) is correct in claiming that, given the extremely permissive attitude of the various social actors in the Latin American periphery, the leadership of multinationals in the main sectors that radiate technical progress ultimately inhibits the development of national entrepreneurship capabilities to "adapt, innovate and compete internationally in a significant range of strategic sectors". It is also correct to reinforce that this attitude does not result from any external pressure or conquest on the part of these global companies, but from the "normative omission of internal agents and the set of social forces that were reflected in public action".

Notwithstanding, ECLAC's economists' critical assessment of the development policies in Latin American, especially those applied at the height of the import substitution model in the 1970s, in no way endorses unconditional adherence to the precepts of neoliberalism, precepts that would ultimately become the guide for the economic policies adopted in the region from the 1990s on. Although ECLAC has since proposed the remodelling of public policies with a view to putting the region's economies back on the path of sustained development, its recommendations have never supported overly rapid trade liberalisation ("shock therapy"), the opening to short-term external financial capital flows, the minimal state, nor even limiting public policies to only correcting market failures.[33] Hence, its public policy proposals were, and still are, completely at odds with the neoliberalism agenda.[34]

33 Neoclassical liberal thought only allows state intervention in situations in which free competition, due to imperfections in the functioning of markets, is unable to produce optimal results in the allocation of productive resources and the distribution of national income. In these cases, the adoption of public policies aimed at correcting market failures is accepted. This subject will be discussed in Chapter 11.

34 The only document in which ECLAC flirts with neoliberalism ideas, yet does not manage to incorporate the set of reforms suggested by this ideology, is *"El regionalismo abierto en América Latina y el Caribe: La integración económica al servicio de la transformación productiva con equidad"*, from 1994, under the coordination of the then executive secretary Gert Rosenthal. In it, some propositions are anchored in the neoclassical approach to market failures. The interested reader can consult ECLAC (1994).

From the abundant theoretical and empirical literature on development produced at ECLAC since 1990, three points should be highlighted: (i) the recognition that the remarkable economic growth observed in the region in the period 1950–1980 was unable to reduce social inequality and eliminate poverty; (ii) the reaffirmation of the centre-periphery model—which sometimes reappears under the name North-South model—on the basis of which the explanatory factors for the persistence of high relative gaps in productivity and per capita income in Latin American economies are investigated; and (iii) the diagnosis that the industrialisation process in the Latin American periphery, in addition to being truncated and incomplete, was prematurely interrupted more than four decades ago. This is why overcoming the prolonged economic stagnation in the region, which persists until today, simultaneously depends on exploring the existing potential for industrial diversification through structural change, increasing investment rates, incorporating technical progress, reducing social inequality and respecting environmental sustainability.

As Fajnzylber (1990: 12) shows, no Latin American country managed to combine an increase in per capita income with a reduction in the level of social inequality ("the empty locker"—"*el casillero vacío*", according to the author) in the period 1965–1984. Argentina and Uruguay, for example, were exceptions in which greater social equity was preserved, but in which per capita income growth was less than 2.4% p.a. Brazil, Mexico and Colombia, on the other hand, exhibited significant growth rates in per capita income, but without having managed to reduce social inequality. The author (op. cit.: 65) points out that the persistence of enormous social inequality in most Latin American countries has its roots in the maintenance of a rentier elite, which "does not seem to care about growth, nor construction projects for the future, but with the preservation of the status quo."

This state of affairs is not irremediable. ECLAC's main orientation, at a time when most of the continent's economies were plagued by external debt crises and chronic inflation, was to restore macroeconomic stability and channel efforts to the creation and diffusion of technical progress such that it replaced the mere imitation of imported technologies, in such a way that the increase in productivity could sustain the expansion of the share of real wages in national income. For ECLAC, it is not the indiscriminate adherence to the precepts of neoliberalism that ensures such results, but the redefinition of the trade protection structure, combined with an industrial policy in which innovation begins to be formulated in a systemic way, i.e., coordinated with other spheres of public policy, such as science and technology, education and training, tax, social and macroeconomic policies.

These are, in fact, the fundamentals of the public policies contained in the influential document "*Transformación Productiva com Equidad*", released by ECLAC in 1990. It proposes "to combine macroeconomic management with sectoral policies, as well as integrating short and long-term policies" (op. cit.: 14–15). With respect to industrial policy, "**gradual and selective** trade opening, the full exports promotion, the incorporation and diffusion of technical progress and support for small and medium-sized enterprises" are recommended (ibid.: 17, emphasis added). However, given the evidence that economic growth does not necessarily ensure a reduction in social inequality, it cautions that "the imperative of equity requires that productive transformation be accompanied by redistributive measures" (ibid.: 15). Anticipating the imperativeness of what would later become unpostponable, it also proposes "the incorporation of the environmental variable into the development strategy" (ibid.: 138).

In a recent document, ECLAC (2020) rightly reiterates that, once the COVID-19 pandemic has been overcome, the significant technological gap of the Latin American periphery from the international frontier could act as a structural barrier to sustaining economic growth in the region. In this document, the institution (op. cit.: Ch. 11) suggests that, in addition to the technological gap, the Latin American periphery must also face the challenge of making its growth rates compatible with two additional gaps: social inequality and the physical limits imposed by environmental restrictions.

Regarding the technological gap, I remind the reader that, as analysed in Chapter 2, Thirlwall's law postulates that in the long run the growth rate of the periphery ($PIB\ \dot{Periphery}$) in relation to the core ($PIB\ \dot{Core}$) depends on the relationship between the income elasticities of demand for exports and imports from the periphery bloc. It is possible to refine equation (2.1), also analysed in the previous chapter, by adding a normative factor, indicated by the expression "development policies" in parentheses in the following equation:

$$\frac{PIB\ \dot{Periphery}_{BP}}{PIB\ \dot{Core}} = \frac{\text{Income elasticity of demand for exports from the periphery}}{\text{Income elasticity of demand for imports from the periphery}}\left(\text{Development policies}\right) \qquad (2.3)$$

To interpret equation (2.3), take the case of Brazil. In the long run, the Brazilian economy's growth rate compatible with its balance of payments (left side of the equation) is limited by the relationship between the income elasticities of demand for exports and imports (right side of the equation, except for the term in parentheses), which, in turn, reflects the current productive structure. According to the results reported in Chapter 2, the income elasticities of demand for Brazilian exports and imports corresponded to 1.74 and 2.01, respectively, in the period 1995–2013.[35] Thus, more robust economic growth rates would tend to be short-lived in Brazil, as they lead to a faster increase in imports than in exports, thereby exposing the country to unsustainable current account deficits in its balance of payments.

Observe also that, as suggested by the term in parentheses in equation (2.3), the ratio between the income elasticities of demand for exports and imports in Brazil is **currently** less than unity. This is because it results from the choices of the short and long-term economic policies adopted in the **previous** period, that is, in the period referring to the estimated series, 1995–2013. As I pointed out in the Introduction to this book, in economics you reap what you sow: the economic performance of a country, expressed in the growth rates of per capita income and the living conditions of its population, results from the choice and combination of public policies adopted in the past. From the perspective, Brazilian economic growth is subject to severe structural constraints.

Not all is lost, however: the expression in parentheses in equation (2.3) suggests as well that appropriate development policies, implemented **from today onwards**, can modify the ratio between Brazil's income elasticities of demand for exports and imports in the **future**, altering their quotient to values above unity. Consequently, more robust growth rates that would position Brazil on a sustained trajectory of catching up, in this and the coming decades, would become possible.[36]

5 Conclusion

The centre-periphery model, far from opposing them, complements the canonical theses of classical developmentalism, according to which the process of economic development is driven by industrialisation and involves structural change whereby productive resources are reallocated from low-productivity sectors to higher productivity ones. By placing greater emphasis not only on economic, historical and social specificities of Latin American periphery countries, but also on the role of planning and public policies in overcoming

---

35 Given the slowdown, crisis and stagnation of the Brazilian economy, which have all persisted since 2014, there is no reason to expect that there have been significant changes in these results since.

36 See ECLAC (2020) and Porcile (2021).

underdevelopment, the centre-periphery model is more advanced in relation to classical developmentalism.

Being an institution for transmitting structuralist ideas in Latin America, ECLAC formulated (and still does) theoretical models of development and elaborated (and continues to do so) recommendations for public policies aimed at promoting and sustaining economic development on the continent. Although the prescribed development policies defend protectionist measures in favour of local industry, conceived under the scrutiny of the theoretical argument for the protection of infant industry, the academic works of ECLAC's principal economists (particularly Prebisch) do not corroborate the criticism that ECLAC's political economy supports a closed development model, entirely focused on the internal market. The range of prescribed policies have included the establishment of selective and moderate protection, measures to minimise technological dependence on multinational companies, the promotion of manufactured exports, among others.

If most of these suggestions were not followed to the letter by Latin American governments, it is proof that, as the popular saying asserts, what you do is what you are: in practice, development policies are influenced by diverse factors, such as pressure from interest groups (lobbies), the power of political oligarchies, the change of governments, cultural aspects, the prevalence of dogmatic thinking, etc.[37] The continent's countries were able to maintain an accelerated pace of economic growth in the period 1950–1980, but at the expense of a heterogeneous, incomplete and microeconomically inefficient industrial system, apart from a few exceptions.

Nevertheless, the finding that, since the beginning of the 1980s, the majority of Latin American countries have been recording low growth rates and secular stagnation in labour productivity does not justify the neglect that has been given to development policies and long-term economic planning on the continent. In any country, developed or not, development policies are subject to hits and misses because they involve a complexity of actors in economic and social interrelations. Precisely for this reason, ECLAC's economists have warned governments that the mistakes of the past can serve as a practical guide for correcting future development policies.

---

37 The author thanks André Lara Resende for remembering this last factor.

CHAPTER 4

Underdevelopment, Development, and Stagnation: Celso Furtado's Theoretical Relevance

1 Introduction

Celso Furtado was one of the founding fathers of ECLAC. He formed part of the institute's research team, which in 1948 comprised a "technical staff that did not surpass ten people".[1] This was even before Raúl Prebisch was appointed as the institute's second executive secretary. The reader may be wondering: why were Furtado's theoretical contributions on underdevelopment, development and stagnation not presented in the previous chapter? Caetano Veloso, a Brazilian songwriter, provides the clue: in his song "*Milagres do povo*", he states that "the one who discovered Brazil was the black man who saw cruelty directly in front of him"; mutadis mutandis, I would say that Furtado "discovered" a theoretically innovative method of analysing economic problems, having been perhaps the Latin American economist who gave the greatest emphasis to the interpenetration of historical and social factors in the dynamics of economic development.

For all his theoretical-methodological originality, Furtado was an "ECLACian", yet "non-ECLACian". Indeed, he did not consider the ECLAC school of thought to have a unified body of theory. On this subject, he writes the following in a letter to Professor Joseph L. Love, dated December 22, 1982, and published in the "Intellectual Correspondence", a posthumous collection of his letters to politicians and intellectuals around the world, which was released in 2021:

> It makes little sense to me to speak of the ECLAC school. On the one hand, there is the work of Prebisch, and on the other, there is what could be called the Latin American structuralist school. The structuralists were characterised by the methods they used (they favoured macroanalysis), valuing the institutional and seeking interdisciplinarity. But the most significant element of this school was the development of works that did not have much in common, and as such exerted little influence on one another. (Furtado, 2021; 330)[2]

1 This information is provided by Furtado himself (1985: 54), in his book "*A Fantasia Organizada*".

2 I thank Rosa Freire D'Aguiar for informing me of this detail.

 DOI:10.1163/9789004734296_007

At any rate, although he did put restrictions on the main theses of ECLAC, as clearly demonstrated in his book "The Organised Fantasy" (1985), like Smith, Marx, Keynes, Schumpeter, Prébisch and Kaldor, who all created autonomous schools of thought, Furtado was Furtado: He did economic theory on development and underdevelopment in his own way and independently.

In this chapter, I analyse Furtado's main theses on underdevelopment, development, and stagnation. In Section 2, I seek to demonstrate how his theoretical propositions on those topics remain relevant for explaining, albeit partially, the stagnation of the Brazilian economy in the last four decades. In Section 3, I discuss how his seminal analysis of the national resource abundance problem in Venezuela, at the end of the 1950s, allowed him to elaborate a refined theoretical framework concerning the phenomena that would later come to be known as the "Dutch disease" and the "resource curse". To round off the chapter, Section 4 contains some brief conclusions.

2 Underdevelopment, Development and Stagnation under Furtado's View

There is no doubt that, although Furtado embraces most of the theses of classical developmentalists, he has reservations on the main hypothesis of Nurkse (1951: 16), also a classical developmentalist, who asserts that "the limited size of the domestic market in an underdeveloped country constitutes an obstacle to development". In a critical essay on Nurkse (1951), Furtado (1952: 10) states that "a market is small in relation to something; and, in the case in question, the market in underdeveloped countries is small in relation to the type of equipment used in developed countries. This is not a fundamental difficulty of economic development, but rather an accidental one." Like Hirschman (1958), Furtado considers the main obstacle to the formation and diversification of a market, which is effectively limited but potentially exists in countries in the early stages of development, is the lack of initiative to integrate and explore it.

In addition, the central theoretical proposition that permeates all of Furtado's academic work is that economic development is strongly conditioned by the historical evolution of each country, which, in turn, influences the dynamics of socio-economic relations, including the formation and diversification of a thriving domestic market. In the above-mentioned essay (op. cit.: 13), Furtado argues that "the problem of economic development has to do with the general problem of social change in our society, and it cannot be fully understood without the historical content". In his classic book "Development and Underdevelopment", from 1961, he reiterates that "a theory of development which limits itself to reconstructing, in an abstract model—derived from a limited historical experience—, the connections of a given structure cannot claim a high degree of generality" (p. 147).

In a development theory framework, which builds upon the specific feature of periphery countries having been historically formed as underdeveloped economies, Furtado (1961) identifies three models, each of them by-products of the industrial capitalism originating in Europe after the Industrial Revolution.

The first, typically European model, emerged from the gradual disorganisation of the feudal mode of production, culminated with the Industrial Revolution and spread to the rest of Continental Europe between the 17th and 19th centuries. This model replicates a typical Lewis-style development process, with the release of surplus labour at a faster rate than the absorption in the initial phase, followed by its exhaustion as soon as the disintegration of pre-capitalist relations becomes evident. From then on, the dynamics of productivity growth becomes endogenously dependent on the generation and diffusion of technical progress.

The second consisted of exporting the European model to Australia, Canada and the United States. The populations that emigrated to those places took the technological base and European consumption patterns with them, in such a way that, when faced with the abundance of natural resources, allowed these "colonies" to reach high levels of productivity and income in comparison with other European countries. For this group, Furtado is right to reject the hypothesis that the phenomenon of underdevelopment is adequate to characterise the situation prevailing in these countries in the phase before the onset of their respective industrialisation processes but is appropriate for the case of the periphery between the end of the 19th century and the middle of the last century. He says (op. cit.: 161, emphasis added): "Underdevelopment is an autonomous **historical** process, and not a stage through which economies that have already reached a higher level of development have necessarily passed."

Branching off from the European model, the third model of industrial capitalism gives rise to the phenomenon of underdevelopment. For Furtado (op. cit.: 171), this "does not constitute a necessary stage in the formation of modern capitalist economies, [but] is a particular process, resulting from the penetration of modern capitalist enterprises into archaic structures". Although this phenomenon has manifested itself in different forms in the global sphere, I will keep to its particularities in Brazil.

The Portuguese colonisation in Brazil was radically different from the British colonization of the United States. In the latter, access to abundant and fertile land, especially in New England, was free and exploitation of this land took the form of settlement colonies, whose cultivation was geared towards community subsistence. Even the southern region of the United States, whose colonisation was similar to that of Brazil's—both being organised as agrarian economies for the export of agricultural products on a large scale and based on slave labour coming from Africa—took a different historical path. In the United States, after independence, the country's dichotomy ended up leading to a bloody civil war in the mid-19th century, which, while not putting an end to the conservative southern social stratification, gave rise to the democratic idea and the project of creating an industrial capitalist nation. As Furtado (1992: 74) points out, "the contrast with Latin American countries is blatant, because in these countries, after gaining political independence, the institutions that were created (being exactly copied from the United States) had no roots in local tradition".

In Brazil, the capitalist development that began after the Abolition of Slavery was *sui generis*, being quite distinct from the classical experiences. At the end of the 19th century, the expansion of coffee monocultures for export, whose agricultural frontier extended from Rio de Janeiro to the São Paulo region, exposed the problems arising from the insufficient labour supply, a problem which had become apparent since the extinction of the slave trade in 1850. The "labour problem",[3] which constitutes one of the fundamental landmarks of the transition from the colonial-type economy to a capitalist economy in Brazil, was eventually resolved through an enormous influx of European wage workers.

Thus, between the end of the 19th century and the beginning of the 20th, as an extension of what came to be called the coffee complex, Brazilian industry gave rise to an integrated and diversified system of economic activities, organised, subordinated and dependent on the production of coffee for export. Within this complex, it had, for example, its own production, financing and marketing of coffee; industries for food, textile and rudimentary equipment used in coffee production; a rail system and basic infrastructure for its storage and transportation; a banking system to finance all these activities and a mechanism for reproducing the capital accumulation in the coffee industry; and so forth.[4]

In the initial phase, in which the growth dynamics was directed "outwards", that is, conditioned by the fluctuations in the demand for coffee and other agricultural products in the international market, the growth of the manufacturing sector proved to be incapable of driving an autonomous process of industrialization in view of two factors: first, the specific nature of the industrial

3 See Furtado (1959, Ch. 23).

4 See Silva (1976).

formation process; and second, the duality present in the evolution of Brazil's productive and social structures.

With respect to the first factor, Brazil inverts the classic industrialisation model. Due to a shortage of labour, the industrial sector embedded in the coffee economy initially had to bear the burden of high real wages. Only after the 1930s, when industrialisation gained momentum and the transport and communications systems expanded, did the fluidity of the labour market begin to shift the workforce, now with unlimited supply, to regions with higher wages. As Furtado (1961: 225) points out, despite the growth in productivity, "the practical consequence of such a situation was that real wages in industries tended to remain stable throughout all subsequent development [until the late 1950s]", so that most of the increase in income was absorbed by profits.

Regarding the dual character of the economy, which is defined by Ignácio Rangel (1957: 298) as a relationship of co-existing duplicity in "permanent conflict" in the productive, social or institutional structure, I focus on the dualities that help to explain, at least in part, the persistence of regional imbalances, social inequality, and the structural stagnation of the current Brazilian economy. The first of these dualities is related to the fact that, since the country developed as a periphery economy and, therefore, dependent on technologies and consumption patterns emanating from the core, the dynamics of capital accumulation is concentrated in the sectors of consumer durables destined for the upper income strata of the social pyramid. This contributes not only to delaying the expansion and diversification of a mass consumption market, but also to increasing levels of regional and social concentration of income in Brazil. As Furtado summarises in his "Theory and Policy of Economic Development" (1967: 185):

> Under the conditions of underdevelopment, this process [the diffusion of technical progress, accompanied by an increase in productivity] is only fully accomplished for a small portion of the population. The remainder of the population is inversely affected because of its integration in the monetary economy and in the manufactured goods market. The weight of the structural surplus of labor means that the penetration of sophisticated techniques in activities linked to the population as a whole results in disproportionate growth in the income of rich groups, whose spending must, as a consequence, increase more than proportionally to continue diffusing new techniques. It is possible, therefore, to conclude that the introduction of new patterns of consumption among rich groups

> constitutes the true primary factor (along with state action) in the growth of underdeveloped economies in the post-import substitution phase.

Armed with empirical evidence, he concludes (op. cit.: 184):

> The practical impossibility of investing in the part of the productive apparatus that is intended to satisfy the needs of the masses emerges. Since it is through the increase in the capital coefficient that technological progress is diffused in the forms of production, it will not be surprising that an intense transplantation of industrial activities linked to the wealthy minority corresponds to a slow diffusion of modern techniques in the other segments of the productive system. This explains why the acceleration of GDP growth has, in some places, led to an absolute drop in the standard of living of large masses of the population, as occurred in Mexico in the 1940s and 1950s, and in the Northeast of Brazil in the 1960s.

The second duality, also highlighted by Rangel (1963) in his classic work "The Brazilian Inflation", and still immanent in Brazilian development, concerns not only the interrelationships between agriculture and the industrial and services sectors, but also the dual structure present within agriculture itself. I will start with the latter.

Mutatis mutandis, the duality of the agrarian structure, although having diminished, is still present. Its origin is found in the era of colonisation, when agriculture was organised into large rural areas (latifundia), which took the form of trading companies involved in the export of monocultures. As Furtado (1961: 228) points out, the evolution of the Brazilian agrarian structure is not conditioned by the relative scarcity of land, a factor which is still abundant in Brazil, but by the "scarcity of capital and entrepreneurial capacity".

In the historical evolution of Brazil, small farms, focused on subsistence production, emerged on the fringes of the latifundia, as those large estates proved incapable of absorbing the surplus of the rural population. Even when the first industrial enterprises were born, under the aegis of the coffee exporting complex at the end of the 19th century, there was no massive displacement, as already mentioned, of labour from the other regions of Brazil to the Southeast. Such a displacement would only occur, albeit chaotically, in the second half of the last century, with the advancement of industrialisation and urbanisation.

The notable exception to the latifundium rule were the settlements based on family agriculture, composing small- and medium-sized farms in the South of the country. However, these were not driven by economic reasons, but by the political interest of the Brazilian government to complete the occupation of the national territory. It was only during the 19th century, with the growth in the demand for food from the United States, that immigration from Central Europe was stimulated in this region. Although initially without great success, the structure of land ownership in the Brazilian South allowed, in the following century, significant advances in productivity and a more equitable intra-regional distribution of rural income.

After 1930, with the decline of the coffee economy and the advancement of industrialisation, the duality of the Brazilian agrarian structure was accentuated. Despite the remarkable economic growth observed until the end of the 1970s, the industrial sector, predominantly using labour-saving technologies, was unable to absorb the rural population surplus. Although the growth in the demand for food, resulting from the accelerated pace of urbanisation, has stimulated the extension of the agricultural frontier to the rest of the national territory, the colossal abundance of land and the unlimited supply of labour acted as inhibitors to the absorption of modern techniques. With the exception of the agricultural export sector and the small- and medium-sized farms in the South, which operated with high levels of productivity, there was a devastating precariousness in the living conditions of rural workers in the poorest regions of the country, especially in the Northeast.

With the duality inherent in the structures of production and employment in the agrarian sectors, on the one hand, and the industrial and services sectors, on the other, this helps to explain the increase in income concentration and the disorderly migratory flows, which led to the spread of *favelas* and the deterioration of living conditions of the poor in urban centres. Without denying that this situation worsened in the years of the so-called economic "miracle" (1967–1973), either because of the repression of unions or due to the wage squeeze imposed by the economic policy of the military dictatorship, Furtado (1992) still attributes one of the causes for the secular concentration of national income to the duality in the Brazilian agrarian structure. He says (op. cit.: 174):

> Brazil's agrarian structure is of significant importance to understanding the strange combination between abundance of natural resources and persistence of low wages. The latifundia-minifundia (large-small farms) binomial enables Brazil's arable land to be underutilised in large areas and, at the same time, forces the rural population to swell in reduced spaces; the appropriation of arable land by a small minority forces the rural masses to accept very low wages in order to survive. Thus, the agrarian structure, on the one hand, and industrial technology that generates

> few jobs, on the other, operate in a way that concentrates income and excludes the masses from the benefits of development. The intensification of demographic growth made possible by advances in prophylactic techniques has aggravated the situation of the masses in rural areas as well as in urban centres.

From the 1970s on, the Brazilian government did begin to adopt a bolder agricultural policy, introducing several measures, especially in the areas of credit (through subsidies and diversification of financial instruments, including derivatives) and minimum price guarantees. This is also the time when the Brazilian Agricultural Research Corporation (*Embrapa*) was created. And later in 1995 came the National Program for Strengthening Family Agriculture (PRONAF), which offered fundamental support for subsistence activities.[5] A range of productive activities was thus created which allowed Brazil to overcome the lack of food, accelerate technological progress in the agricultural sector, extend the agricultural frontier towards the *Cerrado*, especially in the Midwest, and become one of the largest exporters of agricultural products in the world.

While acknowledging the irrefutable advance of agribusiness in Brazil, it is still fitting to ask: did the modernisation of Brazilian agriculture lead to overcoming the structural factors that help explain, at least partially, the enormous personal and regional concentration of national income? The answer is "no". Recent empirical evidence confirms that the Brazilian agrarian structure still retains its dual and extremely unequal character. In a book published by the IPEA [The Brazilian Institute of Applied Economic Research] in 2020, several authors present a broad diagnosis of Brazilian agriculture, based on the 2017 Agricultural Census. Vieira Filho (2020: 37), for example, shows that

> the duality of Brazil's agricultural production still remains. That is, 0.6% of the establishments were responsible for approximately 53% of production, and 69% of the poorest establishments (of which ¾ of this percentage were family producers), for only 4% of the gross value of production, with this inequality increasing slightly between 2006 and 2017.

The author concludes that "the country is still far from solving poverty in the countryside (...), and the main challenge is to reduce extreme poverty, which is firmly located in the Northeast". Souza, Gomes and Alves (2020: 39), when

5 See Guanziroli (2014).

calculating the level of income inequality at the level of agricultural establishments in Brazil, show that "the Gini concentration index [closer to 0, greater equality; closer to 1, greater inequality] at the establishment level jumped from 0.85 in 2006 to 0.90 in 2017".

All this leads me to conclude that Furtado's theoretical propositions on economic development remain relevant today. And to agree with him that overcoming underdevelopment or secular stagnation in economies of continental dimensions that have already reached average levels of per capita income—as is the case of Brazil—depends, primarily, on the formation of a robust market for mass consumption. This, in turn, is only viable if there is a true integration of the domestic market between the different regions of the country. Particularly in the Brazilian case, this depends on the reversal of the draconian concentration of income and national wealth, whose historical roots are related, according to Furtado (1999: 32), to the "considerable potential of unexploited arable soil", and to which access to such land is blocked to rural workers and the "underutilised workforce". The solution to these problems is "of a political nature, before being economic" (op. cit.: 32). Therefore, Furtado rightly suggests that the solution depends essentially on public policies and political concertation, through democratic means, between a diversity of actors across the social classes (industrial and financial capitalists, urban and rural workers, and landowners).

3 The Dutch Disease and the Resource Curse: Furtado's Seminal Analysis

The so-called Dutch disease, as the expression suggests, hit the Netherlands in the 1960s, when considerable reserves of natural gas were discovered. With relatively unregulated markets, the increase in expected profitability ended up inducing a strong reallocation of the economy's productive resources to the non-renewable natural resources sector, thereby reducing investments in the country's manufacturing industry. The Economist magazine, in 1977, coined the expression "Dutch disease" in reference to this phenomenon.[6]

It was treated as a "disease" because the investments concentrated in this intensive natural resource sector, by causing a boom in commodity exports and a significant increase in net foreign exchange earnings, ended up leading to a real appreciation of the Dutch guilder in relation to other currencies.

6 See The Economist (1977).

Ultimately, this succession of events provoked a significant drop in exports of industrialised goods and a weakening of the country's manufacturing sector. In other words, it brought about deindustrialisation.

After the problem occurred in the Netherlands, Corden and Neary (1982) formulated a neoclassical theoretical model to understand the interrelationships of the affected variables and the long-term impacts on economic development. This article started the Dutch disease theory. As stated by the authors, an economy suffers from the Dutch disease when the profitability of one or more sectors is strongly compressed as a result of an exceptional boom in industries specifically producing tradable goods or services, in other words, whose production is destined for both the local and international markets.

In the Dutch case, the tradable good segment in which the boom occurred was natural gas. In addition, Jones and Neary (1984: 25) later show that the manufacturing sector can also suffer a severe contraction if the spending effect, resulting from the boom, disproportionately increases the profitability of sectors that produce non-tradable goods. Since these consist mainly of traditional services (commerce, retail, etc.) with low productivity compared to the manufacturing sector, the phenomenon becomes a "disease" since it adversely affects the trajectory of economic development in the country.

A by-product of the Dutch disease theory is the resource curse theory. The idea is anchored in the hypothesis that many countries with abundant natural resources (for example, oil) are unable to use these resources as a source to diversify their economies and drive industrialisation, be it due to the perpetuation of secularly predatory and corrupt oligarchies, or to the absence of inclusive institutions. The abundance of natural resources can become a "curse" because these economies will begin to stagnate and most of the increase in national income is appropriated by the country's minority elite. The seminal article in neoclassical modelling is that of Sachs and Warner (1995: 7), who, taking a sample of countries abundant in natural resources, make several regressions for the period 1971–1989, in order to explore the correlation existing between the high endowment of these resources and economic growth. The main conclusion is that "the abundance of natural resources depresses economic growth". But does it really?

It turns out that none of the above authors can lay claim to doing the seminal theoretical analysis on the problems of the Dutch disease and the supposed natural resources curse. It was, in fact, Celso Furtado (1957; 1974), in his two essays on Venezuela. In 1957, Furtado theoretically analyses the dialectics of underdevelopment in that country, whose economic performance already depended fundamentally on the oil sector. He identifies (op. cit.: 37–38) the contrasts in the Venezuelan economy which, in the period 1953–1956, is characterised by a high average share of the oil sector in GDP (28%, against only 14.7% for the manufacturing and construction industries, and approximately 11% for agriculture). Although the country had, at the time, "the highest level of per capita income" (op. cit.: 35–36) among economies with similar income levels, it "presented all the structural characteristics of an underdeveloped economy", such as a huge disparity between intersectoral productivity levels, brutal income inequality between urban centres and rural areas, durable consumer goods inaccessible to the majority of the population, high illiteracy rate, etc.

In the late 1950s, the oil sector was already setting the pace of average productivity growth in the Venezuelan economy. Nevertheless, the structural discrepancies observed between the productivity levels of the three basic sectors of the economy (agriculture, industry & construction, excluding oil, and services) were glaring. Even absorbing 40% of the country's workforce, agriculture operated with extremely low levels of productivity. According to Furtado's calculations (op. cit.: 45), the benefits of the significant growth in productivity in the oil sector, around 80% higher than in the other sectors between 1945 and 1956, did not spread to the rest of the Venezuelan economy.

Although the average wage paid in the oil industry was relatively higher than the average wage in other activities, it was the huge structural surplus of labour in the rural area that determined the average wage in the economy as a whole. As the oil industry was (and still is) nationalised, the surplus income was channeled to the government in the form of taxes and royalties. But there was no dynamic impulse emanating from this industry. Given the reduced dynamism of the industrial sector (except, of course, from the oil segment) and the high concentration of income, the structure of total domestic demand was strongly dependent on imports: between 1945–1947 and 1954–1956, the substitution of imports for domestic production was significant, with imports increasing their average share of domestic supply from 51% to 59% (op. cit.: 38–39).

However, differently from the thesis of Sachs and Warner (1995), Furtado (1957) argues that, instead of necessarily signalling a "curse", the abundance of natural resources in poor countries may be a "blessing" as it can enable such countries to overcome economic backwardness. But in the absence of adequate public policies, the inefficient allocation of these resources can perpetuate the condition of underdevelopment and stagnation and make the "curse" a self-fulfilling prophecy. In the late 1950s, Venezuela seemed to follow this path.

Astutely, Furtado (op. cit.: 49) observes that "the expansion of the oil sector was a necessary, but not sufficient, condition for the development of other sectors". This is not because the government was guided by laissez-faire policies, but because it concentrated its investments in conventional infrastructure, that is, in public utility services in which the technologies are very capital intensive, non-reproducible and have a reduced potential to increase permanent employment. Thus, the impacts of public investments, financed mainly by taxes and royalties derived from the oil industry's income, were restricted to the promotion of capital-intensive local industries with low capacity to absorb the surplus of structural, rural and urban labour. In other words, in the absence of programs aimed at diversifying the productive structure and fostering local industrialisation, the indirect impulse emanating from the public sector, far from eliminating structural employment, primarily boosted imports.

It should be noted that Furtado's (1957) theoretical lens had already accurately captured the transmission mechanism of the Dutch disease in Venezuela, even before the phenomenon aroused the academic interest of economists from diverse theoretical perspectives at the later date when it manifested itself in the Netherlands. Whereas in the Netherlands the economic disease led to the destructuring of the manufacturing sector, in Venezuela, by creating barriers to industrialisation and economic development, it condemned the country to stagnation. Furtado diagnoses that the persistent overvaluation of the Venezuelan currency, resulting from the inflows of foreign exchange generated by oil exports, operates as the main fuel that reinforces the conditions of underdevelopment in the country. It is worth describing the transmission channels and deleterious effects of the Dutch disease in Venezuela, as identified by Furtado (op. cit.: 74–75):

> a) the external currency overvaluation in a country with a low level of productivity tends to provoke the disorganisation of important productive sectors, which is sought to be avoided through high selective protection [via import tariffs]; b) an overvalued currency and high protection in the general consumer goods sector imply a high price level—compared to international prices—and very high wages (in relation to productivity) compared to the wages prevailing in those countries that compete in the Venezuelan market; c) the combination of high wages and external overvaluation (low equipment prices) gives rise to a tendency to substitute capital for labour; d) the extreme tendency to save labour has inter alia consequences, such as increasing disparities in productivity between sectors, slower wage growth than the return on capital [i.e., profits] and a relative delay in the occupational diversification of the population and in the expansion of the domestic market; e) from the previous observations, it can be deduced that the benefits of the high productivity of the oil sector tend to be concentrated in the hands of the higher income consumer groups.

As Medeiros (2008: 143) recalls, in the interesting essay "Celso Furtado on Venezuela",

> the essential difference is that in other countries [in Latin America], the currency restrictions created incentives for domestic production, but in Venezuela, thanks to the appreciated exchange rate, these goods were essentially imported, inhibiting domestic production, except for those strongly protected activities.

Furtado makes it clear in his essay that the persistence of the Dutch disease, aggravated by a real appreciation trend of the local currency, can turn into a resource curse. To reverse this trend, the author (op. cit.) outlines a roadmap so that public funds accumulated with net foreign exchange from oil exports are directed to government investment programs, with the aim of diversifying the productive structure, advancing average aggregate productivity, and accelerating economic development. The roadmap combines recommendations inspired by the normative implications of classical and Keynesian developmentalism.

It is worth reiterating that Furtado is more concerned with the dissolution of the factors responsible for the perpetuation of the high level of structural unemployment than with transitory mechanisms of job creation, through Keynesian expenditures in conventional public works. Thus, his Keynesian recommendations stem from the observation that it is in the oil sector where the main dynamic impulses directly reside, since it concentrates the technical progress generated in the country, and indirectly, since it emanates most of the government revenue (taxes and royalties), for the good ("blessing") or for the bad ("curse").

Therefore, it is a matter of redirecting public investments towards projects that, in addition to reducing cyclical unemployment, trigger private investments aimed at driving industrialisation. As highlighted by Furtado (op. cit.: 60),

> they are different things, from the point of view of organisation and management, to build roads or bridges and to operate industrial factories. Unlike current public works, factories need to be planned with very strict economic criteria and their operation requires competent personnel of varying types of specialization (…). The next phase of Venezuelan development will necessarily be a phase of intense economic diversification. That is, either the economy tends to a rapid diversification of its productive apparatus, or the pace of development will tend to reduce. And it will

> not be possible to obtain rapid diversification without extensive investments in the technical and professional training of the workforce and in the creation of collateral services aimed at providing technical assistance, including in terms of organisation, to entrepreneurs.

In line with Lewis and Hirschman, Furtado suggests that, in addition to basic industries (transportation, energy, communications, etc.), public investments should also privilege activities with a high potential for generating positive externalities (i.e., that contribute to increased aggregate productivity), particularly those that accelerate the accumulation of human capital, such as basic education, technical training of the workforce, technical business qualifications and R&D. For Hirschman, government incentives for private investment should focus on industries with the greatest power to create both backward and forward linkages in terms of income generation and employment, initially privileging the most labour-intensive segments. This means that capital accumulation absorbs the structural surplus of the unemployed or underemployed workforce in rural and urban areas and, at the same time, sustains the rate of average productivity growth in the economy. "Achieving maximum social productivity per unit of new investment depends on an adequate orientation for the set of investments [public and private]", concludes Furtado (op. cit.: 59).

But to whom is this important? Afterall, as most of the economic and social problems in Latin America (including Brazil) are rooted in the continent's social and economic history, their solution depends, albeit not exclusively, on political factors. Not by chance, in another essay published almost two decades later, Furtado (1974) was not surprised to find that the abundance of natural resources, by inhibiting the competitiveness of local production owing to the persistent real appreciation trend of the currency, appeared to steer Venezuela on the path of the "curse".[7] The main problems remained untouched: a productive structure in a state of inertia; a higher rate of productivity growth restricted to the oil sector, but insufficient to take the average productivity of the economy out of secular stagnation; and the persistence of a high structural labour surplus, which, by depressing the average wages paid to most workers, aggravated income concentration. In a prophetic and somber tone, Furtado (op. cit.: 121–122) concludes:

7 As Medeiros (2008) points out, with the external financial opening from the 1990s on, the trend towards exchange rate appreciation became a chronic problem not only in Venezuela, but throughout Latin America. This point will be revisited in the next chapters.

> An economic system was created [in Venezuela] that produces little surplus in the form of savings and taxes (not considering the oil industry) and that derives little return on the investments made possible by the oil surplus. It is a socio-economic system fundamentally oriented towards consumption [of imports][8] and waste and in which income is highly concentrated and is likely to be concentrated permanently.

4 Conclusion

Furtado, one of ECLAC's founding fathers, can be considered both a classical developmentalist and an ECLACian. However, in view of the independence and originality with which he analysed the problem of underdevelopment, leading to exhaustion his emphasis on historical, economic and social particularities in the formulation of explanatory theories of development and the tendency to stagnation in periphery countries, it is acceptable to surrender to the pleonasm that Furtado bequeathed a Furtadian theory of development.

As a classical developmentalist, Furtado argues insistently that, due to low levels of per capita income, one of the main obstacles hindering development in periphery countries lies in the reduced dimensions of their domestic market. Yet such restrictions can be overcome with appropriate public policies. As an ECLAC economist, Furtado highlights the tendency towards external imbalance and structural heterogeneity between the core countries and the periphery. But in his own terms, Furtado rejects the claim, which he considered fallacious, that theories of economic development have universal validity.

The theoretical schemes proposed by Furtado, in his rich academic works, remain highly relevant in demonstrating that overcoming underdevelopment and the tendency to stagnation depends, among other factors, on the deep integration of the domestic market, on the diffusion of a mass consumer market, on the reduction of social inequalities and on the efficiency with which economies abundant in renewable and non-renewable resources are able to use these "blessings" of nature in favour of industrialisation and development.

8 Furtado (1974: 123) reports that "in 1972 of the total available goods for consumption and capitalisation, around 40% were imported".

CHAPTER 5

Prologue to New Developmentalism: Notes on the Inflation Targeting Regime and Fiscal Austerity

1 Introduction

Chapters 5 and 6 are dedicated to the new developmental theory. The main contribution of new developmentalism has been to seek to integrate macroeconomics with the theory of economic development. In this chapter, for didactic reasons, I present preliminary notes on the inflation targeting regime and fiscal austerity, topics that, although transversal to new developmental theory, do not constitute its central theses. Accordingly, Chapter 5 can be read and interpreted as a prologue to Chapter 6, where I will return to the central theses of new developmental theory and macroeconomics.

2 Inflation Targeting Regime

2.1 *Inflation Targeting Regime: Theoretical Background*

When it comes to the relatively recent monetary policy practice of a group of countries in the world economy, a refined discussion of the inflation targeting regime would require the analysis of diverse approaches and theoretical controversies that have arisen in the field of monetary economics. Such an analysis is beyond the scope of this book. I, therefore, limit my analysis to the confrontation of two antagonistic approaches to monetary theory and policy: the (neo)classical, with a strong monetarist bias, and the Keynesian. I will further restrict the discussion to what is strictly necessary for understanding, on the one hand, the logic of the inflation targeting regime and, on the other, the problems arising from this monetary policy practice in countries open to free capital flows, according to the new developmental macroeconomics.

I start with the classical interest rate theory. It is a monetarist approach because it accepts the quantity theory of money in the classical version (also known as QTM), whose foundations take root in the mid-18th century, even before Adam Smith's criticism of mercantilism.[1] This doctrine defended a rigid

1 It is worth noting that, even though Milton Friedman rescued several principles of classical macroeconomics, such as laissez-faire, supply side forces as determinants of growth, among

 | DOI:10.1163/9789004734296_008

control over the import flow of manufactured products, under the assumption that the source of national wealth came from the accumulation of precious metals (notably gold). David Hume (1752a; 1752b; 1752c) was one of the first philosophers to oppose mercantilist protectionism and defend international free trade. He based this on the formulation of what came to be known as the quantity theory of money, which thus consolidated the theses for the dissemination of the gold standard as the international monetary anchor until the First World War (1914–1918).

According to Hume, the national currency stock should maintain proportionality with the balance of payments of each country, i.e., with the variation in international reserves. This means that an increase in the quantity of currency in circulation could not be implemented unless the country had a surplus in the balance of payments, which implied a net inflow of gold. The reverse was also defended: if the country had a balance of payments deficit, it should reduce the circulating stock of national currency. Note that Hume worked with the implicit idea that currency, except for its function as a measure of value ("unit of account"), should only serve as a means of exchange for the goods and services produced. Controlling the stock of money supply should correspond to variations in the stock of gold reserves in each country.

In Hume's conception, the trade balance was the indirect thermometer of the creation of national wealth. At a time when there were no methods of accounting for GDP, surpluses in the trade balance were indicative of an expansion in real wealth, expressed in goods and services produced in the country, and therefore, requiring an expansion of the circulating medium in the domestic market. Conversely, trade deficits implied monetary reductions. Hence, Hume's quantity theory of money focuses on the hypothesis that monetary expansion or contraction does not have any real effect, positive or negative, on GDP, only on the price level. In other words, an expansion in the quantity of money causes inflation, whereas a contraction causes deflation. Furthermore, Hume's theory is closely linked to the theory of automatic monetary adjustment in the balance of payments: as countries in deficit should proportionally reduce their quantity of domestic currency, the resulting fall in price level would provide an increase in the real competitiveness of the goods

others, the monetarism inherent to classical QTM is not exactly identical to Friedman's monetarist ideas. Although Friedman (1956) had re-established the importance of QTM, his formulation is completely different and much more sophisticated than the classical version. For more details, see also Rogers (1989), who dedicates Chapter 6 to exclusively analysing the Friedmanian formulation of QTM.

and services produced. This would eliminate, in the long run, the negative foreign exchange balance. The opposite would occur with countries in surplus. The understanding reached from this was that the balance of payments of the world economy would tend to equilibrium in the long run.

After Irving Fisher's (1907/1930)[2] formulation and the refinements of Cambridge's (Marshall, Robertson and Pigou) neoclassical economists, the quantity theory of money became the mantra of "classical" macroeconomics. It was understood as the core of the predominant macroeconomic theory until the publication of Keynes's (1936) General Theory of Employment, Interest and Money. In Fisher's formulation, the famous equation of the quantity theory of money is expressed as:

$$MV = PT \tag{5.1}$$

where M is the economy's money stock; V, the velocity of money circulation (the number of times, on average, a monetary unit circulates to realise transactions of goods and services), P, the price level, and T, the number of transactions.

Assuming some approximation between total transactions and the real value of GDP, equation (5.1) is expressed as:

$$MV = PY \tag{5.2}$$

where V is the income velocity of money circulation (average number of times that a unit of currency circulates as income is generated), which classical macroeconomists assume to be stable (constant) in the short term; and Y is the value of real GDP, i.e., PY is the nominal GDP value, this is, at current prices, which therefore incorporates the variation in the price level (inflation rate) in the period.

Classical macroeconomics assumes that, under laissez-faire and perfect competition in all markets (of goods and factors of production, including labour), along with perfect predictability, the economy can count on automatic forces to guide all sectors to operate at maximum potential production capacity and optimise the use of productive factors. From a macroeconomic perspective, this theory ensures that the economy always operates at full

2 The formulation was made in 1907, but the 1930 edition brings together Fisher's work on monetary theory.

employment, with the actual real GDP (Y) constant and always equal to the potential real GDP (Y^*). What is the moral of this story?

First, it is assumed that there are no business cycles caused by demand factors, nor economic crises! Additionally, if V and Y are, by hypothesis, constant in the short run, variations in the money stock do not cause any change in real GDP (Y), but only in nominal GDP (PY). In other words, according to the quantity theory of money, expansionary monetary policies are useless for promoting economic expansion in the long run. This is because any GDP growth in the short term would only be nominal, since, with full employment and higher inflation, real GDP (in quantum) could not be expanded. In technical jargon, for classical macroeconomics, money is neutral, since variations in its supply do not exert any effect on the real side of the economy—that being GDP, income and employment level—only on the general price level.

So what does this all have to do with determining real interest rates? In classical macroeconomics, real interest rates are entirely determined on the real side of the economy, that is, in the ambit of the decision process of consuming, saving and investing. This is the interest rate theory formulated by Swedish economist Knut Wicksell, in his classic book "*Interest and Prices*" 1898. It's simple: as the economy expands production and income flows (wages and profits), households decide how much to consume and save, and companies decide to invest or save. However, as this approach imagines a completely rosy world, in which there is no type of uncertainty and functions according to the precepts of Say's law ("every supply creates its own demand"), there is no thought of the alternative for entrepreneurs to stop investing.[3] Savings flows (S) generated in the real sector are transmuted into financial flows ("loanable funds"), and from there they flow into the banking system, which uses them as funding to finance ongoing investments (I) in the economy.

Thus, in classical macroeconomics, both savings and investment decisions depend on real interest rates. In the case of savings, the correlation is direct: when real interest rates rise, there is greater incentive to save, because households are stimulated to sacrifice present consumption for greater future consumption. As for investment, it varies inversely with real interest rates, for when interest rates rise, they adversely affect the profitability of capital intended for

3 In the classical model (pre-Keynesian), as I show below, investment also varies inversely with the real interest rate. However, if, for example, the market real interest rate increases in relation to the equilibrium real interest rate, there will be a discrepancy between savings and investment. In this case, the excess of savings in relation to investment demand would cause the free play of market forces to restore the real interest rate to the original equilibrium level.

investment. This happens because it is assumed that the additional accumulation of physical capital reduces the marginal productivity of that same capital. By logical deduction, it is easy to understand why this approach concludes that investment depends on savings: although both depend on real interest rates, since investment flows depend on households channelling resources to banks in the form of loanable funds, this then implies investment depends on savings.

The reader may now be asking: what does all this have to do with inflation targeting regimes? I will get to that, but for now, suffice it to say that, for classical macroeconomics, the functioning of capitalist economies is governed by the law of general equilibrium. That is the one in which, under conditions of full employment, supply and demand for real (goods and services), monetary (currency) and financial (bonds and other securities) assets are equal and simultaneously determine their respective macroeconomic prices (price level, real interest rate and face value of financial assets). That said, given the assumption of full employment, whenever investment is equal to savings, the resulting interest rate is considered real neutral ("natural"), in other words, capable of ensuring real (GDP at full employment level) and monetary (stable inflation) stability of the economic system. Proposed by Wicksell (1901: 193), the concept is defined as follows: "The natural or normal [neutral] real interest rate is that which equates the supply of savings to the demand for loans for investment in new capital, corresponding, more or less, to the expected income [profit] from that same capital". As Rogers (1989: 39) argues well,

> Wicksell's analysis of the natural interest rate lies in the assumption that it represents the equilibrium of the economy that would result if capital were lent in kind [in natural], without the intermediation of money. Therefore, according to the Wicksellian theory of interest rates, savings are investments by definition, because capital is nothing more than saved labour and land.

Wicksell's interest rate theory goes hand-in-hand with the classical quantity theory of money. As Rogers (1989: 23) recalls,

> Wicksell's monetary theory should be understood as an attempt to extend the application of the quantity theory of money to an economy that has moved from the simple use of metallic coins as a means of payment [as it was conceived at the time by David Hume] to the use [and, evidently, dissemination] of credits and loans.

The Wicksellian real neutral interest rate is imaginary, therefore, unobserved, and results from a theoretical model of general equilibrium verified when the actual real GDP equals the potential GDP. In other words, it is a sui generis real interest rate, compatible with equality between savings and investment, but with the economy operating at full employment. Evidently, in the theoretical conception of classical macroeconomics, even though real market interest rates (the observed rates) may be higher or lower than the real neutral interest rate, the free play of market forces is responsible for equalising them through a greater or lesser stimulus to savings. If, by chance, real market interest rates are above (or below) the real neutral rate, the excess (or scarcity) of savings in relation to demand for those savings to finance investment would cause their fall (or rise) towards the equilibrium neutral rate.

2.2 *The Inflation Targeting Regime: in Practice*

It is time to connect the Wicksellian interest rate theory to the inflation targeting regime. In this regime, central banks manage monetary policy not by controlling the money supply, but by setting the short-term basic nominal interest rate (for example, in Brazil, the Selic rate), also known as the monetary policy rate (or policy rate). Economic authorities determine the annual inflation target, which, theoretically, should be equal to the long-term inflation rate compatible with potential GDP and full employment. Evidently, if the economy hypothetically reaches full employment (actual GDP equal to potential GDP) and the observed inflation rate reaches the target, the observed short-term real interest rate (in Brazil, the Selic interest rate minus the inflation rate) equals the real neutral interest rate.

As Lance Taylor (2010) recalls:

> with the deregulation of financial markets in the late 1970s, econometric models found themselves unable to estimate a stable currency demand function, which led central banks to return to Wicksell's focus, managing monetary policy by setting the basic interest rate to the detriment of controlling the supply of money.

Lance Taylor (op. cit.: 234) says that this led "to the idea of an inflation target [regime]". Yet, as the real neutral interest rate is not known, central banks estimate it using econometric models. Conceptually, the real neutral interest rate is identical to that underlying the Wicksellian framework, but with the difference that, as central banks are forward looking, inflation expectations over the specified horizon—between one and three years, or even longer, depending on the monetary framework of the 27 countries that adopted an inflation targeting regime—have greater importance than past inflation.[4]

In practice, central banks manage monetary policy by setting the basic interest rate using a rule known as the Taylor rule. Formulated by the American economist John Taylor in 1993, the rule directs the monetary authority to increase the basic interest rate every time the observed or expected inflation (in Brazil, the IPCA) exceeds the inflation target and/or the actual GDP is greater than the potential GDP, and to decrease when the opposite occurs.

Yet, for monetary policy to be able to affect the general price level, it is necessary that the basic interest rate, in real terms, be higher than the real neutral interest rate whenever observed inflation or inflationary expectations are greater than the target. Not only that: it is also necessary for monetary policy to be able to affect the entire term (i.e., future) structure of interest rates (i.e., the yield curve). Therefore, eventual increases in the basic rate are effective in reducing the inflation rate towards the target only if they are transmitted to short-, medium- and long-term real interest rates, and consequently reducing aggregate demand. Note that the monetary theory underlying the inflation targeting regime implicitly assumes that central banks are fully capable of determining the term structure of interest rates.

As Lance Taylor (op. cit.) emphasises, if inflation is caused by excess aggregate demand, the Taylor rule produces countercyclical effects: when the inflation rate increases, it is understood that the observed unemployment rate is lower than the natural unemployment rate (or NAIRU, meaning non-accelerating inflation rate of unemployment),[5] being that that does accel-

4 According to Araújo and Arestis (2019: 9), "in 2019, the following countries adopted explicit and complete inflation targeting regimes: Armenia, Australia, Brazil, Canada, Chile, Colombia, Czech Republic, Ghana, Guatemala, Hungary, Iceland, Indonesia, Israel, Mexico, New Zealand, Norway, Peru, Philippines, Poland, Romania, Serbia, South Africa, South Korea, Sweden, Thailand, Turkey, and the United Kingdom. Other countries, such as the United States and the European Union, adopted implicit inflation targeting regimes and followed the principal elements of this monetary policy regime" [an inflation target in the medium or long run, the use of the Taylor rule—analysed in the next paragraphs—etc.].

5 The natural rate of unemployment is a concept created by Milton Friedman in his famous paper "The role of monetary policy", 1968. The media tends to treat it, conceptually, as a synonym for full employment, that being a situation in which, at the prevailing wage, there would be no involuntarily unemployed worker, as formulated by Keynes. However, the natural rate of unemployment may or may not correspond to Keynesian full employment itself. This is because Friedman (1968: 8) defines the natural rate of unemployment as "the level of unemployment that results from the Walrasian general equilibrium system [so far, mutatis mutandis, it would correspond to full employment], provided that this level incorporates the

erate the inflation rate over time; if the inflation rate falls, it is assumed that unemployment is high, above the NAIRU. From the concept it was easy to jump to monetary orthodoxy. Lance Taylor (2010: 235) says:

> The Taylor rule would tend to stabilise the unemployment rate around the NAIRU. It is additionally assumed that an independent central bank, understood as not being subordinate to the Ministry of Finance, is capable of ensuring credibility to the market that it is committed to the inflation target.

The problem is that inflation is not always caused by excess demand. If it is caused by supply shocks, such as the oil shock in the mid-1970s or the interruption of production chains during the Covid-19 pandemic in 2020 and 2021, the Taylor rule suggests that the central bank should interpret its effects on inflation as transitory. However, in practice, the most conservative central banks, fearing the secondary effects of the shock on future expectations of price increases, end up increasing the interest rate at this untimely moment, even if unemployment rates are concentrated at significantly high levels. Eventually, inflation falls and converges to target, but at the expense of a greater contraction in economic activity and high unemployment rates. Yet, the central bank argues that monetary policy maintained the credibility necessary to contain inflationary expectations!

It is also necessary to consider the theories of inertial inflation developed by Brazilian economists in the 1980s, namely Arida and Resende (1984) and Bresser-Pereira and Nakano (1984), among others. In the article entitled "Accelerating, maintaining and sanctioning factors of inflation", Bresser-Pereira and Nakano (1984) demonstrate that while the accelerating factors can be demand or supply factors, the maintaining factor is the formal and informal indexation of the economy. The sanctioning factor is the economy's total stock of money, which cannot be completely controlled by the monetary policy instruments of the Central Bank because it is considered endogenous—that is, because it multiplies as a result of the banking system's credit operations and technological innovations introduced into the financial market.

---

prevailing characteristics of the goods and labour markets [for example, bargaining power between unions and business associations], including market imperfections, stochastic fluctuations in the goods and services markets, etc." Therefore, it is the second part of the quoted excerpt that makes the natural rate of unemployment often equivalent to significantly high levels of unemployment.

The Brazilian experience with the inflation targeting regime, in force since June 1999, shows that every time inflation expectations are unanchored—to use financial market jargon—, that is to say every time inflation expectations throughout the specified time horizon (legally, 12 months ahead) exceed the inflation target pursued by the monetary authority, in most cases the Central Bank adopts a cycle of successive increases in the Selic interest rate, even if the output gap is excessively negative[6] and the unemployment rate is extremely high.[7]

As new developmental authors emphasised, maintaining high real interest rates for long periods brings deleterious side effects, which are magnified in view of the wide openness to the movement of external capital.[8] For them, one of the causes of the trend towards long-term real appreciation of the exchange rate in developing countries is very high interest rates.

The following stylised fact, although it replicates the Brazilian case between 2000 and 2015, applies to other developing countries that have adopted inflation targeting regimes in a context of broad external financial opening, such as in Chile, Mexico and Colombia.[9] It is based on the uncovered interest rate parity hypothesis, according to which the difference between the annual domestic interest rate (i) and the annual external interest rate (i^*) must be equal to

---

6 The output gap is measured by the difference between the observed GDP and the potential GDP, in other words, compatible with the full use of the economy's productive resources, considering the available technology. A positive output gap means excess aggregate demand over aggregate supply, which leads to inflationary pressure; a negative output gap reflects excess aggregate supply, the existence of idle capacity and unemployment, which implies deflationary pressure, as long as there are no other factors on the supply side pushing prices up.

7 Compare, for example, the responses of the Central Bank of India and Brazil in the quarter following the collapse of the Lehman Brothers in September 2008, considered by many analysts the mark of the 2008 global financial crisis. Despite India having a higher and faster growth rate in accumulated inflation than in Brazil, the Reserve Bank of India significantly reduced the basic interest rate—notably India did not, at the time, adopt an inflation targeting regime—whereas the Central Bank of Brazil kept the Selic rate unchanged at 13.75% until January 2009, in spite of the dramatic drop in industrial production and exports throughout the last quarter of 2008. For details, see my article [Nassif (2010)], in which I compare the immediate economic policy responses in these two countries shortly after the break of the Lehman Brothers.

8 The reader can verify this emphasis in the works of Bresser-Pereira (2007; 2009; 2020), Bresser-Pereira and Gomes da Silva (2009), Bresser-Pereira, Oreiro and Marconi (2015; 2016), Nassif, Bresser-Pereira and Feijó (2018) and Nassif, Feijó and Araújo (2020), among others.

9 The reader can check in Ffrench-Davis (2015), Ocampo and Malagón (2015) and Ros (2015), who analyse the inflation targeting regimes in Chile, Mexico and Colombia, respectively, and will find that the effects are similar to those described in the stylised fact regarding the Brazilian case.

the expected depreciation of the national currency (e^e, the expected Brazilian R$/US$ exchange rate in the following 12 months), plus the country risk premium (R), which reflects the uncertainty related to the national economy. Mathematically, the uncovered interest rate parity is:

$$(i - i^*) = e^e + R \tag{5.3}$$

Intuitively, it is easy to understand the inter-relationship of the right and left sides of equation (5.3). Assuming that the economy is initially in a situation of relative monetary, fiscal and exchange rate stability, it is assumed that both sides of the equation are also stable in this initial phase. However, if there is an increase in inflationary expectations over the given horizon, the Monetary Policy Committee, in order to maintain credibility with the market, adopts a cycle of basic interest rate increases. The increase in the internal interest differential vis-à-vis the external $(i - i^*)$ tends to attract short-term foreign capital in search of opportunities for financial gains in the country (investments in public and private securities that pay the highest interest currently in force in the country). Depending on the resilience of inflationary expectations, the cycle of rising interest rates may extend over time. Over the period, due to the contraction of aggregate demand, inflation falls and converges towards the inflation target, but the excess foreign exchange provided by the net capital inflow tends to appreciate the currency in nominal and real terms.

For new developmentalism, the real exchange rate in developing countries obeys a cyclical process that keeps it appreciated in the long run. The problem is that if the national currency remains overvalued for a long period owing to additional capital inflows attracted by the high interest rates, there will be a significant loss in competitiveness of goods produced in the country, both for goods suffering from competition from imports and for those destined for export. A significant part of domestic demand ends up being satisfied by imported products. Ergo, at the same time that the monetary authority raises interest rates to reduce inflationary expectations, exchange rate overvaluation winds up producing imbalances in the external sector: trade balance deficits and current account deficits both deepen.

Sooner or later, if external financial agents assess that the current account deficits have reached unsustainable figures or if there is some external or internal economic shock, the overvaluation ends up being forcibly corrected by the market itself. Capital flight and an abrupt increase in exchange rates (sharp domestic currency depreciation) soon follow. It is no coincidence that such episodes culminate in exchange rate overshooting, since in financial crises, nominal devaluations of the national currency, which reach between

30% and 50%, exceed the percentage necessary to restore the real parity of the purchasing power of the national currency in relation to the basket of foreign currencies.[10]

The depreciation of the currency means that local producers, in order to protect their profit margins, seek out a way to pass on the increased cost of imported raw materials and components to prices. At the same time, upon registering an increase in inflation expectations in relation to the target, the Central Bank, being committed to its principal mission of maintaining price stability, implements a new cycle of rising interest rates. In short, the stylised fact replicates a situation similar to that of a dog chasing its own tail: in the long run, under rigid inflation targeting, the country cannot sustain either price stability nor economic growth.[11]

2.3 *Inflation Targeting Regime: a Critique*

Given that the new developmental theory aligns with Keynesian macroeconomics, it would be worth asking: is the inflation targeting regime compatible with Keynes's monetary theory and, therefore, with the new developmental macroeconomic theory? Around 1980, liberal economists finally managed to dislodge Keynesian theory from the economic mainstream. One of the first consequences was that central banks adopted the monetarist policy defended

10 Brazil is, perhaps, the most perfect example of this stylised fact. Between 1999 and 2020, the country recorded several episodes of exchange rate overshooting, such as between 1999 and 2001, due to the speculative attack against the Brazilian real; between 2002 and 2004, during the electoral turbulence owing to the expectation of Luiz Inácio Lula da Silva's victory, at the time seen by the financial market as an unreliable candidate for the interests of investors; and between 2020 and 2021, in virtue of the shock resulting from the Covid-19 pandemic. For the interested reader, see Nassif, Feijó and Araújo (2020).

11 See Nassif et al. (2024) for evidence on developed and developing countries adopting inflation targeting nowadays. Covering the period 2000–2019, we showed that all developed and Latin American developing countries had an RER overvaluation trend, while the European, Asian and African (South Africa) developing countries registered an undervaluation trend in the same period. Our econometric tests also show that (op. cit., p. 1) "in Latin American developing countries, whose ITs are centred on the main objective of pursuing price stability, the RER overvaluation trend, a by-product of this monetary policy regime, is driven by higher interest rate differentials to the US and is harmful to their economic growth; in developed countries, this trend is not explained by their IT framework, but by their high per capita income level, which reflects their high average labour productivity and development pattern. Yet, the trend of real exchange rate undervaluation in Asian and European developing countries and South Africa reflects their governments' ability to combine a more flexible inflation targeting regime with a floating but managed exchange rate system aimed at preserving a competitive and stable real exchange rate in the long term."

by Milton Friedman.[12] But a few years later central bankers, who are generally more pragmatic than academic economists, recognised that this policy led nowhere and replaced it with informally defined inflation targets. As Bresser-Pereira and Gomes da Silva (2009: 25) argued, "the adoption of the target regime resulted from a pragmatic decision, as a consequence of the failure of the monetarist model to justify the new-classical credibility theory." Central bankers began to informally define an implicit long-term inflation target and adopt policies that could bring them to that goal. Unfortunately, being distraught in face of the monetarist failure, neoclassical liberal economists subsequently tried to formalise the theory and fill it with requirements that made it rigid and highly costly for the countries that adopted it.

To understand the failure, it is necessary to compare Keynes's interest rate theory with the classical interest rate theory, examined previously. To start off, Keynes rejects the Wicksellian theory, notably the existence of a natural interest rate. His interest rate theory is anchored in these two hypotheses: the first is the non-neutrality of money, both in the short and long term; the second is that the monetary authority is able to exercise relative control over the monetary policy interest rate (i.e., the short-term basic rate or policy rate), but not necessarily over the interest curve of securities (the yield curve) traded in markets with different maturation periods, be it short, medium or long.

The non-neutrality of money hypothesis is analysed in depth in the famous Chapter 17 of the General Theory, in which Keynes (1936) compares the attributes of money with other assets (commodities and financial securities). According to Keynes, all assets, whether real, monetary or financial, have the attributes of value, profitability, maintenance cost and liquidity. Although money is an asset with zero expected profitability—money per se does not earn interest—and has practically non-existent maintenance costs compared to other assets, it is the one with maximum liquidity premium.

Precisely for this reason, unlike the classical theory view where it is only rational to use currency as a means of exchange, for Keynes money can be retained for the purpose of maintaining wealth over time, that is, it can be used as a store of value, with the benefit that this reserve has maximum

12 Milton Friedman (1968) recommended that monetary policy be managed by controlling the money supply, through one of its main aggregates, such as the monetary base or M1 (currency held by the public plus demand deposits of the public in commercial banks). In practice, Friedman suggested a monetary policy **rule** in which M1 grew at an "automatic" rate of between 3% and 5% p.a. However, in virtue of the endogenous nature of the money supply, central banks soon realised the difficulty of efficiently controlling monetary aggregates and began to manage monetary policy by setting the short-term basic interest rate.

liquidity premium, comparatively to all other assets. Where there is greater uncertainty, agents increase their liquidity preference and, in so doing, significantly intensify the demand for more liquid assets, including very short-term securities and currency. In extreme situations, such as the so-called liquidity trap, only money is retained by agents. For Keynes, it is rational to hoard money in the face of uncertainty, because it allows agents to move between the more or less known present and the completely uncertain future.

When the economic environment is governed by optimism and greater confidence in expectations, the Central Bank, by raising or reducing the short-term basic interest rate, manages to make the interest yield curve follow in the same direction. This happens because the monetary authority, through the purchase and sale operations of very short-term securities on the open market (including as short as overnight), can increase or decrease bank reserves if it is observed that long-term interest rates follow a different trajectory than the pre-fixed short-term basic interest rate.

Suppose, for example, that the Monetary Policy Committee decides to promote a cycle of rising basic interest rates to fight against an inflationary surge caused by excess demand. If the interest rates negotiated in the interbank market do not follow this upward cycle, the Central Bank sells bonds to banks, making the reduction in bank reserves put upwards pressure (in the same direction as the basic interest rate) on not only the interest rates of interbank certificates of deposits (paid at the interbank deposits rate), but also the interest rates on longer maturity bonds. In other words, in financial market jargon, the final effect is an increase in the average market interest rate. In these circumstances, by increasing the short-term basic interest rate, the monetary authority is able to make the yield curve of other financial assets with different maturities follow the same direction, i.e., become steeper—and that monetary tightening leads to the desired objective of eliminating the excess aggregate demand for goods and services, and in so controlling the original inflationary pressure.

The situation changes completely if monetary policy operates in an environment of strong uncertainty. In such a case, the Central Bank may prove incapable of directing the yield curve towards the desired goal. Consider, for example, that in a recessive context with high unemployment, a very negative output gap and an absence of initial inflationary pressure—like at the height of the Covid-19 crisis, between 2020 and the first quarter of 2021—the Monetary Policy Committee adopts a cycle of reducing basic interest rates aimed at stimulating economic recovery. If monetary policy is sufficiently powerful, it is expected that the fall in Central Bank interest rates will be transmitted to the interest term structure of other securities traded on the market and reduce real market interest rates, and thus causing the monetary stimulus to produce positive effects on aggregate demand.

This only happens, however, if the **existing** uncertainty about the economic environment is characterised by high confidence in the monetary authority's action to reverse the negative expectations about the future that **currently exists.** Under more intense uncertainty, the high degree of liquidity preference prompts most agents to demand highly liquid assets, normally very short-term securities, with immediate liquidity. In this case, issuers of longer-term government bonds (the National Treasury) or private ones are only able to sell them if they are willing to pay higher risk premiums, that is, if they are willing to offer them at interest rates much higher than the basic rate set by the Central Bank. This means that, in an environment of much greater uncertainty, the level and direction of the interest spectrum inherent to financial securities of varying profiles and maturity are not under the full control of the Central Bank's monetary policy, but rather under the demand for liquidity by the majority of the economic agents.

In practice, as Keynes (1936: 204) highlights in a well-known passage from the General Theory, the average level of the prevailing interest rate is "highly conventional" since it is determined by a large number of agents whose expectations share the same beliefs about the future. In his own words (op. cit.: 203, emphasis in the original):

> It might be more accurate, perhaps, to say that the rate of interest is a highly conventional, rather than a highly psychological, phenomenon. For its actual value is largely governed by the prevailing view as to what its value is expected to be. **Any** level of interest which is accepted with sufficient conviction as **likely durable will** be durable.

In extreme conditions, wherein the economy is faced with the "liquidity trap", the demand for money as a store of value tends to become widespread via the retention of national or foreign currency for hoarding purposes. In other words, differently from what classical economics postulates, a considerable portion of the money supply, instead of being demanded for the purposes of consumption or investment transactions, starts to be demanded and retained as a store of value. In such circumstances, one can also observe an inversion of the financial yield curve ("interest curve"), in which the interest rates paid on short- and medium-term (between one and two years) securities, even the very low ones, still exceed long-term interest rates.

In these extreme cases, monetary policy becomes ineffective in promoting economic recovery. This task must be commanded by fiscal policy, which, through a government spending programme, particularly government investments, has greater power to reduce unemployment and reactivate increasing aggregate income, as well as reducing the degree of uncertainty and restoring the state of confidence.

The unfolding events described above are not limited to the case where the Central Bank reduces the basic interest rate to promote economic recovery. They can also occur in situations where, despite a recessive environment and high uncertainty, the Central Bank is faced with inflationary pressure caused by various cost shocks, an example being what happened to the world economy throughout 2021, owing to the interruption of global supply chains of inputs and industrial components, the increase in international prices of essential commodities, like petroleum, as well as the significant depreciation of domestic currencies in developing countries.

The initial responses from central banks were completely different. In developed countries, these shocks were treated as temporary, and their central banks avoided raising basic interest rates prematurely, so as not to hinder recovery. Whereas in several developing countries, these shocks were immediately identified as permanent, and the monetary authority preferred to opt for monetary tightening, including the Central Bank of Brazil.

Does complacency in combating inflation caused by temporary supply shocks, at the expense of recession in the short run, also have adverse effects in the long run? In a debate in the Chamber of Deputies (in Brazil), in November 2021, economist André Lara Resende warned that the "highly questionable and mistaken" idea that inflation can be combated by raising interest rates will simply imply an increase in government debt (as a proportion of GDP), with an enormous transfer of resources from the state to holders of Treasury bills. However, some economists aligned with monetary orthodoxy would say "no". Afonso Celso Pastore, for example, in the same debate, peremptorily stated that "the Central Bank cannot close this [contraction in supply with an expansion in demand, according to the economist] on the supply side. **Either you let inflation become unanchored and face a deeper recession later, or you trigger a recession now**" (emphasis added).[13]

Pastore's interpretation is a *non sequitur*, that is, a logical fallacy, because it anticipates an unanchoring of expectations that did not exist at the time. Yet, it illustrates how defenders of monetary anchors ruled with an iron fist tend to consider price stability a sufficient condition to sustain economic growth

---

13 This debate was reported in the Brazilian newspaper *Valor Econômico* on 19/11/2021. https://valor.globo.com/brasil/noticia/2021/11/19/economistas-divergem-sobre-poder-do-juro-ante-a-inflacao.ghtml. Accessed on 19/11/2021.

in the long run. Furthermore, Pastore ignores that the prolonged recessive crisis, which had been going on since the beginning of the Covid-19 pandemic, does produce adverse effects in the long run: it provokes not only a contraction in potential GDP, due to the reduction in the physical and human capital stock—the latter because of the impact of prolonged unemployment on the qualification of the labour force—but also hysteresis effects, meaning the persistence of problems over time and, therefore, greater difficulty in returning to the previous economic and social situation.

I return, then, to the first question in this subsection: are **explicit** inflation targeting regimes, with strict rules, compatible with Keynesian and new-developmental macroeconomic theories? At least in the theoretical field, they are not. This is because this practice of monetary policy is rooted in theories that consider inflation to be a monetary phenomenon ("always and everywhere", to use the famous expression of Milton Friedman, 1963) that manifests itself via an expansion in aggregate demand or a generalised unanchoring of expectations. The Keynesian theory, in contrast, views inflation as the result and not the cause of cost pressure, though it can be caused either by excess demand or shortages in supply.

According to Keynes (1936: 279 and 285, emphasis in the original),

> variations in **demand** act at the same time on costs and on volume" (...), [but] it can only be classified as true inflation when a new increase in the volume of effective demand no longer produces an increase in production [i.e., when the economy is close to or beyond full employment] and only translates into an increase in unit costs, in exact proportion to the increase in effective demand.

The quoted excerpt reinforces my point that monetary policies guided by strict rules, in which the interest rate operates as the only instrument for controlling inflation and anchoring expectations, are not the mechanism to sustain economic growth or price stability in the long run, as previously shown. Particularly in the case of Brazil, the new developmental position, which is correct in my judgment, recommends replacing the current inflation targeting regime, which is governed by rigid rules, with a monetary policy managed by discretionary mechanisms, and not by rigid rules.[14] It also recommends publicly announcing such a change and implementing it in a gradual manner. Following the examples of the Federal Reserve Bank (FED) in the United States

14 At the end of the 2000s, Bresser-Pereira and Gomes da Silva (2009) and Sobreira and Oreiro (2009) proposed that Brazilian monetary policy should move in this direction.

and the European Central Bank (ECB), which use inflation targets with much greater flexibility, focusing on the long or the medium term (the FED and the ECB, respectively) and operate monetary policy in a pragmatic way, simultaneously aiming at price stability and employment levels, the Central Bank of Brazil should be guided by the commitment to keep the inflation rate low and stable in the long run, minimising economic costs (in terms of real output lost) and social costs (in terms of unemployment) in the short and long runs.[15]

3 Fiscal Austerity

In a critical review, Palley (2021) claims that the new-developmental theory defends fiscal austerity. This diagnosis, however, is not correct since new developmentalism, though advocating that the management of the government budget be guided by fiscal responsibility, is totally refractory to so-called fiscal austerity. Even though I return to this controversy in Chapter 7, I will briefly anticipate here the distinct meanings of the concepts of fiscal austerity and fiscal responsibility.

The concept of fiscal austerity is based on the completely counterintuitive hypothesis of "expansionary fiscal austerity", whereby the government's commitment to a programme of contracting public spending would accelerate economic growth.[16] The defence that fiscal austerity expands, rather than contracts, GDP is backed by the supporting argument that the government's commitment to frugality in spending increases the confidence that the stock of public debt (as a proportion of GDP) will remain low and stable over time. With less pressure on the Treasury to issue new bonds, there will be greater stimulus to private savings flows, which previously financed the government, to start financing private investments.

Proponents of this argument sought to support it based on empirical evidence found in broad country databases. The article by Alesina et al. (2017: 5),

15 According to Shapiro and Wilson (2019: 1, emphasis added), "in January 2012, the Federal Reserve announced to the public, for the first time in history, an explicit **long-term** inflation target of 2%." Moreover, as highlighted by Martínez-García, Coulter and Grossman (2021: 1, emphasis added), "as of August 2020, the flexible inflation targeting regime was replaced, in practice, by the **flexible average** inflation targeting regime." The European Central Bank informs on its website its commitment to inflation of around 2% **in the medium term.** https://www.ecb.europa.eu/home/search/review/html/price-stability-objective.en.html. Accessed on 28/12/2021.

16 See Alesina and Ardagna (2010), Alesina et al. (2017) and Alesina, Favero and Giavazzi (2018).

for example, uses data from 17 OECD countries for the period 1978–2009 and concludes that "fiscal adjustment programmes based on tax increases cause much greater losses in real output than those based on spending cuts". The authors (op. cit.: 5) agree that government spending cuts have recessive effects in the short term, but that "permanent spending cuts imply greater transfers to families, allowing the increase in private consumption to partially compensate for the lower government spending." In other words, in the long run, fiscal austerity would be expansionary!

The fiscal austerity argument exerted enormous influence on the adjustment policies of countries with a high level of public debt (as a proportion of GDP) throughout the Eurozone crisis that started in 2009. Five years after the adoption of severe spending-cut measures, especially in the most affected economies like Greece, Portugal and Spain, the countries still showed high unemployment rates and with no signs of solid economic recovery.

Since 2012, several studies have challenged the empirical evidence regarding expansionary fiscal austerity. Auerbach and Gorodnichenko (2012) estimated that fiscal multipliers are greater than 1 in recessions, i.e., an increase in government spending produces a more than proportional expansion of GDP in recessive cycles. De Long and Summers (2012) confirm this result and add that, by promoting faster recovery, fiscal expansion tends to be self-financing. That is to say, for a given tax burden, an increase in GDP generates a greater relative increase in the flow of tax collection, keeping public debt stable over time. They (op. cit.: 234) conclude that "fiscal austerity in a depressed economy can erode the long-term fiscal balance, while fiscal stimulus can improve it."

Furman and Summers (2020: 2), in turn, show that if monetary and fiscal policies are well coordinated, it is possible to maintain average real interest rates lower than real GDP growth. As a result, "fiscal expansions can improve fiscal sustainability per se, by allowing the GDP growth rate to be higher than the increase in the stock of public debt and interest expenses." They highlight, and rightly so, that the government's biggest challenge is to design programmes that promote efficiency in the allocation of public spending, prioritising investments in physical and human infrastructure (sanitation, urban mobility, education, health, R&D, etc.), all of which, in virtue of the significant associated positive economic externalities, tend to "produce benefits considerably greater than the costs arising from any accumulation of additional debt" (op. cit.: 35).

It is worth clarifying, therefore, that the idea of fiscal austerity has nothing to do with that of fiscal responsibility, which is defended by new developmentalists. The former is associated with permanent spending cuts and once public debt has been stabilised at low levels as a proportion of GDP, government expenditures freeze in real terms. An example of the "spending cap" was implemented in Brazil in 2017.[17]

Fiscal responsibility, on the other hand, is perfectly aligned with Keynes's (1982) famous proposal that, to preserve the countercyclical nature of fiscal policy, the government must be guided by two annual budgets: a current budget, which must be permanently balanced and, when possible, in surplus, with expenditures fully financed by tax revenues; and a capital budget (associated with public investments), which should be balanced in the long run, but may be in deficit during recessionary crises.

This proposal is totally consistent with Bresser-Pereira's (2020a) proposal to establish a public savings fund to finance government investments.[18]

In short, new developmentalism is opposed to "fiscal populism", understood as the disorderly growth in government spending to the point of causing a lack of control over public debt. It is, though, completely in favour, as Bresser-Pereira (2007: 174) highlights, of "increasing government savings so that it is possible to finance the necessary public investments" to sustain economic growth.

As proponents, like Wray (1998) and Kelton (2020), of the Modern Money Theory (MMT) claim, governments that issue debt in their own currency never become insolvent. This is a fact, since any repudiation of public debt services payments (principal plus interest) is an eminently political decision made by government authorities. However, the main argument against the lack of

17 The spending cap rule was established by Constitutional Amendment No. 95, on 15 December of 2016. With it, from 2017 onwards, primary government spending in each year began to be corrected to official inflation (IPCA) accumulated in the last 12 months, in force for 20 years and to be revised in 2026. The mechanism has proven to be politically and economically unfeasible since its adoption, since, although it provided for a freezing of total primary expenditures in real terms, the above-inflation growth of mandatory expenditures such as education, health, and social security—guaranteed by a constitutional clause—ended up overly compressing discretionary expenditures, notably public investments. At the beginning of 2023, when this book was a work in progress, the recently sworn-in government of President Luiz Inácio Lula da Silva had managed to approve Constitutional Amendment No. 32 (called "*PEC da Transição*"), promulgated on 22 December of 2022, which in practice revoked the spending cap and, in the second half of that year, provided for the design and submission to Congress of a less draconian fiscal rule.

18 In an article in the Brazilian newspaper *Valor Econômico*, Bresser-Pereira (2020) proposes that "Congress approve a constitutional amendment authorising the Central Bank to purchase, each year, up to 5% of GDP in government bonds to cover spending exclusively on public investments in infrastructure, which must be provided for by the Union budget, with expenditures authorised at each quarterly meeting of the National Monetary Council."

control over government spending and public debt in the long term is that the market may feed expectations, even if unfounded, of future government insolvency. As Skidelsky (1999: 141) recalls, "Keynes was always alert to the effect of politics on business psychology. He understood that excessive government spending would undermine confidence in political relations (...) and put at risk the objective of maintaining real interest rates low in the long run."

Therefore, the defence of fiscal responsibility (but, I reiterate, not fiscal austerity) by new developmental economists is totally consistent with the recommendation that fiscal policy be managed in a countercyclical manner, consequently contributing to ensuring growth and stability in the long run.

4 Conclusion

This chapter showed that countries that adopt monetary policy regimes based on extremely rigid rules, in a context of a high degree of openness to the external capital flows, as in the case of Brazil since 1999, tend to fall into the trap of high real interest rates and of an appreciated real exchange rate trend. I also showed that inflexible inflation targeting regimes, combined with a procyclical fiscal policy—characterised by high fiscal deficits in expansion cycles and reduced fiscal space to expand public spending in recessions—or permanent fiscal austerity, compromise the sustainability of economic growth in the long run. In the next chapter, I will analyse, in detail, the central theses that, according to new developmental macroeconomics, can condemn periphery countries to economic stagnation.

CHAPTER 6

New Developmentalism: Integrating Macroeconomics with Development Theory

1 Introduction

Classical, ECLAC and Furtadian theories of economic development explore in detail, whether on a positive (in strictly theoretical terms) or normative (public policy implications and recommendations) level, how micro- and meso-economic aspects, when combined with historical, economic and social factors of each country or region, condition the way in which underdevelopment is overcome and support a successful catching up path.

However, the reader must have noticed that, in this discussion, practically no emphasis is given to macroeconomic aspects, especially in the theoretical perspectives of development. This does not mean that the "old" developmentalism does not recognise the importance of preserving the reliability of important macroeconomic indicators in order to prevent the development process from being interrupted by chronic processes of stagnation. As I have shown in the previous chapters, developmental authors, such as Nicholas Kaldor, Raúl Prebisch and Celso Furtado, repeatedly highlight how the stability of the balance of payments and the preservation of a competitive real exchange rate (i.e., a real exchange rate level in which the national currency remains slightly undervalued in relation to a basket of foreign currencies) act as supporting factors in sustaining the process of economic development with structural change. Nevertheless, such theoretical analyses do not always explore the interrelationships between micro- and meso-economic conditionalities—like the heterogeneity inherent to the productive structure, the interaction between agriculture and the manufacturing sector, regional imbalances, social inequality, among other factors—and the macroeconomic regime itself.

Aiming to fill in this gap, new developmentalism seeks to integrate macroeconomics with the theory of economic development. This chapter, therefore, summarises the recent propositions of this theoretical current, of which the Brazilian economist Luiz Carlos Bresser-Pereira stands out as the main formulator. The key argument that Bresser-Pereira brought to new developmentalism is that successful catching up trajectories depend on harmonising public policies (particularly industrial and technological policies and the macroeconomic regime) aimed at promoting the diversification of the productive

 | DOI:10.1163/9789004734296_009

structure and export basket. Thus, inadequate economic policy arrangements can cause the initially successful path of catching up in developing countries to be rerouted into long periods of stagnation.

The seminal ideas of new developmentalism are presented in the articles *"Crescimento econômico com poupança externa?"* (Bresser-Pereira and Nakano, 2003) and "The Dutch disease and its neutralisation: a Ricardian approach" (Bresser-Pereira, 2008) and are dispersed throughout the books *"Macroeconomia da Estagnação: Crítica da Ortodoxia Convencional no Brasil pós-1994"* (Bresser-Pereira, 2007) and *"Globalização e Competição"* (Bresser-Pereira, 2009a). The main theses are systematised in the textbook *"Macroeconomia Desenvolvimentista: Teoria e Política Econômica do Novo-Desenvolvimentismo"* (Bresser-Pereira, Oreiro and Marconi, 2016), considered an "improved version" (as stated on the title page) of the original English version, "Developmental Macroeconomics: New Developmentalism as a Growth Strategy", 2014. Despite the relative longevity of this theoretical current, its main formulator considers new developmentalism a "work still under construction" (Bresser-Pereira, 2020a).

The chapter is organised into three sections. In Section 2, I analyse the central theses of new developmentalism. In Section 3, I discuss the critical points that require analytical improvement. In Section 4, I present the main conclusions.

2 The Central Theses of New Developmentalism

As Bresser-Pereira (2020a) highlights, the central theses of new developmentalism do not apply to pre-industrialised economies, but to economies that, although having reached per capita income levels close to the world average, face chronic processes of economic stagnation. In other words, its central theses are based on the stagnation found in the Brazilian economy, but they can be applied to other developing economies that face similar problems.

New developmentalist theses reject the "middle income trap" hypothesis. Introduced by Gill and Kharas (2007) and disseminated by researchers, journalists and multilateral institutions (notably, the World Bank), this hypothesis maintains that, after following a successful path towards catching up for decades, some economies in an intermediate stage of development fall into the "middle income trap" and begin to face almost insurmountable obstacles to overcoming economic stagnation.[1] The hypothesis is based on the

1 For details, consult Bresser-Pereira, Araújo and Peres (2020).

idea that middle-income economies become unable to compete internationally both in labour-intensive sectors, due to the increase in relative wages, and in capital-intensive sectors, owing to the low rate of innovation and inadequate production scales. However, empirical evidence does not corroborate this thesis.[2]

As I initially underscored, new developmentalism seeks to integrate macroeconomic theory with development theory. In this regard, it seeks to demonstrate that the continuity of the catching up trajectory in economies that find themselves in intermediate stages of development is strongly conditioned by the current macroeconomic regime—especially the exchange rate policy and the current account policy of the balance of payments. Different macroeconomic policy arrangements can either induce or block economic development in countries that have reached average levels of per capita income. If the second hypothesis prevails, economic stagnation will tend to perpetuate.

So, which macroeconomic theories is new developmentalism associated with? Developmental macroeconomics aligns with the principle of effective demand, formulated by Keynes (1936, Chapter 3). This principle, central to Keynesian macroeconomics, suggests that insufficient aggregate demand is the main explanatory factor for low growth rates and economic recessions. Before returning to new-developmental macroeconomics, it is worth summarising the foundations of Keynesian theory.

Keynes's main argument (1936, Chapters 5 and 12) is that insufficient effective demand underlies the functioning of capitalist economies since current production (short-term) and investment (long-term) decisions are made with uncertainty about the future. Accordingly, future expectations can be derailed, meaning that the expected demand ("planned demand") by entrepreneurs can be different from the realised demand ("effective demand').

Keynesian uncertainty is considered radical because it cannot be measured by probabilistic calculations. While probable events, like playing roulette, the chance of winning the lottery, or even life expectancy, can be measured probabilistically, uncertain events are incalculable and, therefore, unpredictable. These include the future behaviour of economic variables. As Keynes (1937: 213–214) says:

2 The interested reader can consult the book organised by Huang, Morgan and Yoshino (2018), a work that synthesises the main points of this discussion. In this edition, the articles by Bulman, Eden and Nguyen (2018) and Paus (2018) show that empirical evidence does not support the hypothesis of the middle-income trap, let alone that it is an insurmountable factor to overcoming stagnation in most developing countries, especially in Latin America. Huang, Morgan and Yoshino (2018: 43) categorically conclude that "countries that grow rapidly continue to grow rapidly, and there is no reason for them to be stuck at any specific level of middle income".

> The sense in which I am using the term [uncertainty] is the one according to which the prospect of a European war is uncertain, as is the price of copper and the interest rate twenty years from now, or the obsolescence of a new invention (…). Regarding these problems, there is no scientific basis for probabilistic calculations. We simply know nothing about it.

Keynes argues that decision-making in the face of uncertainty about the future induces agents (entrepreneurs, consumers, financiers, etc.) to use all available information in the present to decide about the future (short, medium and long term). In the General Theory, Keynes (1936: 162–163) refers to the "state of confidence", be it weak or strong, pessimistic or optimistic, in allusion to the "convention", formed by the majority, that "the existing [favourable or unfavourable] business situation will continue indefinitely unless we have concrete reasons to expect a change."

In practice, the construction or breakdown of the state of confidence regarding future economic behaviour does not result from the opinion of a restricted set of agents, but from the opinion of the majority. In the words of Keynes (1937: 214), "we seek to conform to the behaviour of the majority or of the average. The psychology of a society of individuals, each of whom seeks to copy the others, leads to what we may strictly call conventional opinion." However, as uncertainty does not disappear even in periods of enviable optimistic convention, the author (1936: 170) emphasises that, in practice, the decision of entrepreneurs to expand current production or realise investments with a long-term return is, ultimately, driven by "animal spirits", that is, by the deliberate action that, faced with the unknown, leads them to place themselves in inter-capitalist competition, to invest, seek out profit opportunities and accumulate capital.

The breakdown of the state of confidence can happen slowly, as in the transition from expansionary cycles to slowdowns and recession, or suddenly, like in recessions or depressions that last after economic shocks—generally financial ones. In practical terms, when effective demand is insufficient to absorb aggregate supply, the accumulation of unsold inventories causes entrepreneurs, in an attempt to limit the profit fall or avoid economic losses, to reduce the level of productive capacity utilisation. This leads to an economic slowdown and increased unemployment. But when effective demand becomes chronically insufficient, the contraction in GDP and income becomes so pronounced that the economy begins to face depressive cycles—understood as severe and very prolonged recessions—and mass unemployment.

It is, therefore, expectations under conditions of uncertainty and the "state of confidence" of the entrepreneurs associated with those expectations that explain cyclical fluctuations, that is, the alternation between economic expansions, slowdowns and contractions. Furthermore, Keynes (1936: 43) also notes that the full employment of productive factors, especially of the labour force, is a "special" and exceptional situation that is observed in the long-term growth paths of capitalist economies. The situation generally observed, even in expansionary cycles, is having some level of involuntary unemployment.

Additionally, according to Keynes, there are no automatic forces freely induced by the market that are capable of promoting the recovery of GDP and employment levels when expectations about the future are very pessimistic. The main normative implication is that the government must activate the necessary stimuli for monetary, fiscal and exchange rate policies and have coordination between them.

In the case of fiscal policy, especially, the role of public spending in recessions is not to fully occupy the space of private demand, but to replace part of the insufficient spending. This is done notably through public investments in physical and human infrastructure to induce, via direct and indirect impacts on income and employment—i.e., through the fiscal multiplier[3]—the recovery of private demand. In addition, as future uncertainty operates as a cause and effect of economic crises, the management of the aforementioned macroeconomic policies also contributes to stabilising expectations and improving the state of confidence.

In summary, Keynesian theory is anchored in the hypothesis that the rate of GDP growth, both in the short term (that is, throughout the business cycle) and in the long term (economic development) depends, fundamentally, on the growth rate of aggregate demand. However, this does not mean that factors on the aggregate supply side, such as innovations and technical progress, the accumulation of human capital engendered by educational standards and

---

3 The multiplier, a concept introduced by Richard Kahn (1931) and refined by Keynes (1936, Chapter 10), measures the impact resulting from the variation of an autonomous expenditure (for example, total public spending, public investment or aggregate investment) on GDP and aggregate income. In the case of the investment multiplier, for example, Keynes indicates that, "when an increase in aggregate investment is produced, income rises by an amount equal to *k* times the increase in investment" (Keynes, op. cit.: 134). The multiplier mechanism contains a simple logical intuition: if there are idle productive resources (for example, unemployed workers), when aggregate investment increases by a certain amount, income and employment increase in the sectors benefiting from the expansion of this investment, providing an increase in aggregate consumption (although proportionally smaller than the variation in income). This, in turn, induces an increase in income and employment in the sectors also benefiting from the expansion of consumption, and so on. If the *k* multiplier is greater than 1, income ultimately grows in a greater proportion than the initial investment outlay.

technical training, among others, are irrelevant to the behaviour of GDP, especially in the long term. Still, Keynesian models demonstrate that, in the long term, it is not them that limit growth, but the factors linked to the behaviour of aggregate demand.

On the demand side, as already discussed in Chapter 2, the main barrier to growth is imposed by balance of payments constraints, which emerge when the economy is unable to maintain an increasing rate of exports (i.e., external demand) that ensures sufficient net foreign exchange flows to cover import expenditures. In the long term, the growth rate of aggregate supply tends to accommodate the growth in effective demand. As demonstrated by Fazzari et al. (2020: 585, emphasis added), "while economic growth is predominantly induced by effective demand, supply constraints only limit the **maximum possible** rate of growth" in the long term.

André Lara Resende (2015: 34), for example, considers that the world economy will be unable to reach the high growth rates exhibited in the past. In his opinion, two dimensions on the supply side could, henceforth, limit the maximum rate feasible for growth:

> The first is the physical limits of the planet. To continue growing, it will be necessary to change the composition of what is produced towards fewer material goods and more services, health, education and entertainment. The second is the saturation resulting from the increase in productivity in the manufacturing of material goods.

I will now return to new-developmental macroeconomics. This line of thought accepts the Keynesian principle that capitalist economies face a tendency towards insufficient effective demand. Bresser-Pereira (2012; 2015) agrees: for him, insufficient effective demand leads to a reduction in the expected profit rate and, consequently, a drop in productive investments and the GDP growth rate. However, the author emphasises that it is necessary to also consider the behaviour of the real exchange rate. When a currency remains overvalued for some years during the exchange rate cycle (between two financial crises), it begins to occupy "the centre of development theory". According to the author, other schools of economic thought do not do the same because, contrary to what new developmentalism claims, they do not assume that the real exchange rate can remain overvalued in the long term; it would merely be volatile, at times appreciating or depreciating around a long-term equilibrium rate. This means, for new developmentalism, when companies are formulating their investment projects, they consider this exchange rate to be overvalued and generally do no invest.

For Bresser-Pereira, Oreiro and Marconi (2016), the real exchange rate works as a switch that connects or disconnects companies that use the best available technology in their respective markets, confirming or rejecting their **access** to existing demand. Therefore, the greatest challenge for economic policy will be to manage the available instruments so that developing economies can catch up, while preserving internal stability (full employment and stable inflation) simultaneously with external stability (balance of payments). To this end, the authors add (op. cit.: 9), it is necessary for policymakers, when managing the economic policy instruments under their control, to maintain "the five macroeconomic prices (profit rate, exchange rate, interest rate, wage rate and inflation rate)" at adequate levels.

According to new developmental macroeconomics, among the five macroeconomic prices just mentioned, the real interest rate and the real exchange rate are the most important for sustaining economic growth, because: (i) the real interest rate, by measuring the opportunity cost of investments in real ("physical") capital, compared to other assets (including financial), affects the expected profitability of investments, that is, it affects the so-called marginal efficiency of capital.[4] In other words, the higher the real interest rate, the lower the willingness of entrepreneurs to invest and, therefore, the lower the economic growth; (ii) the real exchange rate, understood as the relative price that affects the prices of goods and services traded internationally (the prices of exported, imported and domestic products that compete with the imports), also affects the expected profitability of investments aimed at meeting local and international demands, because an overvalued exchange rate disconnects investment projects that use the best technology in their market. Thus, the lower the real exchange rate—that is, the more overvalued the national currency is in relation to the dollar or a basket of foreign currencies—, the lower the investments directed at meeting local and international demands. In other words, according to new developmentalism, with the domestic currency tendentially overvalued, entrepreneurs tend to face difficulties in **accessing** the existing effective demand. In this same vein, job creation tends to benefit the rest of the world because the expansion of domestic demand ends up leaking, in large part, into imports.

4 The concept of the marginal efficiency of capital, also introduced by Keynes (1936, Ch. 11), is quite simple: it refers to how much a given additional investment (hence the term "marginal") in real capital assets (for example, the purchase of new machinery, the installation of a new industrial plant, etc.) will yield in the future (in terms of profits generated by the sale of the products derived from it) compared to its price today. In addition to the real interest rate, the marginal efficiency of capital is determined by expectations, since it also depends on expected profits.

Although new developmental macroeconomics is suitable for developing countries that have managed to reach per capita income levels around the world average, the theoretical arguments were inspired by criticism of the Brazilian macroeconomic regime from 1995, a time when, having had trade and external financial liberalisation completed, the Brazilian government began to expressly adopt the "policy of growth with external savings", whose framework contributes to sustaining stagnation in the country. In fact, at the time of writing this chapter (November 2021), the arrangement of Brazilian macroeconomic policy can be observed as being guided by external financial liberalisation, based on foreign loans and investments, and by the "macroeconomic consensus" prior to the 2008 global crisis: an inflexible inflation targeting regime, focused almost exclusively on anchoring inflation expectations at the pre-established target level; a floating exchange rate regime with wide openness to the movement of short-term external capital; and a fiscal policy based on strict control of public spending, including investments. In the Brazilian case, this consensus was popularised as the "macroeconomic tripod" and was established between the end of 1998 and June 1999. Although I will return to this discussion in subsequent chapters, it is still worth asking: from a theoretical perspective, what does new developmentalism have to do with this?

The main hypothesis of new developmentalism is that countries whose macroeconomic regime is rigidly subject to the constraints of the "macroeconomic consensus" fall into an iron circle: development becomes impossible because the economy tends to fall into the trap of high real interest rates and an overvalued currency in relation to the dollar or the basket of currencies of the main trading partners.

According to new developmental macroeconomics, this trend is attributed to two policies commonly practiced in the Latin American periphery, especially in Brazil: a strategy of growing with external savings, which, by attracting net inflows of foreign capital, keeps the national currency tendentially overvalued; and maintaining a regime with nearly inflexible inflation targets, which preserves high real interest rates for long periods and causes additional capital inflows that appreciate the real exchange rate in the long term—a practice which is combined with the adoption of an ultra-conservative fiscal policy, based on the idea that the government budget must be permanently balanced, regardless of the economic cycle. These policies, by simultaneously depressing expected profit rates, the investment rate, and capital accumulation, form part of the "macroeconomics of stagnation". In the following subsections, I will discuss each of these policies in turn.[5]

5 While "Macroeconomics of Stagnation" ("*Macroeconomia da Estagnação*") is the title of Bresser-Pereira's 2007 book, the expression "policies as usual" is present in several works by

2.1 *Growth with External Savings*

The liberal argument for poor or developing countries to resort to foreign savings (i.e., "excess" foreign capital) to finance economic growth has a long tradition in neoclassical theory of international trade and economic growth.[6] According to this approach, poor or developing economies generally have a low rate of domestic savings (as a proportion of GDP), understood as the unconsumed portion of aggregate income. Since neoclassical macroeconomics assumes that the expansion of investments depends on domestic savings—unlike Keynesian theory, which reverses this causal relationship—, neoclassical liberal economists consider it natural and advisable that these countries resort to external savings to finance their growth in the long term.

It is argued that foreign savings, by complementing domestic savings, which are considered insufficient in most developing countries, make it possible to increase the investment rate and sustain growth in the long term. In other words, neoclassical economists suggest that developing economies with insufficient domestic savings rates engage in growth strategies with current account deficits and resort to net foreign capital inflows to finance them.[7] As Bresser-Pereira and Nakano (2003: 4) point out:

> The argument that low-income, low-savings countries should grow faster with the inflow of foreign savings seems logical and reasonable. In fact, if capital inflows finance current account deficits due to increased imports of capital goods, and if the investment rate increases, the economy will grow faster. Therefore, this strategy of dependent growth was accepted, without reservations, as true by almost everyone in Latin America and became an inherent assumption in the reasoning of economists, politicians, businessmen and also in all government decisions.

There are at least three counterarguments that invalidate the reasoning that recourse to external savings would increase the rate of investment and growth

---

new developmental economists. See, for example, Bresser-Pereira, Oreiro and Marconi (2014, Ch. 7), Nassif, Bresser-Pereira and Feijó (2018: 356) and Bresser-Pereira (2019: 206).

6 According to neoclassical international trade theory, which assumes the absence of capital flows between countries, a poor country could solve the problem of its relative capital shortage by adopting free trade practices: it would import capital-intensive goods (e.g., more sophisticated manufactured goods, such as automobiles and capital goods) and export labour-intensive goods (primary products and traditional manufactured goods, such as processed foods, clothing, and footwear). As I showed in Chapter 3, the ECLAC school rejects both the conclusions and normative implications of this theory.

7 I would recommend rereading footnote 23 (in Chapter 2), which presents the concept of balance of payments, as well as the meaning of current account deficits.

in developing countries in situations of capital scarcity. First, it is worth reiterating that as Keynesian criticism of (neo)classical macroeconomics maintains, it is not savings that determine investment, but the other way around. In fact, according to Keynes, assuming the existence of unused idle capacity and unemployment, the increase in investments leads to an increase in GDP and income which, given the marginal propensity to consume and assuming everything else constant, divides household income between the decision to spend on consumption and on savings. Therefore, investment precedes income generation and savings, not the other way around.[8] Furthermore, Keynes's (1936) argument is that investment depends simultaneously on the real cost of capital (real interest rates) and long-term expectations.[9] Additionally, as Schumpeter (1911) and Kalecki (1954) have shown,[10] financing is carried out, in practice, by retained profits ("capitalists' savings") and bank credit, which have nothing to do with the neoclassical concept of savings (the part of aggregate income not consumed by households).

Second, in a world of broad openness to the movement of international capital, growth with external savings brings, collaterally, excessive inflows of external capital and, consequently, a tendency towards chronic appreciation of the real exchange rate in the long term. As demonstrated by the Brazilian experience from the second half of the 1990s onwards, the main harmful effect of the

---

8 Neoclassical theory extends the microeconomic validity of the accounting identity between savings and investment to macroeconomic analysis, in terms of the National Accounts. In this case, assuming a "closed" economy (without relations to the rest of the world) and without a government, then GDP and aggregate income (aggregate supply side) are broken down, each year, into household consumption and investments made (aggregate demand side). Savings are understood as the portion of aggregate income not consumed, and therefore they are always equal to the investment already made (ex-post). In other words, although the accounting identity between savings and investment constitutes an irrefutable truth ex-post, considering that the latter has already been made and calculated, it is not so from the outset (planned ex-ante investment). Therefore, from a Keynesian macroeconomic perspective, the investment decision to be made does not depend on savings. For further details, the reader can consult Keynes (1936, Chapters 6 and 7).

9 Keynes (1936, Ch. 12) demonstrates that real interest rates maintained at adequate levels which reduce the cost of capital are a necessary but not sufficient condition for stimulating investment. The sufficient condition is that the "state of confidence" (i.e., a specific level of uncertainty that is quite low and widespread among most economic agents) stimulates the entrepreneurial animal spirits and, with it, investment.

10 In Kalecki (1954, Ch. 9), in particular, investments depend on the availability of one's own financial resources (retained earnings), the variation in profits and the variation in the fixed capital stock.

strategy of growing with foreign savings is the overvaluation of the national currency for long periods, with the exchange rate misalignment being forcibly eliminated by the market only when there are internal or external economic shocks. Anchored in Keynes and Kalecki's investment theory, new developmental macroeconomic theory thus exposes the connections between the real exchange rate and long-term economic growth. Excessive inflows of external capital ("external savings") appreciate the national currency in relation to the basket of currencies of the main trading partners. The persistent overvaluation of the domestic currency throughout an initial cycle of economic expansion **artificially** increases real wages (nominal wages minus the domestic price level) and the income received by rentiers (interest, rent and dividends). This increase is artificial because it results, at least in the short term, from the fall in the level of domestic prices induced by the persistence of the exchange rate overvaluation, and not from the advance in the economy's productivity. Thus, the artificial increase in real wages ends up depressing the expected profit rate and, consequently, the investment rate. Hence, by keeping the currency overvalued for a long period, the main deleterious effect of the strategy of growing with foreign savings is, paradoxically, to reduce growth in the long term.

Third, the strategy of growing with external savings tends to make growth cycles replicate stop and go trajectories that are short and quick, like chicken flights. Consider, for instance, that a developing country begins an expansionary cycle induced by high international liquidity and high commodity prices. As described earlier, excessive net capital inflows overvalue the national currency and **artificially** increase real wages. Consequently, the increase in household disposable income (the real mass of wages minus net taxes paid to the government) causes, for a given propensity to consume, an increase in consumption. However, as the currency is overvalued throughout the exchange rate cycle, most of the increase in aggregate household consumption ends up being used for imports, which become cheaper in the national currency to the detriment of local producers (national and multinational).

Furthermore, in an open economy, a country's total savings results from the sum of its internal savings and external savings, but according to Bresser-Pereira and Gala (2007), in economic terms, as overvaluation makes local companies non-competitive, external savings end up, in practice, replacing internal savings, instead of complementing them. Even if a small fraction of imports are capital goods, these are not capable of expanding and sustaining the investment rate because the exchange rate overvaluation discourages local production that competes with imports and the export sector. Therefore, this result contradicts the neoclassical argument: a significant part of aggregate consumption shifts to imported products, and foreign savings, in practice, **replace** the shortage of savings in most developing countries, instead of **complementing** them.[11]

2.2 *Dutch Disease and Its Neutralisation*

I previously showed how the strategy of growing with external savings ends up leading the economies of periphery countries to stagnation, after making them fall into the trap of high interest rates and a tendency towards currency overvaluation. According to the arguments discussed so far, the broad external financial opening associated with the policy of growth with external savings operates as a cause of the overvaluation of the national currency—making the prices of goods produced in the country (notably manufactured products) expensive, when expressed in foreign currency. Such effects are magnified by the relationship between the inflation targeting regime and the intensity and volatility of international financial capital flows. The new developmental theory, however, adds another explanatory factor for the tendency towards overvaluation: the Dutch disease that was not properly neutralised.

As I showed in Chapter 4, the spread of the Dutch disease, as it manifested itself in the Netherlands in the 1960s, unfolds as follows: initially, the discovery of a natural resource, such as oil or natural gas, attracts the interest of private and/or public investors, causing resources to move from the manufacturing sector to the commodities sector. After the investments mature, there is a boom in exports of the newly discovered commodity, followed by its expansion in the total export basket. The significant increase in net foreign exchange income tends to appreciate the national currency in real terms, consequently leading to the weakening of the manufacturing sector and deindustrialisation.

New developmental theory proposes a third model of the Dutch disease (Bresser-Pereira, 2008; 2019),[12] a model that distinguishes three "equilibrium" real exchange rates: the "current equilibrium", which balances the current account of the country's balance of payments; the "industrial equilibrium", an exchange rate that, because it is higher (that is, more undervalued) than the current equilibrium rate, makes industrial projects competitive that use state-of-the-art technology; and the "external debt equilibrium", the exchange

11 Bresser-Pereira and Nakano (2003) cite the study by Feldstein and Horioka (1980), who, based on a sample of 16 OECD countries, conclude that there is a high correlation between the rates of internal (and not external) savings and investment.

12 As I showed in Chapter 4, while Furtado (1957), based on the Venezuelan case, presents the seminal analysis of the Dutch disease, even before the phenomenon had appeared in the Netherlands, Corden and Neary (1982) propose the second model of neoclassical framework.

rate compatible with a current account deficit, but which does not increase the country's external debt/GDP ratio over time.

According to the new developmental concept, the Dutch disease in the Latin American periphery and in several other developing countries, instead of replicating the classic form that affected the Netherlands, takes on the form originally conceived by Gabriel Palma (2005). In this new concept of the Dutch disease, the increase in the commodities sector's share in the productive structure and in the export basket results from the set of liberalising economic reforms (trade liberalisation, opening to the international flow of short-term capital, etc.) adopted in the form of shock treatment—shock therapy, to use Lin's (2009) expression—given the intensity and speed with which they were implemented from the 1990s onwards.[13]

From this perspective, the new developmental theory conceives the Dutch disease as a structural problem that affects commodity-exporting countries. Those that industrialised were the countries that managed to neutralise this competitive disadvantage; those that deindustrialised were the countries that initially neutralised the Dutch disease, usually with import tariffs and, more rarely, with export subsidies, and after external trade and financial liberalisation, stopped doing so. Bresser-Pereira (2020a: 640) says:

> The Dutch disease is a competitive disadvantage that blocks the industrialisation of a developing country (for example, Venezuela or Saudi Arabia) or causes deindustrialisation in middle-income countries that, from a certain point onwards, implemented trade liberalisation reforms responsible for dismantling the protection mechanisms that neutralised it in the previous phase (the case of Brazil).

The pathway by which this new species of the Dutch disease leads to real appreciation of the domestic currency is similar to the original Dutch disease as described above: the impact of the commodity export boom on the expansion of the net supply of foreign exchange (mainly dollars). The difference is that the new developmental theory incorporates the three concepts of "equilibrium" real exchange rates, around which, in a freely floating exchange rate

13 As I showed in my PhD dissertation, the experience of trade liberalisation in Brazil, for example, runs counter to the recommendations in the literature on foreign trade reform: it was too fast and did not follow the sequence, since the elimination of non-tariff barriers was adopted simultaneously with the reduction of import tariffs, and it was carried out while the Brazilian currency was overvalued. For readers interested in these details, see Nassif (2003).

regime, the nominal exchange rates are negotiated and determined in the supply and demand markets for foreign exchange. Although these concepts involve technicalities and theoretical abstraction, I will try to explain them in the most didactic way possible.

The real exchange rate relevant to conventional economic theory is the exchange rate that balances the country's current account, the so-called real purchasing power parity (PPP). This is an equilibrium exchange rate that would provide identical benefits to the three economic agents that compete in a market economy: exporters, importers and domestic producers that compete with imports. To facilitate understanding, consider that the nominal exchange rate (i.e., the rate quoted daily in the foreign exchange markets) is currently R$5.60/US$ in Brazil. If the equilibrium real exchange rate (estimated by econometric methods) is R$4.20/US$, it can be stated that, in PPP terms, the Brazilian real is neither undervalued nor overvalued in relation to the US dollar; any nominal exchange rate below R$4.20/US$ would indicate overvaluation of the Brazilian real in relation to the US dollar, which would tend (on average) to benefit importers to the detriment of exporters and domestic producers that compete with imports. Therefore, the rate of R$5.60/US$ signals undervaluation of the Brazilian real in relation to the US dollar and, more than that, because it is much higher than the equilibrium real exchange rate of R$4.20/US$, it can be concluded that the Brazilian currency is overshooting (excessively undervalued).

It is important to emphasise that the empirical literature on the inter-relationship of the real exchange rate and economic development records two main conclusions: (i) unless it is reflected in an increase in the economy's average productivity in relation to the rest of the world, the overvaluation of the national currency for a long period of time reduces economic growth;[14] and (ii) all else remaining constant, **slight** (not excessive) undervaluation of the local currency accelerates economic development.[15]

Ergo, the new developmental theory calls the exchange rate corresponding to purchasing power parity the current equilibrium exchange rate. In the new proposed theory, the nominal exchange rate (observed in the exchange market) orbits around the current equilibrium. Yet, it is only the "industrial equilibrium exchange rate" that sustains economic development, because it is the one that makes companies using state-of-the-art technology competitive in each sector in which they operate. If the Dutch disease is neutralised and the

14 The main references are Razin and Collins (1999), Dollar and Kraay (2003); Prasad, Rajan and Subramanian (2006) and Gala (2008).

15 The main references are Rodrik (2008) and Berg and Miao (2010).

nominal exchange rate for goods produced in the country begins to fluctuate around the industrial equilibrium, the country will register current account surpluses.

However, instead of fluctuating around a slightly more depreciated industrial equilibrium, the nominal exchange rate may remain more appreciated than the current equilibrium exchange rate for a long time, and the country will enter a current account deficit in the balance of payments. If, assuming all else constant, the growth of external debt that this current account deficit determines is equal to or lower than the GDP growth rate, this exchange rate will still be sustainable (it will not lead to a balance of payments crisis), but it will be incompatible with industrialisation. The external debt equilibrium rate is the exchange rate that conventional economic theory calls the "fundamental equilibrium exchange rate" (FEER) and the one it recommends to developing countries.[16] And as if it were not enough that this rate is incompatible with economic development, it subjects periphery countries to recurring balance of payments crises.

If the industrial equilibrium exchange rate is the only one consistent with development, then it is important to understand what would redirect the nominal exchange rate from this competitive level. Figure 4 makes it easier to understand the forces that divert the exchange rate level from its "optimal" level ("industrial equilibrium") for economic development.[17] The broken and dotted lines show, respectively, the industrial equilibrium and current equilibrium real exchange rates. Since both show the appropriate **levels** at which the nominal exchange rate (solid line curve) should be maintained to sanction, respectively, technological progress and the balance of external accounts in current transactions, it is assumed that they remain practically stable, in real terms, over time.[18]

---

16 The fundamental equilibrium exchange rate (FEER) was conceived by John Williamson (1995; 2008).

17 In previous articles (Nassif, Feijó and Araújo, 2011; 2017), we defined the "optimal" real exchange rate for development as the one capable of allocating resources to the sectors with the greatest potential to generate productivity gains and sustain growth in the long run. As long as the industrial equilibrium rate is compatible with a slight (and not excessive) undervaluation of the national currency, it is identical to our "optimal" real exchange rate.

18 This is obviously a simplification, because if a country maintains a rate of economic productivity growth that is higher than the world average, its currency will tend to appreciate. In this case, which the economic literature calls the Harrod-Balassa-Samuelson effect, the appreciation reflects economic strength, not economic weakness.

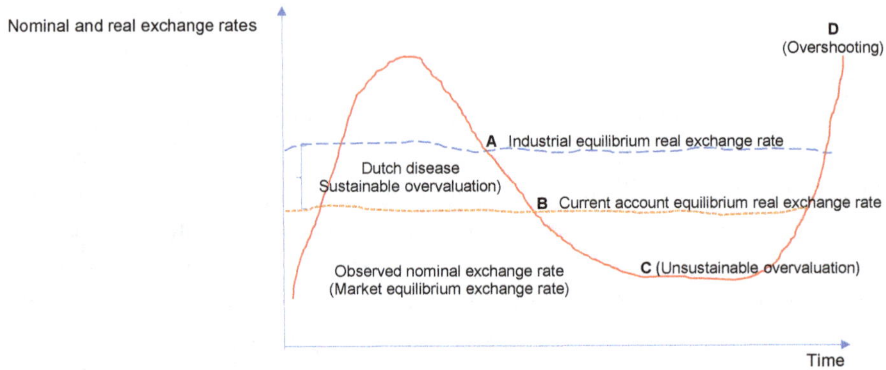

FIGURE 4 Exchange rates determination: New developmental approach
SOURCE: ELABORATED BY THE AUTHOR, BASED ON BRESSER-PEREIRA, OREIRO AND MARCONI (2016: 73)

The new developmental theory identifies two forces that trigger the tendency for the domestic currency to appreciate in real terms, diverting the nominal exchange rate from the industrial equilibrium level and therefore leading to exchange rate overvaluation: one structural and the other induced by market forces. The latter is represented by the debt-led growth policy or by "external savings" and the unneutralised Dutch disease. Assume that, at a given time, the international price of the commodities exported by a country is low and there is no Dutch disease. In this case, all else remaining constant, the nominal exchange rate reaches the industrial equilibrium rate, corresponding to point A.

However, if there is a boom in commodity prices, the nominal exchange rate declines (appreciates), fluctuating around the current equilibrium rate. Since the industrial equilibrium exchange rate has not moved, the Dutch disease causes the nominal exchange rate to tendentially move towards point B. The difference between the industrial equilibrium and the current account equilibrium (between points A and B) is the Dutch disease.

Although this initial exchange rate overvaluation is harmful to the economy's average productivity growth, since it encourages the allocation of resources to the commodities sector, which has lower productivity, it is sufficient to maintain the current account balance in equilibrium—that is, revenues from exports of goods and services, as well as income received from national factors operating abroad, are sufficient to pay import expenses and settle income remittances to foreign factors. Bresser-Pereira, Oreiro and Marconi (2016: 74) argue, in my opinion correctly, that "if we consider the competitiveness of the economy as a criterion, industrial equilibrium is the true [equilibrium], because it is the [desired] rate that the country must seek to develop."

Even so, the country has not yet hit rock bottom: up to point B, the nominal exchange rate does not lead to current account deficits. Let us assume, however, that the country tries to grow with external debt. Up to the current account equilibrium curve (the dotted line), the overvaluation will still be sustainable. Yet, for nominal exchange rate levels below this curve, the external debt/GDP ratio will begin to grow and the country, in addition to not industrialising, will be at risk of bankruptcy in the international financial markets. In this case, what accentuates the process of chronic appreciation of the national currency in real terms are market forces. Induced by the "usual policies" previously analysed, they end up causing an excess of net capital inflow, especially short-term capital, of a highly speculative nature. Though Figure 4 does not highlight the external debt equilibrium exchange rate, it is assumed that, from point C onwards, the level of external debt becomes unsustainable, and the country faces a chronic balance of payments crisis, with capital flight and exchange rate overshooting.

While it can be explained through theoretical reasoning, the exchange rate trajectory illustrated in Figure 4 replicates a stylised fact of what has been happening in Brazil since the end of 1999, after the adoption of the floating exchange rate and inflation targeting regimes. In general, by maintaining chronic levels of overvaluation of the Brazilian real for long periods, unsustainable current account deficits (such as between 1995 and 1998) or the occurrence of unpredictable internal and external shocks (such as the Covid-19 pandemic) trigger abrupt capital flights, high uncertainty and excessive depreciation (overshooting) of the national currency. This steers the country towards a financial crisis and the nominal exchange rate towards point D (overshooting), which is also considered inadequate, as it causes inflation, insolvency of national companies with debt in dollars, a mismatch in the balance sheets of financial and non-financial companies, among other adverse consequences.

3 Critical Points of the New Developmental Theory

There is no doubt that new developmentalism has made progress in positioning macroeconomics at the centre of economic development theory. Since this is still a work in progress, there are some critical points that, in my opinion, deserve to be re-evaluated and revised. I will mention three of them.

The first is to give the impression that new developmentalism considers only the Dutch disease as the triggering cause of the misalignment between the nominal exchange rate and the current equilibrium level. In fact, the difference between industrial equilibrium and current equilibrium is the Dutch disease, but the exchange rate also appreciates due to the debt-led growth policy or "external savings". Although the symptoms of the Dutch disease in Brazil are clear,[19] the brutal deindustrialisation was also caused by market forces resulting from the current macroeconomic policies (rigid framework of the inflation targeting regime, high openness to capital movement, among others), already analysed previously. Econometric studies allow us to identify and measure the coefficients of all the explanatory variables for the tendency towards currency overvaluation, but not necessarily isolate the one that triggers the initial impulse.

There are also normative recommendations aimed at neutralising the impacts of the Dutch disease on the real exchange rate. Bresser-Pereira (2020b) initially suggested the adoption of a variable tax on commodity exports. The tax rate would be zero when international commodity prices reflected the economic cost conditions (costs plus a satisfactory profit margin) of the sector, and positive during boom cycles in these prices. The author (op. cit.: 640) believes that "a variable tax on exports, by increasing the production costs of commodities, provokes the depreciation of the national currency until it reaches the industrial equilibrium level".

More recently, Bresser-Pereira (2020b) has been proposing a "second best" policy, which, according to the author, would be more politically viable in a country with a powerful and diversified commodity export sector: import tariffs and export subsidies. The law should provide for import tariffs to be split into two: a single Dutch disease neutralisation tariff, also variable with commodity prices; and a separate tariff for each product that should be lower than the current one. Recapping the example from the previous section, if the industrial equilibrium and current equilibrium exchange rates are estimated at R$4.40/US$ and R$3.80/US$, respectively, the export tax on commodities or the single import tariff on manufactured goods should be equal to R$0.60 (R$4.40 minus R$3.80) per dollar.[20] Ultimately, neither industrial sector entrepreneurs nor commodity sector producers would be affected: the former

---

19 For example, the share of commodities (primary products plus natural resources-based manufactured goods) in the total exported by Brazil increased from 38.8% in 1990 to 65.8% in 2020! The data are in Nassif and Morceiro (2021: 25).

20 Although new developmental authors estimate the industrial equilibrium rate by comparing unit labour costs (i.e., the ratio between average wages and productivity) in Brazil and its main trading partners, it is assumed that it is only slightly higher than the neutral real exchange rate (R$4.20/US$, as in the example in the previous section), which would hypothetically yield identical benefits for exporters, importers, and domestic producers competing with imports. A real exchange rate that is excessively higher than the neutral rate would accelerate the inflation rate. Readers interested in estimating the industrial equilibrium exchange rate can consult Marconi (2012).

because they would be rewarded by the increase in the exchange rate, and the latter because they would continue to have, in practice, the same exchange rate they had before the Dutch disease neutralisation policy. The burden of the tax, in the short term, would fall on "workers, the middle class and financial rentiers" (op. cit.: 640), because their wages or their interest, rent and dividends would lose some of their purchasing power. In the long term, workers' losses are expected to be offset by the positive effect of a competitive real exchange rate on economic growth.

There are, in my view, reasons to doubt the effectiveness of the variable tax on commodity exports. The main one is that it would only correct the initial exchange rate overvaluation if the increase in production costs discouraged the volume supplied of the commodities affected by the tax. In practice, though, this is unlikely to happen: given the international demand for commodities, producers are unlikely to be willing to reduce production, either because sales are subject to medium or long-term contracts or because entrepreneurs will not risk losing markets. And let us not forget the political difficulties of adopting a tax of this nature, not to mention its administrative management over time, which would be extremely complicated.

The second critical point of the new developmental theory is the excessive emphasis given to macroeconomic variables, especially the real exchange rate, as an (almost) sufficient condition to put countries that have fallen into economic stagnation, such as Brazil, back on a sustainable path towards catching up. In this regard, I reiterate that the best alternative for achieving this objective is to revive the tradition of national development plans, adopted in Brazil in the past and still in force in several Asian countries, including South Korea, China and India, plans in which the long-term economic policy (industrial and technological policy, physical and human infrastructure, etc.) is linked to the macroeconomic regime. Incidentally, in an article published in the *Cambridge Journal of Economics* (Nassif, Bresser-Pereira and Feijó, 2018), we discussed a theoretical milestone regarding the connections between industrial policy (understood as development policy) and macroeconomic policy, something practically non-existent in the literature.

This demonstrates that new developmentalists are not resistant to the alternative given above. So much so that Bresser-Pereira (2020a: 634–635) states that

> new developmentalism recognises that industrial policy is crucial for development, but understands that a country only acts in a developmental manner if, in addition, it efficiently manages the two main macroeconomic accounts—the fiscal and the current account—and if it

> maintains macroeconomic prices [notably, the real interest rate and the real exchange rate] at levels appropriate to sustain economic growth.

The problem is that this position does not always appear with due emphasis in the works of most authors of this theoretical group. For example, in the concluding section of the cited article, Bresser-Pereira (op. cit.: 640) lists more than a dozen policies that, from the perspective of new developmentalism, would be necessary to "sustain growth, financial stability, reduce inequality and protect the environment". All the suggested policies are macroeconomic in nature. It would be highly beneficial to re-evaluate such an undefined position, if only to avoid criticism, such as that recently made by Medeiros (2019: 150), who complains about the lack of a "systemic vision" of new developmental theory.

The third critical point is the defence of an export-led development strategy, even for continental-sized economies, such as Brazil. An export-led growth strategy is appropriate for economies with potentially small domestic markets (South Korea and Chile, for example), where the share of domestic demand components (consumption, investment and public spending) in GDP is lower or not much higher than that of exports. But it is not advisable to use such a strategy in economies of continental dimensions (such as the United States, China, India and Brazil), where the potential for maximising the static and dynamic benefits provided by economies of scale is enormous. I think this conclusion, however, has been settled on since the publication of the seminal articles by Linder (1961) and Posner (1961).

To be clear, export dynamism is crucial to ensuring a successful development strategy. However, I cannot agree with Bresser-Pereira's (2020a: 641, emphasis added) thesis that, although there is "the debate between an export-led strategy versus a domestic-led strategy, **the latter only makes sense if the country adopts an import substitution strategy, which is an outdated strategy**."

My disagreement is based on two reasons: the first is that there is no dichotomy between the dynamism of the domestic market and that of exports (especially of manufactured goods), as evidenced best by the experiences of China and India, both of whom have maintained high rates of investment and growth in manufactured exports in recent decades;[21] the second is that,

21 The difference between investment rates in Brazil, China and India over the last two decades is abysmal. According to data from the World Bank, gross fixed capital formation in relation to GDP between 2000 and 2019 was, on average, only 18% in Brazil, compared to 40.5% and 31%, respectively, in China and India. The same database also records that the average annual growth rate of exports in Brazil, in the period 2000–2020, was lower (6.6%) than that of China (16%) and India (9.3%).

as I have already shown in Chapter 2, Thirlwall's law reinforces that it is crucial to maintain a growth rate of exports higher than that of imports, but this has nothing to do with export-led growth, but rather with the need for the country to be able to count on a sufficient flow of foreign currency to finance the growth of imports.

4 Conclusion

The main conclusion of this chapter is that new developmentalism not only does not oppose, but in fact complements classical, ECLAC and Furtadian developmentalism, relying especially on the three central arguments of the structuralist-developmental school: (i) the manufacturing industry is the dynamic engine of economic development; (ii) periphery countries are subject to external constraints to growth; and (iii) extreme dependence on commodity exports can condemn developing countries to structural stagnation in the long term. However, by integrating macroeconomics into the theoretical analysis of long-term economic dynamics, new developmentalism represents an advance over "old" developmentalism.

CHAPTER 7

Conclusion and Policy Implications of Part 1: in Defence of the Return of National Development Plans

This chapter, acting as a conclusion of Part 1, aims to draw out the main normative implications of the developmental theories analysed in the previous chapters. The main conclusion is that laissez-faire policies, as well as engagement in unconditional free trade practices, and even government interventions directed only at correcting market failures[1] do not provide the way for overcoming underdevelopment or stagnation in countries that successively replicate low growth over decades, as is the case in most Latin American countries, especially Brazil.

This means that there are solid theoretical arguments for the adoption of what is conventionally called "industrial policy". Although the term "industrial policy" covers several definitions, the one I use in this chapter is an adaptation and compilation of the concepts of Chang (1984), Rodrik (2004) and Krugman, Obstfeld and Melitz (2015). It refers to the diversity of government intervention instruments, like import tariff protection, production subsidies, government procurement, a minimum level of local content, among others, with the objective to (i) prioritise activities, segments and sectors, including those outside the manufacturing sector, with a high potential to create and disseminate technical progress; (ii) sustain productivity advancements, in order to boost changes in the productive structure (i.e., promote "structural change") oriented at expanding the share, in terms of value added, of goods and services sectors with high income elasticity of demand; and (iii) consequently promote the economic development of nations.

The ultimate objective is to facilitate the catching up of poor or middle-income countries—stagnate or not—to high levels of per capita income and social well-being. As Erik Reinert (2008) argues, today's developed countries only managed to reach income levels of "rich countries" because, in practice, their governments did not follow the liberal recommendations originating from the Ricardian principle of comparative advantage. Countries

1 This argument will be critically analysed in Chapter 11.

 | DOI:10.1163/9789004734296_010

that are unconditionally guided by this principle "stay poor".[2] Furthermore, as documented by Mariana Mazzucato (2015) in her seminal book "The Entrepreneurial State", even developed countries link their long-term policies to the use of various industrial policy mechanisms. In so doing, they seek to protect themselves against economic regression or falling behind.

I should highlight one caveat regarding political economy: industrial policy, to be successful, must be conceived in a systemic way, whereby it is linked to all other public policies at the micro- (such as tax, regulatory and foreign trade policies, among others), meso- (for example, science & technology, education & training, etc.) and macroeconomic (such as monetary, fiscal and exchange rate policies) levels. Harmony between different spheres of public policy has an effect similar to that between conductor and musicians in an orchestra: the lack of harmony between one or more members compromises the performance of the ensemble. In this perspective, industrial policy aims at the same general objective as national development plans, which is why I will use both terms as synonyms. This means that the arguments in favour of adopting industrial policy, analysed below, serve essentially to defend national development plans (NDPs).

For low-income countries with economies heavily dependent on traditional agriculture, the main argument for adopting NDPs is the need to protect infant industries, as elaborated in detail by List in 1841. The justification is based on the recognition that a backward country, if it unconditionally engages in free trade practices, will be unable to develop its productive forces and converge to average per capita income levels similar to those of advanced countries.

The reason is obvious: with a precarious industrial sector and very low competitiveness, free trade causes the backward country to perpetuate its dependence on manufactured imports. As I have shown in previous chapters, due to the low income elasticity of demand for its main export products (agricultural and mineral products), this country is subject to recurring balance of payments crises.

However, in economies at intermediate stages of development, which have remained stagnant for decades, such as Brazil and several middle-income countries, instead of the classic argument of protecting infant industry, the neo-Schumpeterian argument of technological gaps is the most appropriate to theoretically justify the adoption of NDPs. It is worth noting that, although the argument for protecting infant industry presupposes the existence of technological gaps between countries, the existence of gaps does not necessarily imply

2 The original title of Reinert's book is "How Rich Countries Got Rich … and Why Poor Countries Stay Poor".

that the appropriate argument to justify the implementation of NDPs is that of infant industry. Therefore, the main justification for the adoption of NDPs in countries that have already reached the stage of semi-industrialised economies, like Brazil, is the existence of significant technological gaps in relation to the international frontier—as I illustrated in Figure 3, in the Introduction to this book—and not the protection of infant industry.

The technological gap argument was developed by neo-Schumpeterian economists such as Cimoli, Dosi and Soete (1986), Cimoli (1988), Dosi, Pavitt and Soete (1990) and Cimoli and Porcile (2010). These authors theoretically demonstrate that the most important factors for explaining the dynamism of international trade and economic growth are associated with the absolute technological gaps that exist between productive sectors within each country and also between countries on a global scale—in this case, measured by the differentials in sectoral productivity and per capita income.

These works revisit Schumpeter's (1942) original thesis, analysed in Chapter 1, according to which technological innovations are the preponderant factors in accelerating the process of economic development. They are the ones that, associated with capital accumulation, produce and reproduce the absolute and relative differences between technological capabilities and the growth rates of productivity and per capita income between countries in the global economy.

Technological gap models present a powerful argument for developing countries, especially those undergoing intense premature deindustrialisation—like Brazil—to guide their long-term government policies through the implementation of NDPs. The argument is grounded in two main points: first, is that sectors differ from each other in terms of the pace and potential for generating and disseminating innovations, once dynamic increasing returns are triggered, which, in turn, manifest themselves as a cause and effect of innovations and technological progress. Thus, in the absence of NDPs, technological gaps between sectors and countries tend to become self-cumulative, given the path-dependence and lock-in characteristics of their respective technological trajectories (Arthur, 1989);[3] and second, as industrial sectors differ from each other in terms of returns to scale (static and dynamic) and the capacity to generate innovations and disseminate positive economic externalities throughout

3 According to Arthur (1989), technological change is path-dependent when past events, that is, history, exert a powerful influence on future innovations, learning and technological progress. Change becomes locked-in when historical events subject the economy to the monopoly of a technology, superior or not.

the economy, in the absence of NDPs, signals emanating exclusively from market forces tend to be insufficient to promote an allocation of resources that maximises the potential for social return, expressed in sustainable increases in productivity, growth in per capita income and reduction in inequality.[4]

Cimoli and Porcile (2010) formally demonstrate that the ability of the periphery developing countries of the South, "technology imitators", to catch up with the core developed countries of the North, "innovators", depends on two fundamental conditions to be met by the former: (i) being successful in the strategy of diversifying their productive structure and their export basket in goods and services with high income elasticity of demand in global markets; and (ii) building an export agenda whose income elasticity of demand is higher than the income elasticity of demand for their imports, that is, satisfying Thirlwall's law, analysed in Chapter 2.

To this end, NDPs must prioritise activities, segments and sectors with a high potential to imitate, absorb, launch and disseminate innovations to other sectors and, preferably, to the entire economic system. In other words, appropriate NDPs in countries experiencing economic stagnation, such as Brazil, consist of resuming structural change and diversification of the productive and export structure towards goods and services with high income elasticity of demand in global markets.

Despite the solid theoretical arguments in favour of development strategies being guided by national plans aimed at accelerating and sustaining catching up, the difficulties lie in defining and combining a set of instruments that produce the expected benefits in the medium and long term. As I have mentioned before, this problem is illustrative of the popular saying: "talk is cheap; doing is what matters", or, as Rodrik (2008a) titles one of his articles, referring to the problems concerning the implementation and management of NDPs: "don't ask why; ask how".

Although there is no rule of thumb that explains the successful experiences of the so-called Asian tigers (South Korea, Taiwan, Singapore and Hong Kong), Amsden (1989; 2001), Wade (1990), Mazzucato (2015) and myself in Nassif (2019) indicate the following fundamental requirements for NDPs to be consistent and produce positive results:

4 Krugman (1992: 14) emphasises that "the social return on resources allocated to high-technology sectors exceeds the private return. For this reason, if international competition leads certain countries (that adhere to pure and unconditional free trade practices) to divert resources from these sectors to sectors that operate under constant or diminishing returns, this process will tend to reduce social welfare."

i. *Permanent prioritisation of government investments in physical infrastructure (diversified transportation modes, urban planning and mobility, sanitation, etc.) and human infrastructure (adequate health and education systems at all levels, from early childhood to higher education):* if the role of industrial policy is to produce structural change aimed at diversifying the production of goods and services with greater technological sophistication, it is clear that countries that avoid bottlenecks and deficiencies in physical, health and education infrastructure will be able to generate greater positive externalities to reduce the costs associated with the modernisation of existing activities and the introduction and dissemination of innovations. It is worth noting, however, that investments aimed at creating and maintaining basic infrastructure do not, per se, ensure sufficient conditions for promoting structural change and catching up. To use economic jargon, horizontal policies are not enough; they must be complemented by vertical policies. This means that governments must establish clear strategies regarding which activities, segments and sectors will be prioritised over time;
ii. *selectivity of priority activities, segments and sectors throughout the arduous effort of catching up:* although the principle of comparative advantage implies the misleading normative conclusion that all countries obtain reciprocal gains arising from unconditional adherence to free trade—because it is based on unrealistic assumptions, such as constant returns to scale, perfect competition in goods and factor markets, homothetic demand, etc.—, it contains a practical message of the utmost importance: as no country will be efficient under autarchic conditions, for NDPs to obtain efficient results in static terms (reduction of unit costs) and dynamic terms (increase in productivity and economic growth in the long term), it is necessary that goods and services arising from activities, segments and sectors considered non-priority (notably capital goods and intermediate goods that may not benefit from government incentives) have import tariffs reduced or equal to zero;
iii. *focus on activities, segments and sectors with the potential to trigger and disseminate technological innovations:* this requirement is important not only because technological innovations are the main structural source of growth in the long run, but also because underdeveloped and developing countries already tend to have "natural" comparative advantages in traditional sectors, whether they are intensive in unskilled labour or natural resources;

iv. *creation of mechanisms that enable companies in the manufacturing sector subject to economies of scale, as well as those in the tradable service segments, when applicable, to become competitive in order to reach the global market:* although Linder's (1961) hypothesis still remains valid, according to which obtaining export competitiveness in various segments of the manufacturing sector requires the prior use of a domestic market large enough to exhaust the minimum efficient scales necessary for competition in the international market, the fact is that the government can offer internationally accepted incentives, such as drawback, export credit for manufactured goods, etc., to accelerate the access of potential exporting companies to the international market. With this, they will not only be able to improve technological learning and the quality standards of the goods produced, since they will have feedback from consumers in countries with different levels of per capita income, but they will also contribute to increasing the foreign exchange needed to sustain the balance of payments in the long term;

v. *permanent performance requirements from companies that receive government benefits or have tariff protection:* the government must have institutions and human resources that can monitor the results of companies that receive any form of industrial protection. These results are expressed in increased labour productivity, reduced unit costs and export efforts over time, all of which are considered easy indicators to obtain and calculate. As John Stuart Mill (1848) suggested, if protected companies do not show concrete results over time, incentives should be reduced or even withdrawn, where appropriate;

vi. *policy strategy focused on foreign direct investment (FDI):* following the example of Asian countries, mechanisms for attracting FDI should focus on quantitative aspects, such as stimulating greater investment inflows, and, following the example of China and India since the 2000s, they also need to negotiate conditions for subsidiaries of multinationals to transfer technologies to local firms operating in related activities, segments or sectors;

vii. *use of the most appropriate stimulus mechanism to enable the success of the innovative effort by companies, which means that the choice of each mechanism varies on a case-by-case basis:* in some situations, the most appropriate mechanism may be import tariff protection, in others, the local content policy, or the government's purchasing policy; and in many other situations, the combination of one or more instruments;

viii. *balance between competition and protection:* protection levels should be restricted to those strictly necessary to allow technological learning by local producers;

ix. *deadline for granting import tariff protection and other forms of incentive to local production:* although economic theory has no answer regarding the deadline required for companies, when going through the entire technological learning curve, to be able to make unit costs and quality standards converge to the levels found in innovative countries, the successful experience of some Asian countries shows that the government should gradually reduce the incentives granted until they are completely eliminated. To this end, in each industrial policy program, companies must be informed of these deadlines, so that they can prepare themselves to face external competitive pressure in the future. Even if the deadlines initially planned are exceptionally extended, strict discipline is necessary to prevent entrepreneurs from becoming inactive and continually attempting to obtain unproductive income, the so-called rent-seeking, as emphasised by Anne Krueger (1974);

x. *finally, and probably most importantly, there needs to be a continuous and close coordination of all spheres of industrial and technological policies (science & technology, education & training, customs tariff system, regulatory apparatus, etc.) with macroeconomic policy:* this means, in light of new developmental propositions, that policymakers should make efforts so that the mechanisms of macroeconomic policy, normally managed with the aim of ensuring growth and monetary stability, also serve to anchor the expected ends of the NDPs, especially the increase in productivity and the pursuit of the catching up trajectory. It is worth remembering that the role of macroeconomic policy should be to ensure an environment of stability not only to satisfy the demands of financial markets, but mostly to prolong, as much as possible, the "state of confidence" (to use the term consecrated by Keynes, 1936: 148) necessary for the "animal spirits" of entrepreneurs to be stirred up and to face the uncertainty inherent in expectations of future profits resulting from current investments in physical capital and innovations. With respect to the alignment of industrial and macroeconomic policies, it is worth mentioning Kaldor's (1970) proposition, which, very much in line with new developmentalism, suggests that, all else remaining constant, the undervalued real exchange rate acts as the most powerful instrument for sustaining the goals pursued by industrial policy. In summary, Kaldor (op. cit.: 152) observes that

> of the two instruments for counteracting adverse trends in "efficiency wages"—protection and [currency] devaluation [in real terms]—

> the latter is undoubtedly greatly superior to the former. Devaluation [which produces a slight undervaluation of the domestic currency in real terms], as has often been pointed out, is nothing else but a combination of a uniform ad valorem duty on all imports and a uniform ad valorem subsidy on all exports. (1970: 152)

It must be acknowledged that, in practice, the NDPs of most developing countries (including Brazil) have not met any of the ten requirements listed above. It is true, though, that the results of NDPs are uncertain in any country. Their success depends fundamentally on the skill with which they are designed and the harmony with which their various mechanisms are managed. Such mechanisms include the definition of priority activities, segments and sectors, the establishment of customs protection, the types of subsidies granted, financing mechanisms, the necessary coordination with macroeconomic policy to maintain real interest rates and competitive real exchange rates compatible with productive investments and innovations, among others. As Robert Wade (2015) argues, NDPs, understood as a goal-focused effort to change the productive structure of an economy and accelerate the development process, should be compared to an "inner wheel" whose effects depend on "outer wheels", notably macroeconomic conditions and the consistency of other government policies.

In the case of Brazil, for example, it is worth recalling that the persistence of economic stagnation is generally attributed to the fact that the country has not integrated itself into the so-called global value chains and has no adequate institutions to carry out successful NDPs, points that are repeated, again and again, to exhaustion.

Regarding global value chains, they have been formed in recent decades as a result of the enormous fragmentation of production in the global economy into final products, parts, components and other intermediate goods. However, it is important to remember that global value chains are controlled by large multinational companies.[5] Asian countries have been the most successful in proactively integrating themselves into these global chains, precisely because they have combined gradual trade liberalisation with industrial policies, whose the main objective is **to promote the diversification**, and not the specialisation, of their productive structure.

With respect to the problem of the lack of adequate institutions to carry out successful NDPs—"inclusive political institutions", as Acemoglu and Robinson (2012: 79–83) would say—it is worth highlighting that this criticism would only make sense if institutional modernisation were conceived as an

5 The theoretical foundations of global value chains will be analysed in Chapter 8.

exogenous factor in the development process, according to the neoclassical institutionalist approach, popularised by the seminal work of Douglas North (1990). In the heterodox approach, however, the construction and dissemination of "inclusive political institutions" are endogenous. That is, they emerge with the process of economic and social development itself, which means that institutional modernisation is the result of the very long-term process of learning-by-doing.[6]

---

6 This approach is consistent with the work of several authors, such as Johnson (1982), Wade (1990) and Amsden (2001), among others.

PART 2

The Neoclassical Liberal School

Prologue to Part 2

While developmentalism blossoms from the conceptual roots of Smith, Marx and Schumpeter, the neoclassical liberal school unfolds from the theoretical framework of Ricardo, Mill and Walras. At the macroeconomic level, an immense channel also separates both currents: developmentalism is close to Keynesianism, while neoclassical liberalism extends, first, into monetarism and, later, into the new classical school.

The neoclassical liberal school is characterised by great methodological cohesion, because its theoretical models start from and maintain, as much as possible, the assumption that markets function and achieve ideal conditions of perfectly competitive equilibrium. While this school does not ignore the fact that markets in a capitalist economy are characterised by various types of imperfections, such as monopolies, oligopolies and negative externalities when, for example, carbon dioxide emitting activities are exploited, such imperfections, at the theoretical level, are analysed as mere "market failures", being understood as temporary divergences from the general competitive equilibrium that can be achieved in the long term.

Neoclassical economists do not admit that this analytical perspective is ideologically tainted. On the contrary, they claim that ideology is discarded when they conceive of the functioning of markets in the idealised ("utopian", as Richard Caves, 1960, would say) form of perfect competition. As already defined in the Introduction (see footnote 14), in this form of competition, prices are entirely determined by the market due to the presence of many suppliers and demanders and the absence of economies of scale, as well as any barriers to the entry of potential competitors. Furthermore, the income appropriated by capitalists and workers fully reflects their respective opportunity costs and marginal costs, that is, the income of each reflects only their respective marginal productivity.

In my opinion, this theoretical perspective does not free the neoclassical liberal school from ideological bias. After all, it is impossible for human thought to be free of ideology—also because exempting something from ideology is already, itself, an ideology. In the case of the neoclassical liberal view, above all, the ideological bias is latent when it treats, at least from a theoretical perspective, the existence of oligopolies as failures or temporary departures from perfectly competitive equilibrium. While for the developmental school (especially in the neo-Schumpeterian framework), the existence of economies of scale, externalities, monopolies and oligopolies is the rule in capitalist economies, for the neoclassical liberal school this occurs by exception.

 | DOI:10.1163/9789004734296_011

This theoretical positioning would be less problematic if the confrontation between perfectly competitive general equilibrium and partial equilibrium in a monopoly or oligopoly were proposed to compare hypothetically idealised situations to those prevailing in the real world. Coincidentally, this was the perspective of Marshall (1890), considered one of the founders of microeconomics.

In the macroeconomics field of economic development, however, the neoclassical liberal school preferred to follow the perspective of Walras (1874), who showed, pioneeringly, that if all markets operate under conditions of perfect competition (for goods, services and production factors), the economy reaches general equilibrium, with a single solution for prices and quantities produced. Since competitive general equilibrium would provide a more efficient allocation and distribution of productive resources and income to factor owners, this paradigm is used to radically defend laissez faire practices. The problem is that, since the real world does not replicate Walrasian general equilibrium, the neoclassical liberal perspective reinforces the idea that reality should adjust to theoretical models, and not the other way around.[1]

In the following chapters, I do not intend to exhaust the vast arsenal of neoclassical economic theory, but to focus on the central questions relating to economic development and stagnation. In particular, I will highlight theories developed in the context of economies open to trade in goods and services and to capital flows. The neoclassical theoretical program, although marked by specific differences, has in common the classic proposition that economic development results from the free allocation of productive resources in capitalist economies—this is, in fact, why they are neoclassical: the theoretical development of this school reaffirms the classic postulates of Smith and Ricardo that the free market is the best way to organise the economy. The "invisible hand" coordinates and harmonises such movement through the free fluctuation of supply, demand and relative prices.

---

1 It is no mere coincidence that the title of Walras's main Treatise (1874, emphasis added) is, in the original French, *Abrégé des Éléments d'Économie Politique* ***Pure***.

CHAPTER 8

International Trade Theories and the Case for Free Trade

1 Introduction

As I have shown in previous chapters, in the developmental perspective, economic development is an eminently dynamic phenomenon. In the neoclassical liberal approach, the phenomenon is predominantly understood as a static situation, associated with a specific moment in economic time. It is also viewed as comparative statics in that it compares what occurs at two distinct points in time. In both cases, the analysis is timeless because no changes that have occurred in continuous time are noted. The exceptions—among which are the economic growth models of Solow (1957), Romer (1986) and Lucas (1988), as well as the new endogenous growth models in economies open to international flows of goods, services and knowledge—are islands in the vast neoclassical ocean in which the static approach is dominate.

This chapter thus analyses the theoretical arguments for and against laissez faire practices and free trade in goods and services at the global level. I first discuss how the Ricardian principle of comparative advantage forms the central analytical basis for the defence of this liberal principle. I also show the contribution of the new neoclassical theories of international trade (new trade theories), which incorporate the hypothesis of imperfect competition, notably in the form of oligopoly. Since there are different patterns of oligopolistic competition, the results in each case may confirm or refute the advantages of reciprocal free trade. Since refuting the advantages of free trade offers solid arguments for the practice of protectionist measures, I will mainly explore the case in which a specific form of oligopoly competition, called monopolistic competition, brings benefits to all countries that engage in free trade practices in the international market.

 | DOI:10.1163/9789004734296_012

2 New International Trade Theories and the Reaffirmation of Free Trade

2.1 *Comparative Advantage versus Imperfect Competition: New Theoretical Arguments for Free Trade*

The principle of comparative advantage, both in the original Ricardian view and in the neoclassical Heckscher-Ohlin model, has already been analysed in Chapter 3 (Section 2). Although Ricardo's seminal idea was simply to show that some trade is always preferable to no trade, the price equalisation theorem of goods and factors of production (already discussed in Chapter 3) gave rise to the neoclassical concept of comparative advantage to be used as a theoretical basis for the unconditional defence of international free trade.

There are two problems with the concept of comparative advantage, especially in the neoclassical version. The first is that it assumes both technology and factor endowments in each country as given at a certain moment. The second, and most important one, is that it is based on completely unrealistic assumptions and hypotheses, such as the absence of economies of scale, income-elasticity of demand equal to unity for all goods and services, and perfect competition in all markets. It is no coincidence that the unrealistic nature of the hypotheses gave rise to Prebisch's (1949) strong criticism of the normative implications of the concept, notably the defence that unconditional free trade would be beneficial to the economic development of periphery countries.

The issue changes completely when we characterise capitalist economies as they actually are in the real world: islands of not necessarily perfectly competitive markets surrounded by monopolies and oligopolies on all sides. In truth, the most general case is that markets operate in oligopoly. Such a situation implies that only a few companies produce on a large scale, are responsible for most technological innovations in processes and products, and have a greater capacity to determine prices and hold significant market shares, to the detriment of their actual or potential competitors.

Linder (1961) was one of the first authors to question the general validity of the comparative advantage model. For him, this theory only explains the part of international trade in which the differential in relative costs and prices depends on the factor endowment existing in each country. Thus, countries abundant in natural resources, such as fertile land and mineral resources, tend to export goods that are intensive in natural resources, such as agricultural products, oil and other fossil fuels.

However, the theory of comparative advantage does not show great explanatory power for international trade in manufactured goods. According to Linder (op. cit.), when companies exploit significant economies of scale, compete for product differentiation, introduce brands and modify existing models, prior exploitation of the advantages provided by the size of the domestic market is crucial to enable sufficiently large production scales so that they can compete in the international market. In other words, to achieve competitive conditions in the export of manufactured goods, market size matters. Ergo, countries such as the United States, China and Brazil have, in principle, greater **potential** to produce and competitively sell differentiated manufactured goods in global markets than Chile, Ghana and Costa Rica, for example.

The fact that continental-sized countries have **potentially** large markets does not mean, however, that they can be **effectively** competitive in exporting manufactured products. Linder's model suggests that they should temporarily protect their domestic markets until they reach competitive production scales to exploit global markets. One of the reasons for the proliferation of regional economic agreements that integrate countries with similar per capita income and demand profiles, such as Mercosur (Mercado Común del Sur) and the European Union, is the possibility of expanding the size of the market and, consequently, enabling competitive production scales, so that trade expands within and outside the blocs.

Since the 1970s, several neoclassical models, labelled by Krugman (1990) as "new trade theories", have incorporated the hypothesis of imperfect competition in the international market for goods and services. In addition to this inclusion, the adjective "new" is justified because:

i. In oligopoly market structures, it is much more complicated to determine the trade pattern. It depends on a set of simultaneous variables, such as market size, number of competing companies, factor prices, absence or presence of economies of scale, degree of barriers to entry for competitors, etc. Depending on the combination of these factors, Helpman and Krugman (1985: 86–88; 53–55) showed that the trade pattern (what each country tends to export and import) can be indeterminate or present multiple possible results ("multiple equilibria");
ii. Graham's (1923) original conjecture is valid: in the presence of economies of scale and market concentration under the command of the largest companies, trade globalisation can cause gains from trade to be concentrated in some countries, imposing losses on others. To prove this hypothesis, Helpman and Krugman (1985: 50–55) demonstrated mathematically that, under free trade, if productive resources in a given country are reallocated from sectors operating with economies of scale to traditional sectors, the gains from trade can be fully appropriated by the other trading partner where the reallocation of resources occurs in the opposite direction;
iii. the models of the new international trade theory began to adopt Vanek's (1968) suggestion of estimating each country's trade pattern based on the

> net content of productive factors incorporated in exports and imports. This procedure allowed the traditional model of comparative advantage in the Heckscher-Ohlin-Vanek (H-O-V) form to interact with the new models of international trade, in which the realistic hypotheses of the existence of economies of scale, product differentiation and monopolistic competition are present, as I will show below.

Before analysing the general case, Krugman (1980) demonstrates what determines the pattern of international trade in manufactured goods. His objective is to reaffirm the advantages of free trade, even in the presence of economies of scale and product differentiation. To demonstrate that economies of scale are the main determining element of the capacity to export manufactured goods, Krugman (op. cit.) assumes that two countries, for example, Brazil and Argentina, have identical technologies and factor endowments. I will assume that both are capital abundant. With zero transportation costs,[2] if Brazil and Argentina engage in reciprocal free trade, the trade pattern will be determined by economies of scale and product differentiation. Thus, only one among different goods (imperfect substitutes) will be produced by a single firm in a single country.

In this case, by no longer being governed by comparative advantage, the trade pattern no longer assumes the inter-industry type—in which Brazil, for example, would export automobiles and import dairy products from Argentina. Economies of scale and product differentiation become decisive factors, and the trade structure assumes the intra-industry configuration, in which, for example, Brazil and Argentina would export and import automobiles differentiated by brands and models. Generalising, Krugman (1980: 952, emphasis added) concludes that the gains from (free) trade are preserved because "the world economy is capable of producing a greater **volume and variety** of products [regardless of whether each of them is cheaper or more expensive than in the other country] than would be possible in a single country alone."

In the same article, Krugman (op. cit.) also considers what happens if one of the two countries (for example, Brazil) has a larger domestic market than its partner. In this case, the trade pattern conforms to what is intuitively expected: the country with the highest per capita income has the greatest potential for exploiting economies of scale and, therefore, the greatest potential demand for manufactured goods, as had already been suggested by Linder (1961). Hence, it will be a net exporter of the entire range of differentiated manufactured goods whose production technologies are subject to economies of scale.

2 Krugman (1980, Section II: 953–955) shows that incorporating transportation costs does not change the overall result.

In another article, Krugman (1981) manages to formally integrate the traditional model of comparative advantage in the Heckscher-Ohlin version with the central hypotheses of the new international trade theory, namely, the existence of economies of scale in the industrial sector, the continuous differentiation of products as a strategy for gaining market share and monopolistic competition.[3] That article completes the trilogy that justified the awarding of the Nobel Prize to Krugman.[4] Furthermore, it was also the academic work that reaffirmed the theoretical basis for free trade, although not unconditionally, as in the case of comparative advantage. I will show why.

Krugman conceives a model in which the world economy is composed of several countries differentiated by their respective endowments of productive factors. I will summarise the author's model assuming that there are only two blocs of countries: the developed ones of the "North" ("core"), abundant in capital and scarce in natural resources, and the developing ones of the "South" ("periphery"), abundant in natural resources and scarce in capital. Additionally, world production comes from two sectors: the sector producing primary and manufactured goods intensive in natural resources ("commodities"), and which operates with traditional technology (absence of economies of scale) and under perfect competition; and the sector producing manufactured products intensive in scale, science and knowledge, and which operates with economies of scale, produces differentiated goods and operates in monopolistic competition. With this model, Krugman seeks to answer two questions: (i) what determines the pattern of international trade? and (ii) does free trade still provide reciprocal net benefits for both groups ("gains from trade")? Figure 5 helps to elucidate these questions.

Krugman concludes that the trade pattern will be governed simultaneously by traditional comparative advantages and by the forces of monopolistic competition. The forces of comparative advantage determine the net exports (exports minus imports) of each group—those of developed countries being composed of manufactured goods, the production of which makes intensive use of the abundant factors available in this bloc (capital, science and knowledge), while those of developing countries are commodities, the production of which intensively uses natural resources, the abundant factor of this bloc. Due to the difference in the factor endowments of the two blocs, this trade range is typically inter-industry, since the net exports of each are made up of

3 It is worth rereading footnote 14 (in the Introduction to this book), where I summarise the main market structures and competition patterns, according to neoclassical theory.

4 The trilogy is composed of the articles from 1979, 1980 and 1981. The 1990 article is a more didactic version of the 1981 paper. See Krugman (1979; 1980; 1981; 1990).

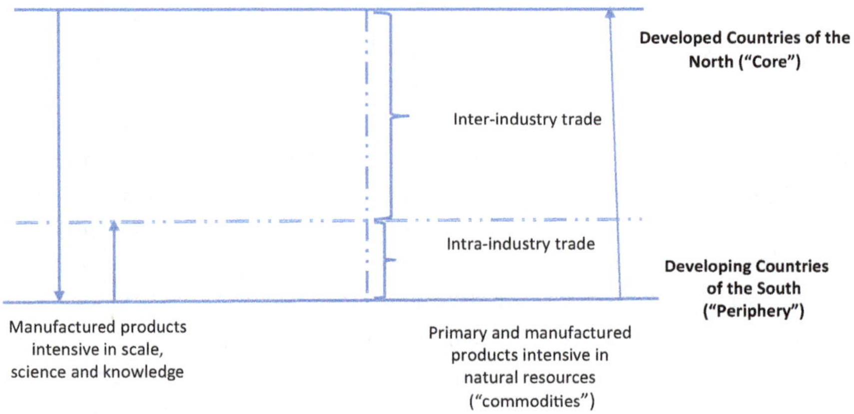

FIGURE 5 Pattern of international trade between developed and developing countries
SOURCE: PREPARED BY THE AUTHOR, BASED ON KRUGMAN (1990: 77)

products from different sectors. It should be noted that the explanatory factor of the trade range governed by comparative advantage is the difference in international relative costs and prices. Developed countries, because they are abundant in capital, science and knowledge, are able to produce manufactured goods relatively cheaper than developing countries. The latter, in turn, produce commodities with lower relative prices.

However, a smaller portion of the total flow of international trade between the two blocs is made up of intra-industry trade: both blocs can export and import manufactured goods, whose trade is no longer explained by the difference in relative costs and prices and starts to be explained by product differentiation. The reciprocal competitive pressure generates a reduction in the total number of industrial plants in the two blocs of countries and a convergence of the largest economies of scale. The result will be a fall in relative prices in the world economy.

So, the questions now: Are there benefits from free trade? And do both blocs obtain reciprocal gains? The joint model of comparative advantage and monopolistic competition conceived by Krugman (op. cit.) ensures that there are, for two reasons. The first is because it endorses the canonical result of the comparative advantage model. By concentrating net exports on products that intensively use the abundant factor and net imports on goods that intensively use the scarce factor, each bloc can import goods relatively cheaper than would be possible if it renounced productive specialisation. The second is because, regardless of the higher or lower relative prices of manufactured goods observed after free trade, the gains from trade are assured by the greater volume and variety of products available to consumers in the world economy.

As Figure 5 shows, the illustrated case suggests that the share of intra-industry trade in manufactured goods in the total trade flow is relatively small. This is because the case exemplified involves trade between two blocs that are quite unequal in terms of levels of technological development and per capita income. Ultimately, if the two blocs had completely identical factor endowments, per capita income and development patterns, the entire trade flow would be intra-industry and would consist solely of differentiated manufactured goods. This is why most of the trade flow between Brazil and the United States is inter-industry: it is governed by comparative advantage. But among the EU's richer partners, the pattern is intra-industry, driven by economies of scale, product differentiation and monopolistic competition. In short, Krugman's model shows that, because they have similar factor endowments and levels of technological development, it is the developed countries themselves that transact most of the trade flows of technologically more sophisticated manufactured goods in the world economy.

2.2 *Global Value Chains and the Liberal Ideological Bias*

The proliferation of models of the new international trade theory coincided with unilateral and multilateral trade liberalisation in the 1980s and 1990s. The completion of the Uruguay Round of the General Agreement on Tariffs and Trade (GATT) in 1994 culminated in the formation of the World Trade Organisation (WTO) and led to the elimination of several non-tariff barriers, in addition to a significant cut in ad valorem customs tariffs among member countries.

In the following decades, the intensification of international competition led to an intense displacement of subsidiaries of American and European multinational companies to Asia and Eastern Europe, especially to countries that had a supply of medium-skilled labour and lower relative wages. This succession of events prompted a trend towards global fragmentation of goods and services production, reflecting the strategic option of multinational companies to specialise in products, parts, pieces and/or components, as a way of maximising the benefits of economies of scale. Economists quickly appropriated the concept originally introduced by Michael Porter (1980; 1989) from the Harvard Business School and began to identify the aforesaid trend as the proliferation of global value chains.

Since multinational companies are the ones that control most of the global production and trade of goods and services, new theoretical models of neoclassical lineage have sought to formally identify the main explanatory factors behind the decision of these companies to establish subsidiaries abroad, especially in the manufacturing sector. The models map three distinct forms of foreign direct investment (FDI), each dependent on the main factors that condition the prospects for maximising profits and/or expanding the market share of multinational companies outside their country of origin.

The first, presented by Helpman (1984), is called vertical multinational FDI. It occurs when the multinational company decides to maintain its main headquarters in the country of origin but directs the activities of production plants for final goods, parts and/or components in different countries according to the differences in the relative prices of production factors (capital, labour, among others).

The second, modelled by Markusen (1984; 2002), concerns horizontal multinational FDI. When a multinational company decides to operate production plants characterised by specific (and generally high) fixed costs in several countries, its choice of country will depend on the difference in transportation costs between the country of origin and the destination.

The third form of FDI, called complex integration, was summarised by Helpman (2011: 147), who was inspired by the classic propositions of Melitz (2003) and Melitz and Treffler (2012). It consists of the combination of simultaneous horizontal and vertical FDI strategies by the multinational company. Its subsidiaries establish factories abroad and allocate part of the production of final goods to the host countries and part to export. However, they import intermediate goods (parts, pieces and components) from affiliates located in other countries, through international trade between the affiliates themselves (intra-firm trade). The portion of the production of final goods destined for export may be carried out via intra-firm trade, or extra-firm when there is a sale to other companies.

Since complex integration has been not only the most widespread form of FDI in recent decades, but also the mechanism that interconnects global value chains, it is worth identifying its main determining elements. Helpman (2011: 148) suggests "analysing horizontal FDI, vertical FDI, and FDI platforms—when FDI is predominantly export-oriented—as interrelated strategies". In what follows, I summarise the author's theoretical model by means of an example.

The global economy is composed of a group of large countries in the "North" (e.g., the United States, Japan and Germany) and small countries in the "South" (the Philippines, Vietnam, and Indonesia). In order to produce a differentiated final good, intermediate goods are incorporated, the location of which in the global economy depends on the relative fixed costs of each country and the productivity levels of the companies involved in the FDI strategies.

Global value chains result from four different types of FDI strategies, illustrated in Figure 6. The first strategy occurs when, assuming the absence of transport costs and some fixed cost in the manufacture of a final good, the

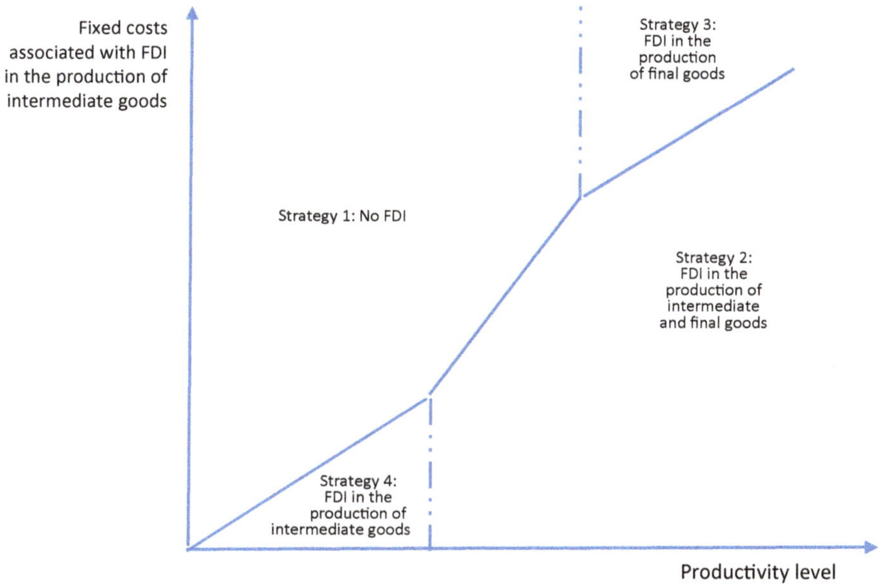

FIGURE 6 The genesis of global value chains: different foreign direct investment (FDI) strategies
SOURCE: HELPMAN (2011: 151)

fixed costs of producing intermediate goods are so high that they make FDI economically unviable in the countries of the South, both in the assembly of final goods and in the production of intermediate goods. In this case, the low productivity levels of companies in countries of the North do not provide sufficient economies of scale to cover the high fixed costs of producing intermediate goods.

The second strategy occurs when the productivity levels of multinational companies from countries of the North are sufficiently significant to offset the enormous fixed costs associated with FDI. In this case, companies tend to invest in the production of both intermediate and final goods in the host countries of the South.

In the third strategy, companies with above-average productivity from the North can engage in FDI aimed at the production of final goods in countries of the South but are unable to provide FDI aimed at the production of intermediate goods in production plants that operate with extremely high fixed costs.

In the fourth strategy, low-productivity firms in countries of the North are only able to engage in FDI for the production of intermediate goods in countries of the South if the fixed costs of the latter are sufficiently low to compensate for the firms' reduced efficiency.

Although they were designed to distinguish the FDI strategies of multinational companies from countries of the North, these theoretical models clearly show that, due to their smaller relative size, companies from the South countries rarely manage to engage in FDI and transform themselves into multinationals. These models also suggest that the extreme tendency towards specialisation inherent in global value chains, although it may bring unequivocal advantages to the large multinational companies that control them, may not necessarily bring the same benefits to the countries that receive them. In other words, while adopting strategies that result in greater productive specialisation is undoubtedly advantageous for multinational **companies**, the Asian experience has shown that the best strategy for sustaining the pace of productivity growth in **nations** is productive diversification, especially in the manufacturing sector. This strategy, pursued by countries such as South Korea, China and India,[5] confirms the validity of the developmental theories discussed in the previous chapters.

Brazilian neoclassical liberal economists, for example, repeatedly state that one of the reasons for the stagnation of average productivity in the domestic manufacturing sector is Brazil's weak engagement in global value chains. Their argument is that Brazil's integration into these global value chains would require a new round of trade liberalisation characterised by a linear cut in customs tariffs.[6] It is alleged that Brazil is a country that is quite closed to international trade. The problem is that, as I showed in an article in the Brazilian newspaper "*Valor Econômico*" in 2018,[7] the concepts of degree of openness—measured by the share of exports or imports in GDP (or even by the sum of exports and imports in GDP)—and levels of protection or trade liberalisation are not identical.[8]

In this article, I argued that, when measured by size criteria, Brazil is in fact a fairly closed country compared to others with similar development patterns. However, when measured by the import/GDP ratio, there is a low degree of trade openness because imports are pro-cyclical and, therefore, have been low because Brazilian GDP has grown at low average rates. If measured by the exports/GDP ratio, the low level of trade openness reflects the stagnation of the average productivity of the Brazilian economy and the absence of structural

5 Empirical evidence can be confirmed in Wade (2015) and UNCTAD (2018), for the case of developing countries in a comparative perspective; and in Marconi, Magacho and Rocha (2014: 125) and Nassif, Feijó and Araújo (2017), for the cases of the BRICS (Brazil, Russia, India, China and South Africa).

6 This is the recommendation of Bonelli (2015: 487) and Bacha (2016: 3).

7 See Nassif (2018).

8 See Nassif (2018).

changes in recent decades. In other words, to transform Brazil into a country more open to international trade, it will be necessary to restore the dynamism of the economy, which would increase GDP and productivity and, thus, expand imports and exports, respectively.

Despite this, it cannot be said that the country is extremely protected, since the average tariff on imported products (11.6% in 2017) is lower than that of India (13%), which is also a developing country, and that of South Korea (14.1%). Even so, it is true that, given the relatively high average tariffs in the Brazilian manufacturing sector, I have argued that a new round of trade liberalisation is legitimate. However, customs rates should not be reduced abruptly and linearly (using the across-the-board method), but rather restructured on a case-by-case basis (using the "concertina" method), in conjunction with the country's development policy. This is, in fact, the recommendation of the literature on trade liberalisation, as shown in the classic books by Bhagwati (1978) and Michaely, Papageorgiu and Choski (1991).

3 Conclusion

Despite the inestimable wealth of the vast theoretical literature that seeks to determine the expected static effects of international free trade on economic efficiency and the well-being of society, the only conclusion that can be drawn is that, since there is no general theory of international trade, it is also not possible to draw a general conclusion. The prediction that free trade **always** ensures an increase in society's total consumption (the "gains from trade"), as well as an increase in the economy's average productivity, depends on several quite restrictive conditions, the most important of which is the existence of perfect competition in all markets.

The incorporation of hypotheses more consistent with market structures and competition patterns prevailing in most productive activities reduces the explanatory power of the traditional theory that trade and its benefits are governed by comparative advantage. The new hypotheses do not, however, guarantee that free trade always improves the productivity and well-being of a given country.

In a world dominated by various forms of imperfect competition, especially oligopolies, it is impossible to reach a general conclusion. Therefore, the analysis must be made on a case-by-case basis. Nevertheless, since in most trade models with imperfect competition the trade pattern becomes indeterminate or presents multiple equilibria, it is equally impossible to ensure that the improvement in economic efficiency, in a broad sense, results exclusively from the free play of market forces.

However, as long as the state of technology is assumed to be a given, the concept of comparative advantage continues to serve to show that, even in a world dominated by imperfect competition, it is unlikely that any country will be able, in practice, to maximise the average productivity of its economy—and therefore accelerate economic development—if it remains almost or completely closed to international trade. In any case, the advantages of the international division of labour and productive specialisation remain valid. Strictly speaking, in oligopolistic markets, the model of monopolistic competition with product differentiation corroborates this old conclusion of classical political economy. Broadly speaking, international trade acts as a mechanism for disciplining competition in highly oligopolistic markets, contributing to the reduction of the mark-up desired by competing companies.

Nevertheless, in all models presented in this chapter, technical progress was assumed as a given. This means that when there are gains from trade, they are of the once-and-for-all type, and no conclusion can be drawn about the change in their structure over time, much less about their impact on the trajectory of a country's economic development. In the next chapter, I will show that once the incorporation of technical progress as an endogenous variable in international trade models is admitted, it becomes possible to evaluate, in greater substance, to what extent this condition affects the efficiency of an economy in dynamic terms.

CHAPTER 9

The Neoclassical Macroeconomics of Growth

1 Introduction

In this chapter, I intend to analyse the likely impacts of international trade on the efficiency of the economic system in dynamic terms. My purpose is to incorporate intertemporal changes, which are absent in the "old" and "new" theories of international trade analysed previously, and to assess whether, and if so to what extent, unconditional adherence to free trade has positive or adverse effects on the long-term growth rate of the economy.[1]

Unlike the structuralist theories of economic development discussed in Part 1, in which growth, in addition to involving structural change, is driven by the dynamism of aggregate demand in the long run, neoclassical growth models, including those "open" to international trade, are all explained by the supply side. The late Professor Fábio Erber, from the Federal University of Rio de Janeiro (UFRJ), used to say, in a colloquial tone, that structuralist economic development models are "more about transformations" since they assume the perspective that growth simultaneously involves structural change. Neoclassical economic growth models, he said, are "more of the same" since they limit themselves to analysing the forces that determine GDP growth in the long run. Hence, the preference of neoclassical authors for the expression "economic growth" instead of "economic development".

For didactic purposes, I divide this chapter into three sections: in the first, I analyse neoclassical growth models from the perspective of economies closed to international trade in goods and services; in the second, I discuss neoclassical models from the perspective of "open economies", which incorporate the hypothesis of a given country to engage in international free trade of goods, services and knowledge; and in the third, I present the heterodox neo-Schumpeterian critique of neoclassical growth models in economies "open" to trade flows of goods, services and knowledge.

1 There is vast theoretical literature that analyses the effects of growth on international trade, but not vice versa. The discussion over this, in addition to being more recent, has been growing in importance in the academic debate. Incidentally, the seminal works of Hicks (1932, Chapter 6), Rybczynski (1955) and Bhagwati (1958), which deal with the impacts of economic growth on international trade, all following the neoclassical approach, ended up being incorporated into traditional textbooks on international economics.

 | DOI:10.1163/9789004734296_013

The reader should be informed that although neoclassical growth models contain complex mathematical formalisation, I will limit myself to capturing their main hypotheses and analysing their conclusions in a descriptive manner. The few equations that appear throughout the chapter should not discourage the reader, as they will be interpreted textually.

2 Growth Models in Closed Economies

2.1 *Keynesian Theoretical Background*

Despite the revolutionary nature of Keynes's General Theory, published in 1936, its emphasis is on the factors that determine fluctuations in GDP, income and employment in the short run. In the language of conventional macroeconomists, the General Theory focuses on the analysis of the business cycle in the short run, supposedly placing less emphasis on long-term growth.

Keynesian economists, however, soon sought to incorporate into their analysis the factors that determine the behaviour of aggregate demand in the long run. The first major contributions to the theory of economic growth, from a Keynesian perspective, date back to the classic essays by Roy Harrod (1939) and Evsey Domar (1946), from which the Harrod-Domar equation, found in most macroeconomics textbooks, was derived. It is the starting point for long-term growth models, including the neoclassical ones. Although the focus of this chapter is on neoclassical models, it is worth recapitulating the essence of the Harrod-Domar Keynesian model.

In general terms, this model suggests that equilibrium in the real sector of a closed economy requires that planned investment be equal to planned savings, that is:

$$I = s_y \, Y \tag{9.1}$$

where I is investment, Y is aggregate income and s_y is the marginal propensity to save, that is, the proportional increase in savings S as income Y varies. In dynamic terms, I can be interpreted as the capital stock, K, since investment increases the stock of K over time. Equation (9.1) does not violate the Keynesian principle that investment decisions depend fundamentally on the long-term expectations of entrepreneurs. This is a long-term relationship in which investment tends to vary *pari passu* with the growth rate of real output and income Y (accelerator principle, according to which the growth of income Y itself induces additional investment).

To avoid possible misunderstandings, Harrod (1939: 19) warns that:

> the equation is consistent with Keynes's proposition that [in a closed economy] savings necessarily equals investment—but investment ex-post [already realised]. Savings does not necessarily equal investment ex-ante [planned, to be realised], since machinery, equipment and other investment capital goods may have been produced in quantities above or below those needed.

Dividing equation (9.1) by K, we find the Harrod-Domar equation, denoted in (9.2):

$$g = \frac{s_y}{q} \tag{9.2}$$

where g is the growth rate of the capital stock (in mathematical terms, $\dot{K}/K$) and q is the capital-output ratio (i.e., K/Y). The Harrod-Domar equation suggests that the long-term growth rate depends on the savings rate and the capital-output ratio.[2] However, if this relationship remains constant, economic growth will depend entirely on the marginal propensity to save in the long term.

Harrod (1939: 16) calls the long-term growth rate the "warranted" growth rate. This is the rate that would generate a sufficient level of output to satisfy all business owners with what had been planned to meet a certain expected demand, without resulting in a lack or excess of unsold stock. Thus, the warranted rate consistent with entrepreneurs' ex-ante planning is the one that makes the planned output level equal actual aggregate demand.[3] Aggregate supply will also equal aggregate demand in this case because if entrepreneurs

2 The capital-output ratio measures the capital stock needed to generate each unit of real output (GDP). The inverse of this ratio is nothing more than the average productivity of capital. Note that Harrod's model implicitly assumes the Keynesian principle that, in the long run, growth depends on the investment rate. In a numerical example, if the economy's propensity to save is 10% of income and the capital-output ratio is equal to 4, the annual GDP growth rate in the long run will be 2.5% (since 0.10/4 = 0.025).

3 It should be noted that the warranted rate of growth is not necessarily the rate of growth compatible with full employment. This is what Harrod (1939: 30) calls the "natural rate of growth, [which is] the maximum rate of output growth compatible with the rate of population growth, capital accumulation and technical progress on the assumption that the economy is operating at full employment".

expected a certain aggregate demand, they produced an equivalent aggregate supply to meet it.

However, the warranted (planned) rate may not correspond to the realised (or the actual) rate. In Harrod's model, in particular, business cycles are inherently unstable because ex-ante investment may exceed or be lower than ex-post investment. In the first case, there is a stimulus to economic expansion, since the investment made is lower than the planned investment. Entrepreneurs, as a whole, underestimate the growth in demand for goods and services—which indicates a lack of stock. In this case, the warranted growth rate is lower than the realised one.

In the second case, there is overproduction and there will be a stimulus to economic contraction, since the investment made is greater than planned. Entrepreneurs, as a whole, make a mistake when estimating the growth in demand for goods and services, which indicates unsold production and, therefore, excess stocks. This is what happens when the warranted rate exceeds the realised rate. In short, there are business cycles because, due to uncertainty about future effective demand, investments fluctuate and mean that the warranted rate of output growth does not necessarily equal the growth rate of actual output. The main message of Harrod's model is that capitalist dynamics do not ensure any tendency towards equilibrium in the long run.

2.2 *Neoclassical Growth Models in Closed Economies*[4]

In the 1950s, Harrod's model was criticised by the neoclassical school. The conclusion that long-term growth depends on savings was questioned. But what was most disturbing was the demonstration of the Keynesian thesis that capitalism is an inherently unstable system. Solow's neoclassical model, still one of the most influential in academic circles today, directly criticised Harrod's. Developed independently by Robert Solow and Trevor Swan in 1956, it is often known as the Solow-Swan model.

The Solow model (1956) completely ignores the role of aggregate demand, attributing the fundamental determining force of long-term growth to supply-side factors. It is the first influential model that sought to explain the differences between the levels and growth rates of per capita income across countries through an aggregate production function. For the individual firm, the production function is defined as a technological relationship in which the product depends on the combinations of different productive factors and inputs, such as capital, labour, land, and elements such as the state of technology, managerial and labour efficiency, etc.

4 The formulas described in this subsection combine the notations of the original authors referenced and those contained in the excellent textbook by McCombie and Thirlwall (1994).

In the Solow model, however, the production function is defined in aggregate terms and is restricted to three factors: capital, labour, and the state of technology. The model is that of a non-monetary economy that produces a single good that is representative of the economy as a whole. The firms that produce it operate in perfect competition. Solow (1956: 85) expresses the aggregate function as follows:[5]

$$Q = K^{1-\alpha}L^{\alpha}A(t), \tag{9.3}$$

where Q is the level of output (GDP), K is the economy's capital stock, L is the labour force, $A(t)$ is the state of technology at the time t, and $1 - \alpha$ and α are technical coefficients that represent the returns to the capital and labour factors, respectively.[6]

Two assumptions of the model are ad hoc and unrealistic, but crucial for its main results: the first is that the aggregate production function is subject to constant returns to scale. This means that if all factors vary according to a certain multiplicative, the level of aggregate output Q varies in exactly the same way, keeping the average productivity of the economy unchanged. The second is that, since the rate of change in the labour force grows at the same rate as the population growth, the capital factor is the only one to vary and presents diminishing returns. This means that the growth rate of output varies in smaller proportions than the growth rate of the capital stock. Note, then, that the Solow model gives the three basic sectors of the economy (primary, secondary and tertiary) the same importance in the process of economic growth. Therefore, it ignores the crucial role of the manufacturing sector as an engine of growth, so emphasised by developmental economists.

Through various mathematical manipulations,[7] we arrive at the growth rate of real output in the long term:

$$q_t = (1 - \alpha)_t k_t + \alpha_t l_t + \lambda_t \tag{9.4}$$

5 Solow expresses equation (9.3) in exponential form $Q = K^{1-\alpha}L^{\alpha}Ae^{\lambda t}$. However, the function expressed in equation (9.3)—known as the Cobb-Douglas production function—is the one most used in nearly all empirical studies that use the growth accounting method to estimate the parameters of the Solow model.

6 Returns to scale measure the combined impact of all factors of production on the total produced.

7 For the reader interested in the mathematical demonstration, equation (9.4) is reached through the following steps: equation (9.3) is differentiated with respect to time t; then all terms on the left and right sides are divided by Q; and, finally, this last result is rewritten in instantaneous rates of change.

where lowercase letters indicate instantaneous growth rates of the model's variables, $(1 - \alpha)$ and α are the shares of capital and labour in total output, respectively, and t is the time.[8] Equation (9.4) shows that the long-term growth rate of real GDP (q) depends on the growth rates of the capital stock (k) and the labour force (l), as well as on technical progress (λ). As McCombie and Thirlwall (1994: 149) point out, "both long-term output growth and capital accumulation depend on (and are equivalent to the sum of) the increase in Harrod-neutral technical progress [i.e., which increases incorporated employment] and the increase in the labour force".

In view of the unrealistic nature of its assumptions, the model cannot explain why per capita income levels between countries are so disparate. Given that in the Solow model technical progress is exogenous (given) and the labour force grows *pari passu* with the increase in population, if growth is sustained only by capital accumulation, the growth rate of the economy tends to converge to zero, since the capital factor is subject to diminishing returns!

Furthermore, as McCombie and Thirlwall (1994) point out, the Solow model leads us to believe that there is "unconditional convergence" between the per capita income levels of all countries in the long run. This means that, regardless of their different initial per capita income levels, as all countries experience the same rates of technical progress—because they all have free access to the same technology, which is considered exogenous—, population growth and capital depreciation, the model predicts that they will all converge to the same capital-labour ratio (K/L). Therefore, all countries will converge to the same per capita income in the long run. This eliminates the distinction between poor and rich countries! It is clear that this conclusion violates the results observed in the real world, since the possibility of convergence, when it exists, is not absolute, but relative.

Solow correctly concludes that technical progress is the only driving force capable of diverting the economy from the tendency toward stagnation in the long run. But theoretically this conclusion is problematic because technical progress, the fundamental force of development, is not explained in the model, since it is exogenous. For this reason, technical progress has been considered theoretically and empirically as a residual (the so-called "Solow residual"). Suggestively, Moses Abramovitz (1993) called it the "measure of our ignorance".

Despite theoretical limitations, the Solow model is the main basis for estimating aggregate productivity. Instead of calculating it using the classical labour productivity indicator, many economists prefer to estimate it using

8 While equation (9.3) expresses the determinants of GDP in the long run in terms of level, equation (9.4) expresses these same determinants in terms of rates of change.

total factor productivity (TFP), linking it directly to the Solow growth model. The rate of change of TFP in each period t is estimated as the residual of equation (9.4) and is expressed as follows:

$$tfp_t = \lambda_t = q_t - [(1-\alpha)_t k_t + \alpha_t l_t] \tag{9.5}$$

In this form, TFP is the difference between the variation rate of aggregate output growth and the variation rates of the labour force and capital stock, weighted by the respective shares of these two factors in total output. The growth rate of labour productivity is $p_t = q_t - l_t$, that is, the difference between the variation rates of the output and the labour force.

One of the most hard-hitting criticisms of the Solow model, as well as of TFP as a reliable measure of productivity estimation, is related to the fact that it is not possible to calculate the economy's aggregate capital stock. This criticism has its roots in the famous Cambridge controversy over the concept and estimation of capital, which pitted leading Keynesian economists from the University of Cambridge in the United Kingdom (Joan Robinson, Luiggi Pasinetti, Nicholas Kaldor and Piero Sraffa) against those from the Massachusetts Institute of Technology (MIT) in Cambridge in the United States (Robert Solow and Paul Samuelson). In short, economists at the British university emphasised that, because capital has heterogeneous technical specificities and is continually subject to technological change, it is not possible to find units of measurement for capital in different sectors and, in the end, aggregate such measures into the same common unit.

Many developmental economists turn a blind eye to the reliability of capital stock estimation and still defend TFP as the most appropriate criterion for estimating productivity. McCombie and Thirlwall (1994: 23), for example, prefer TFP, arguing that it

> allows the contribution of the capital stock to the total productivity of the economy to be incorporated separately. A limitation of labour productivity is that it would be only a partial criterion for evaluating efficiency. For example, a significant increase in labour productivity can only be the result of a significant increase in the number of machines available to workers.

It is interesting that, despite the impossibility of finding reliable measures to calculate the capital stock, TFP indicators do not have the tendency to estimate absurd results. Herbert Simon (1979) and Anwar Shaikh (1974), who had demonstrated the mathematical inconsistency of the aggregate production function, argued that this paradox occurs because estimates of aggregate production functions reflect the accounting identities that underlie them. Although the estimated indicators are quite close to the observed ones, Shaikh (1974) showed that TFP estimates are based on theoretical tautologies.[9]

At the theoretical level, the Solow model (1956) carries the totally unrealistic and counterintuitive result that, once the steady state of the economy is reached, the investment rate does not affect growth in the long run. However, this result is only possible because of the assumption that the capital factor is subject to diminishing returns. This defies Piero Sraffa (1926), who, in a very rigorous essay published 30 years earlier, demonstrated that the Ricardian law of diminishing returns is not valid to explain the dynamics of capital.

By abandoning this hypothesis, endogenous growth theories, which came to fruition from the end of the 1980s onwards, sought to save the neoclassical approach by preserving supply-side forces as the main drivers of growth and by insisting on conceiving the level of output and its long-term dynamics through an aggregate production function. The two most influential models in this line are those of Romer (1986) and Lucas (1988). Both value mathematical elegance, but in order to obtain equilibrium solutions they continued, to some extent, to use unrealistic assumptions, even though they assumed the much more realistic hypothesis that the state of technology and technical progress are endogenous and, therefore, explained by the model.

I begin with Romer's model (1986), which is based on a Cobb-Douglas type aggregate production function expressed as follows:

$$Q = F(K, L, E)\, G(E') \tag{9.6}$$

where Q is the level of aggregate output; K is the capital stock, L the labour inputs (normally expressed in hours); E is the stock of technological knowledge held by the firm; and E' is the stock of knowledge of the economy. The model assumes a representative firm, which replicates the characteristics of all other firms that compete in the economy, whether in the same or different markets.

In order to obtain a mathematical equilibrium solution, the function F is characterised by two ad hoc assumptions: (i) it is concave; and (ii) it is homogeneous of degree 1 in K, L and E (which means that the level of output varies in the same proportion as the variations of these factors). The novelty is that the E' factor is subject to increasing returns to scale, so growth depends

9 For those interested in the mathematical proof, see Shaikh (1974).

fundamentally on the accumulation of aggregated knowledge resulting from technical progress.

But how can we obtain a result in equilibrium if one of the factors is subject to increasing returns? This is possible because the model introduces another ad hoc hypothesis: that economies of scale are external to the firm, which causes externalities emanating from the stock of "public" knowledge to leak to all other firms, whether they are innovators or imitators. This assumption is essential and is made ad hoc to ensure general competitive equilibrium (Walrasian general equilibrium).[10]

The model is then calibrated to allow considerations of its possible outcomes. It is assumed that K, E, and E' grow at the same rate in the long run, which makes equation (9.6) become:

$$Q = F(L, K)\, G(K) = L^{\alpha} K_t^{(1-\alpha)} K^{\psi} \tag{9.7}$$

Since $\psi > 1$, K^{ψ} can be interpreted as the capital stock amplified by the accumulation of technological knowledge. However, if $(1 - \alpha + \psi) < 1$, there will be diminishing returns to capital, so the investment rate will not have a positive effect on the GDP growth rate in the long run. To escape this Solow-like result, Romer (op. cit.) works with the hypothesis that $(1 - \alpha + \psi) \geq 1$. However, if $(1 - \alpha + \psi) > 1$, the output growth rate would be explosively high in the long run. Since such a result is very unlikely, Romer began to work with the hypothesis $(1 - \alpha + \psi) = 1$ and concluded that, due to constant aggregate returns, but increasing in K^{ψ}, the growth rate of output is proportional to the rate of increase in investment. With these juggling acts, Romer managed to explain the nature of economic growth from the neoclassical perspective.

Translating expression (9.7) into logarithmic form, it becomes possible to present growth accounting according to Romer's model:

$$Q = \alpha l + (1 - \alpha + \psi)\, k \tag{9.8}$$

Unlike the Solow-Swan model, Romer-based growth accounting does not contain any residuals to be estimated, since technological progress is endogenized in the model.

Lucas's (1988) model is similar to Romer's. The difference is that, instead of technology being expressed as a stock of knowledge, it is conceived as an

10 If the hypothesis were that of economies of scale being internal to the firm, which would be much more realistic, a case of competition under oligopoly would be configured, making modelling in general equilibrium impossible.

accumulation of human capital, assumed to be the main driver of economic development. The aggregate production function is composed of the conventional factors K and L, plus the human capital available to each individual (H) and the stock of human capital available in the economy as a whole (H').

Both forms of human capital have positive effects on the long-term growth rate of productivity. The "individual" rate increases the productivity of the individual worker. Together with that of other workers, it also increases the productivity of the firm. In other words, individual human capital has internal effects, while the human capital accumulated by each worker generates positive external effects, reciprocally benefiting all workers in the economy. Similar to E and E' in Romer's model, it is assumed that $H' = H$. Furthermore, it is assumed that each worker spends a part of his/her working time u in conventional productive activities and another part $(1 - u)$ forming individual human capital.

Thus, the aggregate production function is the expression

$$Q = (uH^{\Theta}L)^{\alpha} K^{(1-\alpha)} \tag{9.9}$$

where $\Theta = \alpha + \gamma/\alpha$ measures the contribution of both sources of labour productivity—productive effort and human capital—to total labour productivity, part of which comes from the individual's efforts in production and part comes from the effect of the total human capital stock.[11] With u constant, the growth rate of H is also constant, so the aggregate production function can be rewritten as:

$$Q = (uLe^{lt})^{\alpha} K^{(1-\alpha)} \tag{9.10}$$

where Le^{lt} is the stock of human capital that reproduces itself exponentially over time. To translate its long-term growth trend form, (9.10) is transformed into logarithmic form:

$$q = \alpha\,(\lambda + l) + (1 - \alpha)\,k = \alpha\,l^{*} + (1 - \alpha)\,k \tag{9.11}$$

where l^{*} is the growth rate of labour inputs expressed in efficiency units.

11 Labour efficiency could be expressed as efficiency unit $L^{*} = H^{\Theta}L$. According to Lucas (1988), to make growth endogenous, human capital varies and is acquired by the individual worker at the rate $\frac{dH}{dt} = H^{\zeta}\delta\left(1-u\right)$, where δ is constant; and ζ cannot be < 1, which would lead to decreasing returns in human capital formation and negatively affect the growth rate.

Unlike Solow's exogenous growth model, neoclassical endogenous growth models suggest that it is no longer possible to ensure absolute convergence between countries' growth rates in the long run. In the words of Romer (1986),[12]

> since the model assumes that the rate of investment and return on capital can now increase, levels of real output per capita across countries do not necessarily converge in the long run; growth may be persistently lower in less developed countries or even non-existent in most of them!

In addition to the use of an aggregate production function, Lucas's model suffers from another serious criticism. McCombie and Thirlwall (1994) comment that, even if K and L remain constant over time, the model demonstrates that the accumulation of human capital is capable of ensuring economic growth indefinitely in the long run. To illustrate, Scott (1989) in the noteworthy book "A New View of Economic Growth" refutes this conclusion. He argues that, given that the stock of human capital is associated with the growth of both the stock of physical capital and the stock of knowledge accumulated by workers, human capital per se does not have sufficient strength to ensure economic development.

3 Neoclassical Growth Models in Open Economies

3.1 *Fundamentals of the Models: Innovations, Technological Spillovers and Product Variety*

In the neoclassical field, the most notable work extending Romer's endogenous growth model to the context of economies open to international flows of goods, services and knowledge is Grossman and Helpman's 1991 book, "Innovation and Growth in the Global Economy". Given the mathematical complexity of the various models analysed, I will limit myself to summarising them in textual form.[13]

Grossman and Helpman (1991) argued that their academic work was influenced by the Schumpeterian view,[14] according to which technological

12 Lucas (1988) draws a similar conclusion.

13 Mathematical understanding presupposes knowledge of dynamic optimisation. The interested reader can consult Chapter 11 of my PhD dissertation (Nassif, 2003).

14 This perspective had already been explicitly assumed by the authors in an article previously published in the *American Economic Review—Papers and Proceedings*, May 1990 (notably on page 87).

innovations are the main engine of long-term growth. Technical progress is the endogenous variable of growth, since companies, when seeking new opportunities to make extraordinary profits, not only spend large amounts of financial resources on research and development (R&D) projects but also consequently cause changes in the allocation of economic resources, especially human capital, to innovative sectors that produce technological services (blueprints).

However, the assumptions and methodology of the theoretical models, typically neoclassical, differ from Schumpeter's (1942) original view, for whom technical progress occurs as creative destruction and tends to produce permanent intertemporal imbalances. Ergo, in the original Schumpeterian perspective, there are no unique equilibrium outcomes. Returning to the models of Grossman and Helpman (1991), with respect to technological innovation and knowledge, the basic assumptions are:

i. Innovative firms spend money on R&D because they seek extraordinary profits ("monopoly profits");
ii. There is free entry to the R&D process, but the conditions for this cease when the sector starts to generate only normal profits ("perfect competition profits");
iii. As a corollary, technology, understood as a service resulting from R&D activities (blueprints), is incorporated into the model as a good whose essential characteristics are related to non-rivalry and non-excludability. This means that innovators, although protected by legal barriers that guarantee their respective intellectual (brands) and/or technological (patents) properties, are unable to completely prevent the unauthorised use of their innovations, nor are they able to block other producers' free access to the technological blueprints that disseminate throughout the economy. Consequently, technical progress allows the diffusion of Marshallian external economies (spillover effects)[15] on a national or international scale.

The particularities of technology expressed in (iii) are essential for the core assumption of the new endogenous growth models, that is, the formulation of an aggregate production function that exhibits increasing returns to scale, attributable, in turn, to the accumulation of knowledge. Grossman and

15 The concept of "agglomeration economies", traditionally used in Regional Economics and reintroduced by Krugman (1991), refers to the results of the combination of Marshallian external economies with the concentration of industries and productive resources in a given region (especially in "nations"). Although Krugman (1989, 1992) places restrictions on the use of the concept in international terms, it is perfectly in tune with the central hypothesis of Grossman and Helpman (1991) of the possibility of transmission of technological spillovers in an economy open to international trade.

Helpman (1991, p. 18) demonstrate the existence of a virtuous circle between technical progress and growth. The trajectory of economic growth in the long term tends to be sustained by the increase in the marginal productivity of knowledge. This, in turn, results from the effects of technological spillovers that feed the growth process itself.

The method of analysis is neoclassical in two senses: in terms of partial equilibrium, it is implicitly assumed that the prevailing market structures are those of monopolistic competition à la Chamberlin. Innovative firms realise extraordinary profits in the short term, but these tend to be dissipated in the long term, as free entry conditions allow potential producers access to the R&D-producing sector (blueprints). In terms of general equilibrium, since the authors' purpose is to analytically focus on the interrelationship of technical progress, trade and growth in a global perspective, the basic trade model used is explicitly that of comparative advantage à la Heckscher-Ohlin.

Before analysing the impacts of free trade on long-term economic growth, it is worth noting that the model supports the central hypotheses of the new theory of international trade. The combined forces of economies of scale, product differentiation, and monopolistic competition tend to expand the variety of differentiated products in the manufacturing sector. In the standard model proposed by Grossman and Helpman (1991), innovations tend to generate self-sustaining growth, under the strong assumption that the blueprint-producing sector exhibits increasing returns to scale. In this case, what guarantees the long-term growth process is the existence of a greater variety of products resulting from technical progress and the spillover effects triggered by the diffusion of technological knowledge.

This standard model of product variety expansion contemplates two distinct cases: in the first, technology is conceived as a good whose results are entirely appropriated by innovators. There is no possibility that non-innovative agents can have access to technological knowledge as it accumulates over time. In this case, since there are no spillover effects, the R&D sector operates with a production function subject to constant returns to scale, whereas economic growth continues as long as there is an incentive to create new product varieties. In the second case, this hypothesis is relaxed and technology is seen as a good that, due to its non-rivalrous and non-excludable attributes, can be partially appropriated as knowledge by other producers.

I will start with the first case. As noted, the key hypothesis assumes the impossibility of diffusing the effects of technological spillovers as innovations are introduced, which only increase the variety of products ("horizontal differentiation"). In this model, consumers and producers behave economically in a conventional manner. They seek to maximise their utility and profit functions, respectively, over an intertemporal horizon.

In dynamic equilibrium, the model predicts the existence of an optimal number of product varieties. Below this optimal quantity, the initial incentives to promote R&D expenditures will cease as the firm's profitability rate decreases. This increases the opportunity costs of the innovative sector. Quantities above the optimal number are not sustainable in the long run because they configure infinite levels of varieties and an infinite value for the innovative firm. From an economic point of view, this trajectory is unfeasible because, as the variety of products expands in the market, companies are faced with a reduction in the sales volume per good produced due to competition with other firms that produce differentiated goods.

The second case configures the hypothesis that the authors consider to be more realistic. Although innovators appropriate a flow of monopoly profits as a reward for successful results derived from investments made in R&D, part of these services (blueprints) overflows into the economic system, either as a flow of ideas, techniques and methods, or through the products themselves. This enables innovation through reverse engineering and therefore expands the stock of knowledge accessible to any private agent in the economy. Since the proliferation of innovations results from external economies created and disseminated from the original innovations (technological spillover effects), the technological knowledge "sector" becomes subject to dynamic increasing returns to scale, which disseminate Marshallian external economies.

In this instance, the increase in the innovation rate triggers a reallocation process of the economy's productive resources and leads to a steady state trend in the long run. Thus, as the rate of innovation accelerates, workers in the manufacturing sector move from segments producing differentiated final goods to the R&D sector. As the model assumes full employment, the result will be a lower supply of final goods from the manufacturing sector and an increase in the wage rate in this sector, due to the lower availability of potentially available workers.

The model shows that technical progress is the factor responsible for sustaining growth in the long run. However, what guarantees the acceleration of technical progress is the expansion of available productive resources, the increase in the average productivity of these resources, the lower degree of risk aversion on the part of savers and the greater potential for product differentiation.

3.2 *Trade and Growth in Open Economies: Impacts of the Free Flow of Goods, Services and Knowledge*

It is now time to analyse the dynamic interrelations of innovation, free trade and growth according to the models proposed by Grossman and Helpman (1991, Chapter 9). The impact of trade on the long-term growth trajectories of two economies that are internationally integrated results from three simultaneous effects. First, through the "externality effect", trade facilitates the mutual transmission of technological knowledge. Second, through the "competition effect", it stimulates the introduction of innovations, whether in processes or products, avoiding the duplication of goods, ideas and production techniques. Third, through the "economies of scale effect", it generates ambiguous results on growth. If the expansion of the international market increases the degree of specialisation, leading to an increase in sales and profits for firms, given the pre-existing market share, confrontation with a greater number of competitors tends to reduce the rate of innovation and, consequently, economic growth.[16]

Grossman and Helpman (1991) argue that global economic integration tends to exert ambiguous forces on the growth process: with the expansion of the market, international trade provides greater opportunities for profit and growth. Nevertheless, greater capitalist competition on a global scale tends to curb the search for greater product variety, which reduces potential profit opportunities and, consequently, the growth rate. The long-term growth trajectory results from the net effect of both trends.

I will summarise the impacts of trade on growth in two relevant cases: free trade between countries with similar productive structures; and free trade between countries with different productive and technological structures, a particularly important case for extracting useful lessons for developing countries. I will illustrate both cases assuming that there are two countries in the global economy: Belporto and Belmonte. A fixed division of resources allocated to the manufacturing and R&D sectors is assumed, so that the aggregate value of the stock market in each country remains constant. In addition, it is assumed that each country holds a constant share of the total differentiated products existing in the global market.

Initially, I assume that Belporto and Belmonte have the same productive resource base and identical technologies. What impact, then, will it have on the long-term growth of both countries if they engage in free exchange of goods, services and knowledge ("flow of ideas and information")? The dynamic equations of the model lead to a surprising result: if there is no duplication of efforts in the research laboratories devoted to the creation of new products in both countries, the market expansion resulting from economic integration has no net effect on the long-term growth rate of the nations! It is a hypothesis that seems to be quite plausible as a long-term trend, since competition, in global

16 It is no coincidence that these three effects are present in the methodology for empirically estimating changes in total factor productivity based on data from production plants, proposed by Tybout and Westbrook (1995).

terms, tends to make firms choose to launch products that were previously non-existent on the world market, instead of behaving as simple imitators of their rivals.

Are there gains from trade? Yes, but they are not dynamic. Gains from trade are largely static and are provided by consumers in the world market having access to a greater variety of products. But in dynamic terms, both countries will continue to grow at the same rate that prevailed before trade liberalisation. Although the result of this model is surprising, it is not counterintuitive, since it suggests that, all else being equal, countries with identical levels of development will continue to maintain the same growth patterns.

In the second case, following Grossman and Helpman (1991, Chapter 9), the flow of knowledge does not overflow beyond national borders, which makes it impossible for its accumulation to produce spillover effects in global terms. Even though the world economy is characterised by similar productive structures—an assumption that is unacceptable according to the heterodox neo-Schumpeterian approach, as I will show later—the stock of knowledge is privately appropriated by the entrepreneurs of each country.

I will also consider that Belporto maintains a faster pace of innovation than Belmonte. The idea is that the higher rate of innovation in Belporto further encourages firms in that country to introduce new cost-reducing techniques and new products to the market. Consequently, greater international oligopolistic competition not only reduces the market share and incentive for innovation by Belmonte firms, but also further widens the technological gap between their industries and those of Belporto.

Since the rates of technological innovation are unequal in both countries and one of them dominates the state of the art, the respective shares of each in the global demand for differentiated goods are different. The mathematical manipulations of the model lead to dynamic equilibrium results that are not very encouraging for Belmonte. If the faster pace of technical progress allows Belporto to dominate the market for innovative goods, in a situation of pure free trade, this larger country tends to present the same long-term growth rate that it would achieve in the absence of international trade ("autarky").

However, the expansion of the market via foreign trade means that Belporto is growing faster than if it were isolated from the global exchange of goods and services. Note that the gains from trade are typically Schumpeterian (dynamic) rather than Ricardian (static). They provide Belporto with higher long-term GDP growth rates than those obtained by Belmonte.

And what can be said, according to the model by Grossman and Helpman (op. cit.) about the future of Belmonte, the country with the smallest market, in terms of growth and well-being? The model's dynamic equations demonstrate that this country not only sees a loss of market share in the world market, but also has a lower long-term growth rate in free trade than in a hypothetical situation of autarky. As Grossman and Helpman (1991, p. 250) argue, the alternative hypothesis that Belmonte increases its international market share would be a contradiction in terms. This is not possible, for the simple reason that this country does not innovate!

Is everything lost, then, for Belmonte? Not in the short term at least. Confirming the conclusions of the models of the new theory of international trade, in static terms consumers in this country can obtain immediate gains (once and for all). These may come from the possibility of greater access to differentiated goods from Belporto or from the increase in the rate of product variety compared to the situation of autarky.

Although Grossman and Helpman are not emphatic, my conclusion is that, in the long run, there are losses for Belmonte in dynamic terms. And it is not difficult to understand why. Because of the reduced incentives for research and development directed at the manufacturing sector, trade reduces the level of well-being of Belmonte society in the long run. After all, while Belporto diversifies its production structure into manufactured products with high technological intensity, generally with high income elasticity of demand, Belmonte specialises in "commodities". In other words, in a situation where technological knowledge is retained in the innovating country, but there is a flow of trade in goods and services between the countries, the static gains obtained by the non-innovating country may be gradually diluted, due to the effect of potential dynamic losses in the long term. This unquestionable result is the core of the heterodox neo-Schumpeterian critique of neoclassical endogenous growth models in economies open to international trade, the point of the next section; and a warning about accelerated processes of trade liberalisation in developing countries, as already discussed in Chapter 7.

4 Neoclassical Growth Models: the Developmental Critique

Despite the immense neoclassical theoretical effort to elucidate the impacts of dynamic increasing returns on the long-term growth trajectories of capitalist economies, this school of thought fails to convincingly show how the process of knowledge generation effectively transforms into the introduction and/or incorporation of innovations. Furthermore, even when the possibility of knowledge spillovers at the international level is assumed, the condition of free entry into the R&D sector ends up obscuring the more evident fact that the high risks inherent to this activity, arising from uncertainty regarding future returns, greatly restrict the possibility of innovative catching-up in technologically more backward countries.

Heal (1998), for example, recognises the interesting results presented by the neoclassical literature in this regard, but does not hide enormous frustration with this line of research. He says (op. cit.: 4): "Although they present clear and robust results, neoclassical growth models end up avoiding the real implications of the existence of dynamic economies of scale, thus diverting the analysis from the path originally traced by Adam Smith" (as I discussed in Chapter 1). He rightly suggests that when the world becomes dominated by dynamic increasing returns, the very possibility of equilibrium, even partial equilibrium, becomes extremely compromised, since at any given price there may be excess demand for some sectors and excess supply for others.

In the theoretical analysis of the interrelations of technological change, international trade and development, the neo-Schumpeterian approach seeks precisely to free itself from the traps present in the general equilibrium literature on the subject. As Dosi, Pavitt and Soete (1990) warn, although Schumpeter is the original source of inspiration—especially because he was the pioneer in analysing the role of innovations and technological progress as foundations of economic change and the process of creative destruction—this line of research also incorporates the contributions of all authors, liberal or not, who analysed the problem of development from an eminently dynamic perspective. Since almost all of these authors of developmental lineage (including the neo-Schumpeterians themselves) dared to break with the general equilibrium paradigm, Dosi, Pavitt and Soete (op. cit.) call them "heretics".

I thus summarise the "heretical" model proposed by Dosi, Pavitt and Soete (1990), whose starting point is the "different technological and innovation capabilities between countries, which also impact, in a differentiated way, the patterns of international trade and growth".[17] In the proposed approach, although the relative differences in technologies between countries determine the pattern of foreign trade in the short term, the mechanisms that act dynamically in the innovation process exert a preponderant influence not only on **changing** the trade pattern, but also on the **potential for future growth** of the economy.

17 In contrast, in traditional trade models, analysed in Chapter 3, comparative advantages are determined by different relative labour productivities, the causes of which are related either to different relative technologies (as in the Ricardian case) or to different relative factor endowments (as in the H-O-S model). In both cases, the technologies are not explained but taken as given. Incidentally, in the second part of the book, Dosi, Pavitt and Soete (1990) present ample empirical evidence related to the world economy.

Since technological change permanently interferes with the coordination and interdependence mechanisms of domestic and international economic agents, the analytical approach of Dosi, Pavitt and Soete (1990) is preferably dynamic. From this perspective, issues related to international trade and long-term economic growth, despite their recognised complexity, are treated using the evolutionary method.[18] Its assumptions are as follows:[19]

a. technological differences between countries and their distinct innovation capacities are dominant factors in explaining the causes and flows of trade, as well as the respective levels of national income;
b. the abandonment of the Walrasian general equilibrium method in favour of another that prioritises the role of technological change in the flow of international trade and in the dynamic adjustment of economies, whose growth rates are conditioned, hypothetically, by balance of payments constraints;
c. the existence of absolute advantages specific to each country, generally reinforced by technological progress, which influence its market share, both sectoral and total, in the global market for goods and services;
d. a refusal to identify technology as a good freely traded on the market, as in neoclassical models of endogenous growth;
e. the pattern of specialisation can have cumulative effects (positive or negative) in the long run.

Based on these assumptions, I will illustrate with a simplified model (two countries, two goods and only labour as a factor of production), to demonstrate how theoretical conclusions distinct from the neoclassical approach to the pattern of international trade, technological change and economic performance in dynamic terms can be drawn.[20]

Let us imagine that the manufacturing sector of the two countries that make up the world economy, Belporto and Belmonte, consists of the computer and

---

18 The evolutionary concept, which is closely aligned with Schumpeter's original vision, was introduced by Nelson and Winter (1982). The authors abandon the neoclassical hypothesis of profit maximisation, assuming instead that in a world of uncertainty and under permanent competitive pressure, companies seek to make important decisions, whether short-term (for example, the degree of utilisation of installed capacity) or long-term (such as investment decisions, R&D expenditures, etc.), which reflect a routine aimed at achieving the primary objective of expansion in the market in which they operate. This routine, paradoxical as it may seem, reflects a state of permanent change, so that, according to Nelson and Winter (Ibidem, p.18), "the central problem of evolutionary theory consists in analysing the dynamic process through which the firm's behaviour patterns and market results are simultaneously determined over time".

19 These assumptions are in Dosi, Pavitt and Soete (1990, p. 26).

20 The model presented is an adaptation of that of Dosi, Pavitt and Soete (1990, pp. 29–30).

automobile industries. Let us assume that both countries have identical technologies, the same relative costs and prices, the same consumer preferences, and that the exchange rates between their currencies are equal to one. Let us also consider that both economies operate with some level of involuntary unemployment. Given these assumptions, even if Belporto and Belmonte were to open up to free trade, according to traditional theory, no trade exchange would take place, since international trade would only take place if there were differences in relative costs (classical Ricardian case) or relative prices (standard neoclassical case).

Let us then assume that a certain technological innovation in both industries in Belporto gives it an absolute cost advantage but leaves relative labour productivity and relative prices intact in both countries. According to the predictions of the Ricardian and Heckscher-Ohlin-Samuelson models, there would also be no reason for trade exchange to be triggered between the two countries, since, in these models, the specialisation pattern is always determined by the difference in relative costs and/or relative prices, regardless of the absolute differences in the technological profiles of their industries.

The above result is what should be expected according to the traditional model of international trade. In the neo-Schumpeterian dynamic approach, however, Belporto has more advantageous absolute costs and tends to increase its relative share in the flow of exports to Belmonte in both industries. Belporto would consequently increase the net volume of foreign exchange received. In dynamic terms, as it managed to sustain economic growth rates higher than those of its partner, the technological gap favourable to Belporto's industries would enable them to increase efficiency in the production of both goods, due to the presence of increasing returns, via an increase in the international market share, even though relative efficiency levels were preserved.

If we incorporate the hypothesis that both industries operate with economies of scale internal to the firm and compete in an oligopoly, it is possible for there to be multiple equilibria, even if there is some intra-industry trade flow between the two countries. However, once the existence of a technological gap favourable to Belporto is considered, economies of scale would only reinforce it, through a self-cumulative movement, given the greater delay in Belmonte's technological capacity, as well as the lock-in nature of technological trajectories, according to the definition by William Brian Arthur (1989), set out in Chapter 7.

Considering the strong influence of technical progress on international trade and economic growth rates, Dosi, Tyson and Zysman (1989) introduced the concept of *Schumpeterian efficiency*. It consists of evaluating the dynamic effects of resource allocation on the trajectory and direction of technological change, as well as on the random, i.e. unpredictable, outcome of the innovative process. Additionally, they present as a complementary criterion *Keynesian efficiency*, which relates the maximum possible growth rates of the economy, given the restrictions of the balance of payments (Dosi et al., Ibidem: 13).[21]

The authors do not oppose evaluating economic efficiency using the static criterion of comparative advantage theories, as seen in the Ricardian-neoclassical perspective, where gains from trade are of the once and for all type. However, they warn that by subjecting the economy's resource allocation process solely to this requirement, there will be an effective trade-off between Ricardian efficiency and Schumpeterian efficiency. Dosi, Tyson and Zysman (ibidem: 14) explain the problem in the following terms:

> If the dynamic growth potential of economic activities differs between them, then a pattern of national specialisation that is efficient at a given time in terms of a given set of market indicators may not maximise economic welfare in the long run. If private agents and government authorities allocate resources according to these indicators, the future development trajectory of the economy may be adversely affected. A nation may engineer an efficient allocation of resources by specialising in those industries and activities where opportunities for growth and technological development are minimal.

To demonstrate analytically how the aforementioned trade-off could emerge, Dosi, Tyson and Zysman (1989)[22] align themselves with the developmental tradition. Thus, they move away from three assumptions normally implicit in neoclassical models of international trade: the first, that income elasticities of demand are identical between products and countries; the second, that price elasticities of demand are similar and high for all products;[23] and the third, that technology, generally taken as exogenous data, is easily transferable internationally.

Regarding the inversion of the first hypothesis, Dosi, Tyson and Zysman (1989) argue that income elasticities of demand are not only unequal across products and countries but are also higher for goods from high-technology industries

21 Both concepts also appear in Dosi, Pavitt and Soete, 1990, Chapter 8, especially on p. 240.

22 See also Dosi, Pavitt and Soete (1990: 250).

23 As a basis for supporting opposing hypotheses, Dosi, Pavitt and Soete (1990: 250) cite empirical studies by A.P. Thirlwall, G. Lafay, J. Cornwall and, in the tradition of development literature, R. Prebisch.

and services.[24] They assume the general Keynesian rule that the economy is faced with underutilised productive resources and therefore operates, with few exceptions, below full employment. Thus, short-term economic growth depends fundamentally on the expansion of aggregate demand. Extending the idea to the world economy ("considering the world as Keynesian", Dosi et al., ibid.: 15), they conclude that

> the efficiency of growth of a specific pattern of production and international specialisation depends in part on the income elasticities of demand for different products in the world market (…); and (therefore) the greater the expansion rate of external demand for a nation's products relative to the variation in world income, the greater the possibilities for growth of this economy, ceteris paribus.

The question remains: why do market signals alone (via relative prices) tend to fail to promote efficient resource allocation in terms of long-term economic growth? One of the main reasons lies in the uncertainty of agents regarding the future return on their investment decisions. Uncertainty, combined with the imperfections in the capital market, means that financial resources are not always allocated to industries that offer the highest private and social returns in the long run. In this case, according to the authors (Dosi et al.: 16–17),

> firms are able to increase the demand for financial resources for investment in industries that offer high rates of return over relatively short periods, but are unable to increase the demand for financial funds for investment in those sectors whose private return, given the conditions prevailing in the world market, is not only uncertain but also only realised in the longer term. If national capital markets are "impatient" and risk-averse, then investment projects whose returns are highly uncertain and involve high risk would hardly be implemented, despite their great potential for long-term growth.

The inversion of the third hypothesis is methodological in nature and is related to the neo-Schumpeterian research program, which assumes that technological change is endogenous. However, different from neoclassical models,

24 Although there is no precise definition, high-technology industries and services can be conceptualised as having the greatest growth potential among other sectors of the economy (see Dosi, Tyson and Zysman, 1989: 14). They are also characterised by higher expenditures on R&D (generally well above the economy's average) and by the greatest potential to generate positive economic externalities, both intra- and inter-sectoral.

technology is conceived as an asset that is not easily transferable between companies, sectors and, much less, countries. Unlike scientific knowledge, which is transmitted more easily in international relationships, technological knowledge, because it basically depends on the specific skills and experiences of firms, the existing technical capabilities and the institutional characteristics of each country, does not flow freely across national borders!

In this case, since the technological capabilities of companies are closely related to the effective production patterns in the same sector or in related sectors, technical progress becomes strongly conditioned by the **current** process of resource allocation and production in a given country (Dosi et al.: 20–21, emphasis added). Considering also that opportunities for technological change are differentiated between products and sectors, Dosi, Tyson and Zysman (1989: 22) suggest that the allocation of resources entirely guided by market signals may be efficient in static terms (Ricardian efficiency), but inefficient in dynamic terms (Schumpeterian efficiency), that is, in terms of realising the technological potential and long-term growth of the economy. This trade-off is best understood by describing the particularities inherent in technical progress. According to the evolutionary approach, innovative activities, due to their highly selective and cumulative characteristics, are processed through static and dynamic increasing returns, which operate in several dimensions. First, due to the high entry costs and because a significant part of the resources mobilised are classified as sunk costs, technological innovations imply significant static economies of scale when introduced into the production process. Second, as greater experience is gained in their use, dynamic economies of scale emerge resulting from greater technical improvement. Third, because of their non-ergodic and cumulative nature (path-dependence), the success of innovative search efforts is largely dependent on the results already accumulated by companies and countries in relation to technological change. Finally, high-technology industries and services are primarily responsible for generating technological spillover effects in the economy.

In sum, as sectors of the economy present different capacities to realise their potential for growth and technological development, market signals tend to prove insufficient to promote the allocation of resources that maximise the potential for social return. In this case, the trade-off between Ricardian and Schumpeterian efficiency tends to emerge as "correct" relative prices, imposed by free international competition, revealing the country's static comparative advantages. This happens, however, at the expense of a resource allocation process that is "incorrectly" diverted from the sectors with the greatest potential for long-term economic growth. The inability to count on sustainable and relatively stable growth rates will eventually lead the country to stagnation and the impoverishment of its population in the long run.

5 Conclusion

In an explicit general equilibrium approach, Grossman and Helpman (1991) presented several dynamic models in which the conditions for appropriation of technological knowledge vary from total private retention by innovators to complete international spillover, thus allowing catching-up by imitators. It is true that the transmission of knowledge is neither entirely fluid, as neoclassicals suppose, nor almost entirely insurmountable, as more radical heterodox economists suppose.

However, the assumption of total appropriation of the knowledge stock by innovators is too strong to be taken as a proxy for the real world. To some extent, international knowledge transfer is possible. This hypothesis can be corroborated by recent technological changes, which, with the revolution in microelectronics and the telecommunications industry, have led to greater speed, ease and reduced costs of information transmission.

Even so, the greater possibility of access to the stock of technological knowledge does not necessarily ensure the incorporation of technology services (blueprints, to use the neoclassical term) related to the state of the art. Grossman and Helpman (1991, Chapter 9) even suggest that the deepening of economic integration and technological knowledge in global terms may not translate into a higher rate of innovation in countries with a lower relative endowment of human capital. This restriction could be explained because of the greater abundance of unskilled labour in these countries that ends up reducing their opportunity cost and consequently encouraging activities that intensively use low-skilled labour.

With a radically different analytical framework, neo-Schumpeterian developmental models, such as those of Dosi, Pavitt and Soete (1990), reach very similar conclusions. However, due to the adoption of the single and irrevocable assumption of the existence of absolute gaps between countries, even before trade takes place between them, the theoretical conclusions of the neo-Schumpeterian dynamic models are much more incisive than those of the neoclassical models. In particular, the model by Dosi, Pavitt and Soete (1990) concludes, in a compelling manner, that between two countries with highly unequal productive and technological structures in absolute terms, trade liberalisation can generate mutual static benefits for both in the short term. However, it will always end up favouring the most advanced in terms of greater opportunities to realise its potential for technical progress and, therefore, long-term growth.

Although they did not point out probable normative implications arising from the theoretical conclusions they reached, these authors suggest that the process of trade liberalisation in developing countries must be accompanied by compensatory industrial and technological policies. In fact, both theoretical approaches highlight the importance of government incentives for private R&D activities. Grossman and Helpman (op. cit.: 339), for example, go so far as to state that "by strengthening incentives for private research, the government of a technologically backward country can level the playing field." It is obvious that it is also not possible to guarantee that national programs that support R&D spending will definitively eliminate technological gaps accumulated in the past. However, they do help to reduce them and, nevertheless, accelerate the long-term growth rate of developing countries.

CHAPTER 10

The Washington Consensus and the Ideology of Neoliberalism

1 Introduction

Liberalism encompasses not only economic aspects, but also political, sociological and philosophical ones. Since it is beyond the scope of this book to analyse all of these aspects, I will restrict myself to the main economic features. In this respect, liberalism is strongly linked to the defence of laissez faire—that is, the absence of government intervention at the domestic level—and free trade in goods and services at the international level. It should be noted that classical liberalism defends free trade in goods and services but is resistant to the total liberalisation of financial capital flows on a global level.

Between the British Industrial Revolution (18th century) and World War I (1914–1918), capitalism was strongly influenced by classical ideas in defence of laissez faire and unregulated international trade. In practice, however, as amply documented by Chang (2003), the United States and the emerging powers of Continental Europe adopted measures to protect their infant industries. In Hobsbawm's (1994) interpretation, the crisis of the gold standard and the enormous political, economic and social disorganisation observed in the interwar period (1914–1945)—hyperinflation in Germany and Hungary, Nazi-fascism, the Great Depression and mass unemployment in the 1930s, etc.—reflected the reckoning between the old liberal capitalism commanded by British imperial power and the new international order under the hegemony of the United States in the post-war period.

The new international economic order, resulting from the Bretton Woods agreements (1944), was based on a set of explicit multilateral rules (and not tacit, as in the gold standard system) in the trade and financial spheres, whose main objective was to ensure global financial stability. In essence, Bretton Woods represented the reorganisation of the international monetary system based on fixed but re-adjustable exchange rates in relation to the US dollar, which became the standard currency in global trade and financial transactions. In order to maintain a system of fixed exchange rates at a global level, two rules were established: the commitment of the convertibility of the dollar into gold by the US government, in order to ensure the fixed parity of US$35 per ounce of gold, and capital controls.

 | DOI:10.1163/9789004734296_014

Several multilateral institutions were created within the Bretton Woods System, such as the General Agreement on Tariffs and Trade (GATT), to encourage the liberalisation of trade transactions in goods and services, the International Monetary Fund (IMF), to ensure international financial stability, and the World Bank, designed to provide long-term financing for physical and social infrastructure projects in developing countries. The Bretton Woods system, which operated between the immediate post-war period and 1971, essentially sought to establish multilateral rules and cooperation mechanisms between countries, which would strengthen economic liberalism.

The Bretton Woods system collapsed in 1971, when Nixon, in reaction to attempts at a speculative attack on the US dollar, abandoned the commitment to convert the dollar into gold and adopted a floating exchange rate regime, followed by the governments of other developed countries. Thus, the 1970s marked the transition to the phase of what has come to be known as neoliberalism, understood as the extension of laissez faire practices to all markets in a capitalist system (of goods, services, production factors and financial capital). Neoliberalism reached its peak in the 1980s and 1990s, with the liberalisation of short-term financial capital flows on a global scale. With the exception of a few countries, namely China and India, most developing countries adopted full external financial liberalisation.[1]

Although the rise of neoliberal economic programs was rooted in the ideology and rhetoric of United States President Ronald Reagan (1981–1989) and British Prime Minister Margaret Thatcher (1979–1990), whose speeches emphasised belief in the self-regulatory power of the free market, its diffusion in the Latin American periphery accelerated under the political pressure of the so-called Washington Consensus. This expression, coined by John Williamson (1990), refers to the series of neoliberal recommendations addressed to the governments of Latin American countries in the mid-1980s. They came with the consensus of the main institutions based in the US capital city (the United States Treasury, the World Bank and the International Monetary Fund—IMF), and aimed at supposedly overcoming the tendency towards stagnation and restoring sustained economic growth in these countries. The original recommendations included measures such as trade liberalisation, privatisation, exchange rate flexibility, liberalisation of the domestic financial market and deregulation.

1 India, previously resistant to even productive investments by multinational companies, liberalised the flow of foreign direct investment and equity capital from 1991 onwards, but continued to prohibit short-term capital inflows, especially those of a speculative nature. For more details, see Nassif (2007) and Subbarao (2014).

Subsequently, as Rodrik (2006) emphasises, the "expanded" Washington Consensus added recommendations such as central bank independence, inflation targeting regimes and liberalisation of capital flows. The adherence of Latin American countries to the Brady Plan, a restructuring program designed by the US Treasury and coordinated by the IMF between the end of the 1980s and the first half of the 1990s, and which provided for the forgiveness of a significant portion of the external debt of the countries of the continent, was conditional on the adoption of many of the measures provided for in the two configurations of the Washington Consensus. In other words, in practice, the adoption of neoliberal reforms was clearly imposed by the US political power.

This chapter contains two main sections. In Section 2, I analyse the era of liberalism under Bretton Woods (1944–1971), a period in which efforts to liberalise trade in goods and services in global markets did not impede the adoption of autonomous national policies for economic development. In Section 3, I discuss the rise and hegemony of neoliberalism, showing how the adherence of periphery Latin American countries to the economic policy practices emanating from the Washington Consensus, from the 1990s onwards, significantly reduced the degrees of freedom of governments to adopt autonomous economic policies. The normative implications arising from the main theoretical formulations of the neoclassical liberal school will be discussed in the following, concluding chapter.

2 The Bretton Woods Era and Regulated Liberalism

The Bretton Woods system was the result of multilateral negotiations coordinated by the governments of the United States and the United Kingdom, represented by Harry Dexter White and John Maynard Keynes, respectively. The main objective of the negotiations was to formulate a new world economic order, guided by rules and institutions that would avoid the destructive protectionist practices that prevailed in the interwar period, but that would also preserve the autonomy of governments to adopt public policies in favour of national economic development.

After three weeks of intense debates and negotiations, the Bretton Woods architecture produced, in summary, the following rules: (i) a system of fixed exchange rates pegged to the parity of the US dollar in relation to gold (US$35 per troy ounce); (ii) capital controls; (iii) the possibility of adjusting exchange rates when countries faced "fundamental disequilibrium" in the balance of payments; and (iv) use of the US dollar as the standard currency in global trade and financial transactions.

The first two rules, proposed by Keynes, aimed to ensure international financial stability. After all, with fixed exchange rates and capital controls, each country is able to adopt autonomous policies to achieve the objectives of growth with full employment and price stability. However, Keynes was aware that these objectives would be compromised if the dissemination of the dollar as an international reserve currency were to remain outside the control of a supranational financial institution. For that reason, instead of the dollar, Keynes advocated the creation of a quasi-currency (the bancor), which would serve exclusively to mediate global trade transactions and the operations of a central bank that would function as a clearing house for creditor and debtor positions between member countries. This proposal was rejected by the American representative. An intermediate solution was then adopted, which was to create the International Monetary Fund (IMF), which would be responsible for monitoring the operations of the monetary system and providing compensatory financing to countries with balance of payments problems.

As Rodrik (2006) notes, the main characteristic of the Bretton Woods system is multilateralism, meaning that economic relations between countries would be coordinated by rules based on the principle of non-discrimination. The triad of multilateral institutions created within this system (IMF, World Bank and GATT) should, at least in theory, reinforce and legitimise the principles of reciprocity and non-discrimination—although they were not entirely independent of American political power. Hence, Bretton Woods sought to avoid the resurgence of "beggar thy neighbour" policies, so in vogue in the 1930s. During this period, countries did not hesitate to resort to widespread protectionist policies and competitive devaluations of their currencies, with the aim of transferring their internal unemployment problems to other countries—and thus aggravating and prolonging the depressive cycle.

Regarding trade multilateralism, the negotiations at Bretton Woods provided for the establishment of the International Trade Organisation (ILO). In the face of a veto by US Congress, which feared the intrusion of this organisation into US domestic policies, the intermediate solution was the creation of the GATT, which, according to Matsushita, Schoenbaum and Mavroidis (2006: 3), was already weakened from the start, as it did not have the legal power to impose sanctions against countries that violated the negotiated rules. Despite this, the general assessment is that, of the eight Rounds of multilateral trade negotiations sponsored by the GATT between 1947, the year of its official establishment, and 1994, when the creation of the World Trade Organisation (WTO) was approved, there was a significant effort to promote the liberalisation of international trade based on the Most Favoured Nation Clause (MFN). According to this principle, a contracting party to GATT, when granting a trade preference via a reduction in import tariffs or another benefit to one partner, must extend it to all the others.

Furthermore, at least until 1995, when the WTO began to act as the highest regulatory body for international trade, the GATT was not guided by fundamentalist views on free trade. Its purpose was to encourage contracting parties to reduce import tariffs, while refraining from applying quantitative barriers to trade, such as quotas, for example. The GATT was also successful in introducing "anti-dumping" codes and countervailing duties (anti-subsidies). As Rodrik (2011: 75) points out, "the purpose of the GATT was never to maximise [pure] free trade, but to achieve the maximum volume of trade compatible with the different levels of development among the participating nations." It is no coincidence that, before the establishment of the WTO, the multilateral treaties negotiated by the GATT preserved ample space for developing countries to use industrial policy instruments (import tariffs, subsidies for domestic production, export subsidies, etc.), aiming at advancing industrialisation and economic development.

Despite all the rules that came into force after World War II, designed to govern international economic relations, the Bretton Woods system contained contradictions that led to its collapse in the early 1970s. The main inconsistency was identified by economist Robert Triffin of Yale University in the early 1960s. As I have already mentioned, the system, according to its design, should operate based on a fixed parity between the US dollar and gold. All other currencies would fix their respective exchange rates in relation to the dollar. However, the reliability and stability of the international monetary system depended on a fundamental condition: the Federal Reserve (the American central bank) had to ensure dollar-gold convertibility, offering the metal when there was pressure to devalue the dollar or buying it when the American currency was pressured to appreciate.

As Triffin (1960) showed, the system could only remain stable during the period of European reconstruction and dollar shortages in the immediate post-war period, when the United States concentrated most of the global current account surpluses. From the mid-1960s onwards, the rise in current account deficits and inflation in the United States (in both cases aggravated by its involvement in the Vietnam War), the European economic expansion, and the formation of the Eurodollar market in the main financial centres of Western Europe—that is, the spread of financial assets denominated in dollars and other convertible European currencies—exposed the main contradiction of the Bretton Woods system: since the United States's current account deficits were the main source of international liquidity, their exponential growth led to an uncontrolled abundance of dollars on the international market, undermining confidence in the stability of the US currency at the parity of US$35 per troy ounce.

What's more, while other countries could adjust their exchange rates in relation to the dollar, the same could not happen with the exchange rate of the US currency in relation to other currencies, unless the golden rule of the system (fixed dollar-gold rate) was violated. Despite the overvaluation of the dollar, the United States's current account deficits did not need to be adjusted via exchange rates, as they were financed by the rest of the world through net capital inflows. Such a passive attitude was established because, in the expression coined by French Prime Minister Valéry Giscard D'Estaing in 1960, the United States already enjoyed the "exorbitant privilege" of being the issuer of the international reserve currency.[2]

This problem became known as the "Triffin dilemma" because the US government felt pressured to either reduce current account deficits, which would lead to a decline in global growth, or to find another mechanism for creating and controlling international liquidity. As Gilpin (1987: 137) notes,

> acting as the world's leading provider of international currency gave the United States enormous power and independence (...). Over the years, European and Japanese governments began to realise that the American government was abusing the political and economic privileges afforded by the supremacy of the dollar (...). They showed growing concern about inflation and monetary instability resulting from the enormous expansion of international liquidity. They also perceived that the United States sought to transfer to the rest of the world the significant costs of its domestic and foreign policies (...). The United States, on the other hand, adopted an accommodating position of "benign neglect" until 1971.

Triffin's (1960) warning, which initially aroused mere academic curiosity, became a self-fulfilling prophecy in 1971, when Nixon, in response to several attempts at speculative attacks against the American currency, ordered the suspension of dollar-gold convertibility and thus unilaterally imposed a new international monetary system based exclusively on the dollar as a reserve currency. It also adopted unorthodox measures, such as increasing import tariffs and controlling prices and wages, to curb ongoing inflation. Despite the failed attempt to revive the system through the Smithsonian Agreement (December 1971), by which the dollar was readjusted to US$38 per troy ounce

2 The expression became the title of one of the economist Barry Eichengreen's books (2011).

and devalued in relation to European currencies, Bretton Woods officially came to an end in 1973, when the United States let its currency float freely against other convertible currencies.

It is important to highlight that, after the rupture of the Bretton Woods system, the technological decline of the United States compared to Japan was notorious, which apparently challenged American economic and financial hegemony. In her classic essay "The Resumption of North American Hegemony", Maria da Conceição Tavares (1985) comments that

> speculative capital movements always denominated in dollars, which gave rise to a non-system, continued to undermine the dollar as a reserve currency, periodically destabilising the pound and strengthening the Deutsche [German] mark and the Japanese yen as international currencies. Thus, the international monetary order was rapidly heading towards chaos, especially after the first oil shock and the American recessive policy of 1974.

Hence, the external events that characterised the 1970s—the definitive rupture of Bretton Woods in 1973, two oil price shocks (in 1973 and 1979) and the sudden and violent increase in interest rates in 1979, unilaterally decided by Paul Volcker, Chairman of the Federal Reserve—in addition to being extremely disturbing, delimit, above all, the transition period for the resumption of American hegemony and the ideological rise of neoliberalism from the following decade onwards. As I will show below, unlike the regulated liberalism of Bretton Woods, which granted a wide degree of freedom to periphery countries to implement public policies in favour of economic development, neoliberalism and adherence to the reforms recommended by the Washington Consensus greatly reduce, and in some spheres eliminate, the autonomy for the adoption of national development policies.

3 The Washington Consensus and the Spread of Neoliberalism

3.1 *The Original and Expanded Washington Consensus*

After the two oil shocks of the 1970s, Reagan and Thatcher were responsible for the rise of the ideology of neoliberalism in the following decade. Through liberal measures such as the deregulation of markets, notably the financial market, the flexibilization of the labour market (including through legislation to reduce the power of unions), the privatisation of state-owned enterprises (in Thatcher's case) and the reduction in government spending (except military spending), among others, Reaganomics and Thatcherism put into practice measures long advocated by radical liberals such as Milton Friedman and Friedrich von Hayek. Neoliberalism must be understood as a radical economic ideology because it advocates the extension of the practice of laissez faire to all markets (of goods, services and factors of production, including financial, exchange and capital markets) at national and international levels.

Let us be clear: neoliberalism, whose start was lubricated by the rhetoric of Reagan and Thatcher, has a strong ideological bias because, in practice, not all the recommendations directed at the rest of the world, notably developing countries, were followed to the letter. In the case of Reaganomics, for example, although part of the economic policy was influenced by the classical and monetarist approach of supply-side economics, in practice the explosion of domestic interest rates, resulting from Volcker's ultra-contractionary monetary policy, allowed the United States to absorb almost all of the international liquidity in dollars coming from countries with current account surpluses (Japan, Germany and oil exporters grouped in Organization of the Petroleum Exporting Countries – OPEC) and from the repatriation of external debt services from the Latin American periphery. The immediate consequence was that the overvaluation of the US currency and the restoration of strong dollar "diplomacy" made it possible to reverse the inflationary acceleration inherited from the oil shocks of the previous decade.

At the same time, Reagan's military defence program (Star Wars), while promoting a technological revolution in the industry supplying war equipment for American military defence, operates, in practice, as an undeclared industrial policy, with incentives for massive investments in the electronics, aerospace and telecommunications complex. Aware of the "resumption of North American hegemony" at the beginning of the 1980s, Maria da Conceição Tavares (1985: 5; 9) observed, presciently, that

> The United States is now investing heavily in the tertiary sector and in the new high-technology industries. One need only look at the structure of investment in 1983 and 1984 to see the extreme concentration of investment spending in the areas of information technology, biotechnology, and sophisticated services. The United States is not interested in maintaining its old structure. It also knows that it does not have the capacity to achieve a huge boom from reforms in the industrial sectors that led the world's post-war economic growth. Instead, the United States is

> concentrating its efforts on developing cutting-edge sectors and subjecting the old industry to international competition from its partners.

As Mariana Mazzucatto (2013) shows, with detailed documentary evidence in her seminal book "The Entrepreneurial State: Debunking Public vs. Private Sector Myths", the American government, by allocating a large amount of subsidised financial resources to various areas of cutting-edge technology, such as advanced defence, the pharmaceutical industry, nanotechnology, information technology and telecommunications, and innovations in small and medium-sized enterprises, in practice bears the business risk underlying the uncertainty associated with investments in technological innovations. In the words of the author (2013: 79–80), the various initiatives in these areas share

> a proactive approach, in which the State encourages and shapes the market with the aim of accelerating innovations. This suggests that, in addition to configuring an entrepreneurial society in which it is culturally natural to start and develop a business, the United States is also an economy in which the State, by investing in new areas that trigger radical innovations, also assumes an entrepreneurial role.

Furthermore, to expand markets in strategic sectors, the United States government frequently applies Section 301 of its Trade Act, which allows for trade retaliation against partners reluctant to open markets to exports and foreign investment by American companies. Section 301 was applied quite frequently against developed and periphery countries throughout the 1980s and 1990s, a period in which the US's companies were sparking the technological revolution in the microelectronics, computer and telecommunications sectors.

With regard to Latin America, the major turning point at the end of the 1980s was the formulation and almost immediate implementation of the Brady Plan, conceived by James Brady, the United States Treasury Secretary at the time. It provided for the discount of a significant share of the external debt stock of the continent's countries, which represented, in practice, the cancellation of almost all payments for debt services due (principal and interest). However, there was a sine qua non condition for joining the agreement: governments had to commit to adopting "structural economic reforms", expressed in a ten-step set of recommendations from the US Treasury, IMF and World Bank.

The ten original recommendations, described in the first column of Table 2 below, were decoded by John Williamson, who called them the "Washington Consensus". Subsequently, Latin American countries, either on their own initiative or under pressure from those institutions as they adhered to the Brady

TABLE 2 The Washington Consensus and the genesis of neoliberalism

Original		Expanded	
1.	Fiscal discipline	11.	Corporate governance
2.	Government spending redirected primarily to education, health and infrastructure	12.	Anti-corruption measures
3.	Tax reform	13.	Liberalisation ("flexibilization") of the labour market
4.	Domestic financial liberalisation ("financial de-repression")	14.	Adherence to the multilateral rules of the WTO
5.	Unification and exchange rate flexibility (floating exchange rate regime)	15.	Financial standardisation
6.	Trade liberalisation	16.	Opening of the balance of payments to financial capital flows (including short-term)
7.	Openness to foreign direct investment (FDI)	17.	Total flexibility of the foreign exchange market
8.	Privatisation of State-owned enterprises	18.	Central Bank independence
9.	Market deregulation	19.	Social protection network
10.	Property rights	20.	Mechanisms to combat poverty

SOURCE: WILLIAMSON (1990) AND RODRIK (2006: 978)

Plan, adopted several measures of the "expanded Washington Consensus", which are listed in the second column of Table 2.

It is true that some of the recommendations outlined are irrefutable. After all, few analysts would be against fiscal discipline, as long as it is understood not as the adoption of permanent fiscal austerity, but as a practice in which the government budget, on the revenue or expenditure side, follows policy priorities, and that fiscal policy be managed in a countercyclical manner, as discussed in Chapter 5. Few would also be resistant to the recognition of property rights, the existence of social protection networks and the application of corporate governance, anti-corruption and anti-poverty mechanisms. Nor would they oppose the adoption of tax reform in which the tax burden is compatible with the country's per capita income level, and that the criteria of progressiveness and distributive efficiency be adopted, such that the highest direct tax rates reach the highest income brackets, and the lowest indirect tax rates apply to essential goods, with the rentier class paying taxes on dividends and large fortunes.

However, the Washington Consensus contains two glaring weaknesses: the first is that, driven by the ideology that the free play of market forces and a strategy oriented towards external markets are sufficient to promote and sustain economic growth with price stability, it recommends a single recipe for public policies for all countries on the Latin American continent, ignoring their historical, economic, social and cultural particularities; the second is that it was precisely the recommendations with the greatest lack of theoretical or empirical support that, by having reduced the autonomy of economic policies, are indirectly responsible for the long economic stagnation of the Latin American periphery since the 1990s.

Since "Washington does not, of course, always practice what it preaches to foreigners", as John Williamson himself recognises (1990: 17–18), I will restrict myself, in the following subsection, to the critical discussion of the Consensus measures subject to the second block of weaknesses described in the previous paragraph.

3.2 *The Main Weaknesses of the Washington Consensus*

Proposals to liberalise domestic financial markets—including the gradual reduction, until the total elimination, of credit managed by state-owned development banks and other public banks—and external financial capital flows are at the heart of the weaknesses of the Washington Consensus and neoliberalism.

These recommendations are inspired by the theses of Ronald McKinnon (1973), according to which the mechanisms of "financial repression" tend to adversely affect economic growth in the long term, by inhibiting the free allocation of savings flows ("loanable funds") in financing investments. For McKinnon (1973), at the domestic level, the intervention of Central Banks in determining market interest rates and the practice of subsidised interest rates on financing provided by public banks discourage savings and act as one of the main causes of the high cost of capital, especially in developing countries. Ultimately, "financial repression" would be the main factor responsible for the low rates of gross investment (as a proportion of GDP) in developing countries.

As Arestis and Sawyer (2005) note, McKinnon's arguments on financial repression are based on the assumption that credit flows cause ("precede") growth, and not vice versa. The authors survey the empirical literature and conclude that, although the development of the financial system and economic growth are strongly correlated, there is no single direction of causality between the two. Credit flows are both a cause and an effect of economic growth. Furthermore, financial liberalisation in developing countries in the

1990s and 2000s led to a significant increase in demand for credit from households and businesses, without any increase in savings rates (as a proportion of GDP). And the high real interest rates practiced during the period, as Arestis and Sawyer (op. cit.: 11) point out, "completely failed to increase savings or stimulate investment—in fact, both contracted as a proportion of GDP over the period".

The defence of financial liberalisation was not restricted to the functioning of the domestic financial market. McKinnon's (1991) theses were extended to the global financial market. In this case, it is necessary to consider that the flows of financial capital between countries encompass both short-term and long-term capital. The latter include, in addition to foreign direct investment aimed at creating and/or expanding production capacity abroad, long-term loans and financing. Short-term capital, in contrast, is highly speculative in nature and highly volatile, as it is intended for investments in portfolios of securities, financial bonds and shares with a maturity of up to 1 year. Neoclassical theory seeks to provide theoretical support for the liberalisation of global capital flows, including those of a speculative nature.

The argument for liberalising long-term capital flows, especially those destined for productive investment, is rooted in the neoclassical theory of capital. Take the example of two countries: one rich, with plenty of capital, and the other poor, with plenty of labour. If the production functions of the same product in these countries occur under similar conditions (constant returns to scale and identical technologies, that is, the same capital/labour ratio), the labour productivity in the rich country is still greater than in the poor country. This happens because the marginal productivity of capital in the latter (which is scarce in capital) is greater than that of the former. Therefore, the rate of return on capital in the poor country is, at the margin, higher than that in the rich country.[3] That said, neoclassical theory predicts that under free mobility of international capital flows, capital will flow from rich countries to poor countries in search of higher rates of return on investment. But can it?

Note that, up to this point, the theory refers to international capital flows in the form of foreign direct investment, embodied in the decisions of multinationals to establish factories and other operations abroad. Since not all poor or developing countries are able to attract satisfactory flows of foreign

3 According to neoclassical international trade theory, which assumes that there are no capital flows between countries, a poor country could solve the problem of its relative capital shortage by adopting free trade practices: it would import capital-intensive goods (e.g., more sophisticated manufactured goods, such as automobiles and capital goods) and export labour-intensive goods (primary products and traditional manufactured goods, such as processed foods, clothing, and footwear). As I showed in Chapter 3, the ECLAC school rejects both the conclusions and the normative implications of this theory.

investment, Lucas (1990) conjectures about why long-term capital flows do not flow to these countries. Based on a neoclassical theoretical model, the author applies data observed in an abundant country (the United States) and in some capital-scarce countries (India, Indonesia and Ghana). By incorporating the effect resulting from the significantly higher level of qualification of the workforce ("human capital") in the country with abundant capital (the rich country), Lucas demonstrates that labour productivity in this country becomes significantly higher than that observed in countries with scarce capital (physical and now also human). In other words, due to the greater stock of human capital in rich countries, the marginal productivity of capital and the respective rate of return on capital fall considerably in poor countries. In short, Lucas attributes the lower potential for attracting foreign investment in many poor or developing countries to the scarcity of human capital.

It should be noted that the previous work was done at a time when international capital mobility between developed and developing countries was concentrated on long-term capital. That is, Lucas's conjecture was made before the liberalisation of short-term capital flows, oriented towards investments in short-maturity securities and bonds, of a predominantly speculative nature, as already mentioned. So, what does neoclassical theory have to add to the defence of the liberalisation of this last modality of capital?

As John Eatwell and Lance Taylor (2000: 2) note, the liberalisation of global short-term capital flows was initially a consequence of the collapse of the Bretton Woods regulated system, and so, not something that was theoretically elaborated first. In their words,

> under the Bretton Woods system, foreign exchange rate risk was borne by the public sector [since, after all, the fixed exchange rate system freed the private sector from exchange rate risk]; when that system collapsed, risk was privatised [and borne by households, companies, financial funds, etc.].

Eatwell and Taylor (op. cit.: 2) report that, as early as the mid-1970s, governments were pressured to liberalise short-term financial capital flows. They say (op. cit.: 2):

> The incentive to deregulate international capital flows was driven by the overwhelming need to hedge against the costs that fluctuating exchange rates imposed upon the private sector. To reduce risk, those who traded in foreign markets needed to be able to diversify their portfolios at will, changing the mix of currencies and financial assets both at present and in the future in line with the changing perception of foreign exchange risk.

This suggests that the beginning of the process of global financial deregulation was not preceded by theoretical support. Yet, it was not long before theoretical arguments, be them old or new, appeared in its favour. The main one is the recovery of the hypothesis of efficient financial markets, by Eugene Fama (1970), according to which an individual agent is not capable of anticipating the expected returns of a given financial application, but the financial markets contain all the important information (i.e., they are efficient) to provide all agents with returns equal to the average expected by the market.

More recently, as Ajit Singh (2002) points out, the efficient market and rational expectations hypotheses began to go hand in hand. The rational expectations hypothesis implies that economic agents are able to anticipate the average expected value of the variables relevant to their economic decisions. As Singh (op. cit.: 196) observes, "orthodox economists subscribe to the efficient markets hypothesis, in which asset prices are the results of the collective actions of a multiplicity of individual economic agents, whose behaviour is guided by the maximisation of utilities and rational expectations". This means that, if both hypotheses are valid, the interaction of the prices of all assets leads to efficient prices and the observed average values will coincide with the results expected by the agents. Nothing could be more unrealistic than to account for the movements observed in domestic and global financial markets. Unrealistic hypotheses are only acceptable if they are used to compare abstractly extreme situations with those that actually exist in the real world, such as, for example, perfect competition with monopoly and oligopoly.

In the case of the modus operandi of deregulated financial markets, it is essential to analyse reality as it is. And the most powerful analytical insight continues to be that of Keynes (1936), who, in the much-mentioned passage from Chapter 12 of "The General Theory of Employment, Interest and Money", compares the inherently speculative tendency of financial markets to the beauty contests sponsored by popular London newspapers in their Sunday editions. Keynes suggests that readers take part in a competition in which they are presented with one hundred photographs. The winner of the competition will be the one who indicates not the six most beautiful faces, according to his or her individual opinion, but those that coincide with the average preference of all readers. Since all readers face the same problem, Keynes (1936: 156, emphasis added) notes that it is not a question of choosing the six faces that the average opinion judges to be among the most beautiful, but "anticipating what average opinion **expects** the average opinion to be".

Keynes contrasts (op. cit.: 158) the terms "speculation activity" and "enterprise activity". He argues that the nature of financial markets is essentially speculative. While in speculation agents seek to "estimate the psychology of the market", in enterprise activity agents seek to estimate the expected returns of a real [productive] asset over its useful life. Even though both cases involve non-probabilistic expectations, whose effective average values are impossible to calculate a priori, in a capitalist economy with deregulated financial markets, he says (op. cit.: 158), "it is by no means always the case that speculation predominates over enterprise". This does not mean that markets remain permanently unstable, but that their stability depends not only on economic fundamentals (growth, low inflation, public debt under control, etc.), but mainly on the convention established by the majority. As Eatwell and Taylor (2000:13) point out,

> for substantial periods of time markets may be stabilised by convention—everyone believes that everyone else believes that the economy is sound and financial markets are fundamentally stable. But if convention is questioned or, worst of all, shattered by a significant change in beliefs, then the values of financial assets may soar to great heights or collapse to nothing (…). Financial stability is eminently a problem of convention. But the convention of stability contains the seeds of its own destruction.

The cited excerpt uses the concept of convention, proposed by Keynes, and alludes to the hypothesis of financial instability developed by the post-Keynesian economist Hyman Minsky. In his classic study, Minsky (1982) argues that it is precisely during periods of stability that the patterns of behavior which ultimately cause future instability are sown. This is because it is during the boom phase of the business cycle that entrepreneurs maintain the belief that average profits inherent in productive activities will remain robust and so speculators tend to hold long positions in financial assets, believing that their future prices will continue to rise, which leads to the formation of speculative bubbles. This implies, argues Minsky (op. cit.: 66), that "the fundamental instability of the capitalist system occurs in the boom phase" ("stability is destabilising"), because if the expectations of the average opinion are abruptly reversed in the face of the forecast of a fall in asset prices, the majority changes their portfolio to short positions, causing their prices to collapse. This is how systemic financial crises are generated in deregulated financial markets.

The liberalisation of global capital flows in deregulated domestic financial markets leaves virtually the entire world economy at the mercy of financial crashes and panics, because, as Minsky (1986: 48) warns in his remarkable book "Stabilising an Unstable Economy",

> financing arrangements in which borrowing is necessary to repay debt is speculative finance. Over a run of years in which serious depressions are avoided and in which banks and other financial institutions prosper, the weight in our economy of units that depend on speculative finance increases. In an economy characterised by privately owned capital assets, uncertainty, and profit-maximising behaviour by business, good times induce balance sheet adventuring. The process by which speculative finance increases, as a proportion of the total financing of business, leads to higher asset prices and to increased investment. This leads to an improvement in employment, output, and business profits, which in turn proves to businessmen and bankers that experimenting with speculative finance was correct. Such deviation-amplifying reactions are characteristic of unstable systems-and thus of our economy.

The problem is that when asset prices collapse in the main financial centres, as was the case with the New York Stock Exchange crash in 1929 and the subprime crisis in the United States in 2007–2008, the shock is transmitted, in a practically synchronised manner, to almost the entire global financial system. The harmful effects are well known: while, on the one hand, the worsening of uncertainty, an increased liquidity preference and the rise in long-term interest rates lead to a dramatic contraction in aggregate demand and GDP, in addition to a sharp increase in unemployment rates, on the other hand, the drastic reduction in cash flows of non-financial companies compromises their effective capacity to pay commitments assumed in the past.

As deregulated banking systems encourage financial positions with excessive leverage (i.e., with an excessive proportion of loans in relation to equity) and generate a huge mismatch between the amount of financed resources, concentrated in the long term, compared to the amount of financial resources raised, predominantly in the short term, the abrupt and sharp drop in cash flows of non-financial companies tends to produce cascading effects throughout the financial system. To prevent financial crises from turning into major and prolonged depressions, Central Banks and national Treasuries have no alternative but to operate, respectively, as lenders ("lenders of last resort") and buyers ("big governments") of last resort. As Minsky (1986: 21) notes, rescue operations for "too big to fail" companies and banks emerge to avoid the enormous social cost of economic depressions.

So far, we have shown how the liberalisation of short-term capital flows creates economic instability in the global economy. But what about its impacts on developing countries? I will recall what is suggested by the liberal theoretical interpretation, developed independently by economists Robert Mundell (1960) and J. Marcus Fleming (1962) and widely celebrated in undergraduate economics courses. The Mundell-Fleming model seeks to elucidate how the balance of payments adjustment works in countries, while taking into account the exchange rate regime (fixed or floating) and the degree of openness to capital movement (low, high or perfect). For what concerns us here, I will focus on the case in which a country adopts a floating exchange rate regime and has a high degree of openness to international capital flows, a situation characteristic of most developing countries today—including Brazil.

The model considers the different combinations of real interest rates and aggregate income levels that allow the economy to reach its general equilibrium. These are points that ensure, simultaneously, internal equilibrium (investment equal to savings and money supply equal to money demand) and external equilibrium (balance of payments). If the economy deviates from any situation of macroeconomic equilibrium, automatic forces in the goods and services, monetary and foreign exchange markets are triggered to facilitate adjustment to a different equilibrium point from the original one. Although changes occur between periods, the model is typically static ("comparative statics"), since there is no room for dynamics that occur over time. Nor does it play any role for expectations, since agents expect the current situation to continue indefinitely into the future.

The model assumes that, with broad openness to the flow of foreign capital, monetary and exchange rate policies operate independently. Yet, is this true? According to the logic of the model, while monetary policy aims to maintain full employment and price stability, exchange rate policy, anchored in a floating exchange rate regime, promotes adjustment and preserves the stability of the balance of payments in the long term.

I will take, as an example, the case of Brazil, which since 1999 has adopted inflation targeting and floating exchange rate regimes and, since the beginning of the 1990s, has granted broad freedom to the entry and exit of foreign capital. Consider a period of prosperity and high international liquidity such as that which occurred between 2005 and mid-2008. Suppose that, faced with an inflationary outbreak, the Central Bank increases interest rates to anchor expectations of future price increases and reduce inflation to the centre of the target. The increase in the domestic interest rate differential in relation to international interest rates tends to increase the net inflow of foreign capital, part of which will be short-term and speculative in nature. This movement increases the country's balance of payments surpluses, contributing to the real appreciation of the domestic currency in relation to the currencies of the main international partners. According to the logic of the Mundell-Fleming model, real appreciation should reduce net exports (exports minus imports) and, assuming all else constant, immediately promote the adjustment of the balance of payments by eliminating the surplus. Moreover, according to Mundell's (1962) argument, policymakers are faced with a "trilemma": with free access to external capital flows, it is only possible to preserve monetary independence and stability if, and only if, the exchange rate regime is floating, but even then, at the expense of exchange rate stability. These are the outcomes the theory predicts.

In the real world, however, the adjustment of the balance of payments is not immediate and automatic. As already discussed in Chapter 6, the tendency towards real appreciation amplifies current account deficits, increasing the country's dependence on foreign capital financing. Such a trend can continue throughout the financial boom cycle, so that when it reverses, there is capital flight, intense currency depreciation and an increase in inflation. To contain a new outbreak of inflation, the Central Bank finds itself compelled to establish a new cycle of rising domestic interest rates, which proves that, in practice, its autonomy is quite reduced and monetary policy is totally dependent on exchange rate policy, contrary to what the Mundell-Fleming model postulates.

In a celebrated article, Helènne Rey (2015) points to abundant empirical evidence that the global financial cycle, whether it be a boom or a burst of speculative bubbles, is strongly conditioned by the Federal Reserve's monetary policy. This implies that the financial cycle is determined in a countercyclical manner: in periods of low US basic interest rates (Fed funds), there is a tendency for international credit flows and asset prices to expand, as well as for the formation of huge speculative bubbles; then the increase in Fed funds triggers a reverse movement, causing most of the international liquidity to flow back to the main hegemonic centre (the United States). As Rey argues (op. cit.: 18; 21), referring to the world of financial globalisation,

> although it is not possible to have monetary independence in relation to the core economies throughout the global financial cycle when there is free capital mobility, the trilemma [elucidated by Mundell] becomes a dilemma: regardless of the exchange rate regime adopted, it is only possible to achieve monetary independence if, and only if, there are capital controls.

Even with relatively solid economic fundamentals, as was the case of Brazil on the threshold of the 2008 financial crisis, the reversal of the global financial cycle means that periphery countries face the worst of all possible worlds: greater uncertainty, increased liquidity preference and country risk, capital flight and intense depreciation of their national currencies (overshooting). The immediate effect is an acceleration of inflation. Since central banks react by increasing basic interest rates, in the medium-term economies end up facing a slowdown or recession.

Even when major global financial crises originate in developed countries, as was the case in 2008, it is periphery countries that suffer the greatest adverse impacts. The main reason for this contradiction is that, as noted by Barbara Fritz, Luiz Fernando de Paula and Daniela M. Prates (2018), the international monetary system works in a hierarchical manner, in which currencies are ranked from the top (the dollar, followed by the euro and the yen) to the base of the pyramid (the currencies of periphery countries), according to their capacity to be internationally accepted as a medium of exchange, unit of account and store of value. While in the boom phase of the international financial cycle, foreign agents compensate for the almost zero degree of liquidity of periphery currencies with the high financial rates of return provided by securities and bonds denominated in these currencies, when the cycle reverses, the high uncertainty causes these same agents to flee from these currencies like a bat flees from hell.

From what has been revealed in this subsection, it is possible to draw an important conclusion: developing countries that promoted openness to the free movement of foreign capital and entered firmly into financial globalisation should never have embarked on such a strategy. Or, at least, they should have done so gradually, simultaneously imposing controls on entry in the form of a quarantine (a minimum period of stay) on all capital flows, including long-term modalities.[4] Full convertibility of the capital account should only be adopted when the economy reaches a level of economic and financial strength that allows free access to its stock, security and bond markets for non-residents. It is for no other reason that countries such as China and India have not put

4 The imposition of controls on all capital flows is justified because, in the case of Brazil, for example, multinational companies often internalise foreign capital as "intercompany loans", which are recorded under the heading of foreign direct investment, although these resources can be invested in the market for short-term securities and bonds denominated in domestic currency. Unlike portfolio investments, which are directly influenced by the difference between domestic and international interest rates, long-term capital tends to be much less affected by barriers in the form of quarantine.

their cart before the horse and continue to impose restrictions on the entry of short-term foreign capital.[5]

4 Conclusion

The Bretton Woods system, established near the end of World War II in 1944, consisted of several mechanisms for multilateral regulation of international trade and financial transactions, negotiated between the official representatives of 44 countries, led by John Maynard Keynes of the United Kingdom and Harry Dexter White of the United States. At Bretton Woods, the prevailing understanding was that, because capitalism is inherently unstable, it requires regulation of the markets for goods, services and factors of production.

In the context of international trade, instead of the uncompromising defence of pure free trade, associated with laissez faire, efforts to reduce barriers to transactions of goods and services predominated, but by creating retaliatory mechanisms against anti-competitive practices, such as dumping and subsidies, and leaving ample room for the adoption of national development policies guided by the criterion of protecting infant industry, as already analysed in Chapter 7.

In the area of international finance, the adoption of a fixed exchange rate regime, which could be adjusted in cases of fundamental imbalances in the balance of payments, was only possible due to controls on capital flows. In general, foreign trade policies and mechanisms for regulating international capital movements were subordinated to national development plans, and not vice versa.

The main distinguishing feature between regulated liberalism and neoliberalism is that the latter, as the term itself suggests, seeks to recover the spirit of laissez faire that characterised global capitalism until World War I. Since the defence of the liberalisation of trade and financial transactions is based on completely unrealistic assumptions, such as the prevalence of perfect

5 The imposition of barriers to the free movement of capital is well known in the case of China. In India, the opening to the flow of foreign capital was limited to foreign direct investment and the stock market. In the security and bond market, non-resident investors face several institutional barriers. Even so, Duvvuri Subbarao, former governor of the Reserve Bank of India (the Indian Central Bank), complains, in an article in the Financial Times on 21/06/2021, about the pressure exerted by the significant inflows of international capital destined for the country's stock market on the appreciation of the Indian rupee. This article can be downloaded at https://www.ft.com/content/30652b8d-8aff-444a-a703-fd8582058c69. Accessed on 14/07/2022.

competition and the existence of efficient financial markets, neoliberalism has a strongly dogmatic and ideological bias.

The adherence of Latin American countries to neoliberalism, from the mid-1980s onwards, far from reflecting unilateral choices by the region's governments, was in fact imposed by the expanded Washington Consensus, which conditioned the restructuring with a discount on the countries' external debts, within the scope of the Brady Plan, to the liberalisation of domestic financial markets and the opening up to the movement of short-term capital. In this chapter, I showed how external financial opening has greatly increased the vulnerability of periphery countries and extremely reduced the autonomy of macroeconomic policies aimed at sustaining economic development and improving the well-being of the population.

CHAPTER 11

Conclusion and Policy Implications of Part 2: Market Failures as a Criterion for Adopting Public Policies

A Critical Evaluation of the Neoclassical Liberal Argument

In Chapter 7, I drew the main normative conclusions related to the theoretical approach of the developmental school. This chapter is also conclusive and presents a note on the public policy implications of the neoclassical approach.

1 Market Failures as a Criterion for Adopting Public Policies: the Neoclassical Liberal Argument

The neoclassical perspective is eminently liberal. Its theoretical framework is constructed and sustained based on the hypothesis that all markets (of goods, labour and capital) function under ideal conditions of perfect competition. As I have shown in previous chapters, neoclassical models are formulated with a high degree of mathematical sophistication and treat the functioning of capitalist economies as if they were "pure" economies, without giving great importance to class conflicts and ideological influences.

If the real world replicated the conditions required by perfect competition models, the free market and relative price mechanisms would be able to provide private agents (firms and households) with all the information necessary to allocate productive resources efficiently and equalise private and social marginal costs and benefits. Under these circumstances, capitalist economies would reach a state of general equilibrium, with all markets reaching unique and stable solutions for prices and quantities. In standard economic jargon, this is said to be Walrasian general equilibrium, in reference to León Walras (1874), the French neoclassical economist who originally envisioned such a situation.

Having reached this ideal condition, economies would also reach optimal levels of social welfare. In standard economic language, they would reach "Pareto optimal", in reference to the understanding that economist Vilfredo Pareto (1909) gave to the issue. In short, the neoclassical approach concludes that if all markets operate under perfectly competitive conditions, capitalist

 | DOI:10.1163/9789004734296_015

economies generate the Pareto-optimal pattern of income distribution. This is the situation of maximum social welfare. In it, an improvement in the welfare of one individual would only be possible at the expense of at least a worsening of the welfare of another.[1]

In addition, neoclassical theory considers that if the world economy replicates the ideal conditions of perfect competition, **only** free trade and the specialisation of each country in the production of goods in which it holds a comparative advantage provide an optimal configuration of international equilibrium consistent with maximum social well-being under the Pareto criterion ("social optimum"). Thus, neoclassical liberal economists argue that if Walrasian general equilibrium provides both the optimal allocation of productive resources and the best standard of social welfare at a given point in time (whatever the distribution of national income), there is no theoretical argument that justifies government intervention, either to produce an improvement in the welfare situation or to accelerate the growth of the country's per capita income over time. This means that laissez faire and free trade are the best economic policy strategies (the first-best approach) and there is no reason to adopt national development policies similar to those proposed in Chapter 7.

However, the question that arises is: how does the neoclassical liberal view deal with the unquestionable fact that the prevailing competitive pattern in capitalist economies is not perfect competition, but imperfect competition, especially oligopoly? Since this theoretical school of thought favours formalism to the detriment of the realism of hypotheses, the problem is not faced directly. It is circumvented through the somewhat imaginative idea that monopolies, duopolies and oligopolies are temporary deviations of the capitalist system from Walrasian general equilibrium. In neoclassical lexicon, they are market failures that tend to produce divergences between private and social marginal costs and benefits. In these cases, and only in these cases, the neoclassical liberal view admits the possibility of government intervention in markets. Even so, such intervention occurs under sizeable restrictions, according to the position of neoclassical economist James Meade (1955): policies to correct market failures are always second best in relation to laissez faire and free trade.[2]

Neoclassical liberal economists treat most public policies as second best because they believe that, compared to the private sector, the government lacks sufficient information to correctly identify the source of market failures.

1 It should be noted that this Pareto-optimal pattern determines maximum social well-being for a given income distribution but is not necessarily associated with greater or lesser social inequality.

2 Meade (1955) developed the second-best theory.

Consequently, it is unable to choose the most appropriate economic policy instrument (subsidies, government procurement, import tariffs, etc.) to correct them. In his treatise on trade policy (*"Trade Policy and Economic Welfare"*), Corden (1974) argued that if the divergence between private and social marginal costs and benefits has a domestic origin, the appropriate economic policy instrument should correct this failure in the domestic market (a production subsidy, for example). If the divergence originates in the international market, the appropriate instrument must correct this failure whose source is foreign trade (an import tariff, for example).

I will illustrate the problem with an example based on Corden (op. cit.). Let us assume that Brazilian producers of PVC, a basic raw material for the chemical industry, are facing a significant loss of market share in the domestic market due to a sudden increase in imports from China. Following Corden's reasoning, this loss of market share can have several causes, such as a temporary drop in competitiveness of national producers, real wages higher than productivity, dumping by Chinese producers (i.e., predatory prices lower than those practiced in the Chinese domestic market), among others.

It is also assumed that the government, upon suspecting the existence of dumping, opens an investigation process and concludes that, in fact, there has been unfair competition on the part of China and that, following WTO rules, a retaliatory import tariff (anti-dumping) can be adopted against Chinese imports of PVC. However, if, in fact, the damage to the domestic industry resulted from wage cost pressures rather than dumping, neoclassicals would argue that the government failure which led it to misjudge the existence of unfair competition may outweigh market failures.[3] Thus, **divergences** ("market failures") caused by imperfect competition become **distortions** (worsening of "market failures") created by the government itself.[4] In the case illustrated, instead of increasing the import tariff, the most appropriate instrument should have been a domestic subsidy, even if it did not affect the total value of production but only the cost of labour, considered the primary source of the divergence between private and social marginal costs and benefits.

In short, neoclassical economists are almost unconditional defenders of free trade, which they consider the "first-best" strategy. Considering the existence

3 For example, due to information failures, the government may assess the existence of dumping based on inaccurate data on domestic and international prices, which are essential for identifying anticompetitive practices.

4 In neoclassical literature, **divergences** between private and social marginal costs and benefits naturally result from market failures themselves. **Distortions**, on the other hand, result from the adverse impacts of government economic policies adopted to correct these same market failures. In this regard, the seminal reference is Meade (1955).

of market failures, for each divergence between private and social marginal costs and benefits there would be a hierarchy of suboptimal economic policies (second-best, third-best, and so on).[5] As Corden argued (op. cit.: 28–31), the more inappropriate the instruments used to correct market failures, the greater the government failures, which aggravate distortions in production, or consumption, or the labour market, or the export sector, etc.

2 Market Failures: a Critique of the Neoclassical Liberal Argument

It is time to ask whether the theoretical argument of market failures is an accurate criterion for shaping public policies. The answer is a resounding **no**. For two reasons: First, imperfect competition is not a mere temporary departure from perfect competition in capitalist economies, a sine qua non condition for achieving Walrasian general equilibrium and Pareto optimality. Imperfect competition in the form of monopolies, duopolies and, especially, oligopolies is the norm of contemporary capitalism, not the exception. Second, neoclassical economists see the elaboration and implementation of public policies as if they were implicitly sufficient to promote the return of capitalist economies to a position of general equilibrium. However, this perspective makes no sense at all. I have to agree with Mário Possas (1996, p. 78), who identified, critically and with great precision, the weak point of the market failure theory:

> We arrive at the paradoxical situation that the theoretical relevance of the [general equilibrium] model is not dictated by its adherence to reality, and the respective market "imperfections" or "failures" are overwhelmingly more frequent than the hypothetical situation that corresponds to the ideal model. If the theory always finds "failures", generally significant ones, in the application of its ideal model, would it not be the case to recognise that the fault lies with the model?

5 The reader should be informed, however, that this ordering is associated with the set of hierarchies of available economic policies (internal and external), but not with the ideally expected results in a possible situation in which the economy achieves efficiency in the Pareto sense (the utopian solution, in Meade's original terminology (1955, p. 8). In other words, in the second-best theory, the use of active economic policies always produces results that are inferior to those that would be achieved in a possible laissez faire, a sufficient condition—albeit utopian—under which the economy can maximise efficiency in a manner compatible with the Pareto criterion.

The neoclassical argument is so paradoxical that liberal economists even accept the argument for protecting infant industries, but only if, in the spirit of John Stuart Mill (1848), the relative delay (lagging) of a national industry in relation to that of another country is assessed as a result of market failures.[6] In this case, the use of import tariffs, subsidies and/or other complementary instruments could, in principle, eliminate the disadvantage of the backward country, if there are expectations of cost reduction over time, as knowledge accumulates dynamically through learning by doing. However, given the risks of possible non-internalisation of learning by doing and the emergence of new market failures that could lead the protected industry to failure, such occurrences end up opposing, as in Corden's argument (1974, Chapter 9), the protection measure.

Furthermore, the criterion of market failures as a requirement for government intervention is eminently static. It is associated with the improvement in the allocation of productive resources between two specific moments (comparative statics). Neoclassical liberal economists have as their main motivation the achievement of equilibrium and the maintenance of stability. The developmental school, on the other hand, as I showed in Chapter 7, justifies the adoption of public policies through protection, subsidies or other government incentives with eminently dynamic arguments.

This is because, as Schumpeter emphasised and as I extensively explained in Chapter 1, capitalist development has a form of reproduction that continuously and non-linearly revolutionises the technical-productive base. Thus, technologies, enterprises and productive systems are created and destroyed. For this very reason, in addition to being intrinsically unstable, capitalism's tendency is to produce and reproduce imbalances in the long run, with innovations being the main driver of the process of "creative destruction" in the national and global spheres.

As if that were not enough, the effects of capital accumulation and technical progress tend to produce technologies subject to significant economies of scale and to make oligopoly, with a high degree of concentration of production in favour of the largest companies, the standard of competition usually observed. Therefore, it makes no sense to expect government interventions to correct market failures and promote the convergence of capitalist economies towards general equilibrium simply because this aim is impossible to achieve.

---

6 As I showed in Chapter 3, the argument for infant industry protection was pioneered by the German nationalist economist Friedrich List (1841) and later recognised by the classical liberal economist John Stuart Mill (1848).

As Mariana Mazzucato (2013) has shown, governments mobilise and subsidise large amounts of public resources destined for private financing of innovations precisely because, due to the enormous uncertainty and risks associated with future profitability, the expected social returns tend to fall short of the private returns associated with them. In this case, the need to correct market failures is not the main justification for the state to subsidise innovations, especially in high-technology segments. As Mazzucato emphasised (op. cit.: 32), the main reason is the urgency to induce the private sector to "shape and create new markets". For this reason, I believe that the arguments proposed by the developmental school in favour of state intervention are much more consistent than the neoclassical liberal argument of market failures, because they conceive of capitalism as a dynamic system.

Conclusion

With this book, I intended to contribute to the debate that is taking place between the developmental and neoclassical liberal thinking, also including their respective normative implications and economic policy recommendations. From everything I have analysed, to a reasonable degree of detail, I venture to draw a general conclusion.

Developmental economists agree with the assumption that capitalist economies operate according to certain general laws. However, for this group, such laws are not absolute, but relative, because there is also the influence of the dynamics of history, conflicts between social classes, ideology, culture and other non-economic factors. Moreover, these general laws are not immutable, as they are subject to changes driven by the history of societies. Neoclassical liberal economists, in turn, are more attached to the idea that the functioning of the capitalist system obeys, or at least should obey, the general laws of markets and free competition.

From an exclusively theoretical perspective, the starting and ending points of neoclassical liberal analysis are always perfect competition and Walrasian general equilibrium. These models are idealised and because they are mere abstractions without any connection to the real world, they are irreconcilable with the developmental approach. Even when neoclassical theoretical models recognise and incorporate structures of imperfect competition (monopolies, duopolies and oligopolies), such deviations are analysed as temporary departures from idealised situations. Therefore, this ideal scenario is both the starting point and the destination of the neoclassical liberal view: in theory, this is where the economy should converge, even though there is no economic experience that reproduces this ideal situation *ipsis litteris*.

For this reason, a huge channel separates these two currents of thought in the normative field: developmentalists defend an active state intervention, whether to revive the entrepreneurial animal spirits in supporting physical investments and technological innovations, or to stimulate productive segments that induce technical progress. Neoclassical liberals are enthusiasts of laissez-faire and free trade. They accept, at most, occasional and passive state intervention, restricted to correcting market failures. I repeat: correcting market failures. The problem is that, on a theoretical level, the idea of correcting market failures is associated with the objective of redirecting the economic system towards the ideal situation of general equilibrium. This means that the ideology in defence of the "minimal state" is being disguised as theoretical arguments, of which I unravelled in Chapters 10 and 11.

 | DOI:10.1163/9789004734296_016

The impossibility of reconciliation between developmentalists and neoclassicals, whether in the theoretical or normative field, thus arises from several reasons, among which I will mention and summarise the main ones below, as I have discussed in this book.

i) Developmental economists follow the theoretical tradition of Smith, but place special emphasis on Marx, Keynes and Schumpeter, who conceived of capitalism as a dynamic system, subject to continuous imbalances and structural changes. Neoclassical liberals follow the tradition of Ricardo, Mill and Walras, who understand capitalism as a static system in which the solution to economic problems depends on the optimal efficiency with which productive resources (labour, capital, land, etc.) are allocated to produce situations of equilibrium between supply and demand in all markets.

ii) Developmentalists ("classical", ECLACian, Furtadian and new developmentalists) conceive of economic development as a process of structural change resulting from capital accumulation and technical progress. The manufacturing industry, increasingly integrated with high-tech services, operates as the main source responsible for the generation, dissemination and reinforcement of technical progress, and thus sustains the growth rate and the increase in the economy's average productivity in the long term. But not only that: development, when it materialises as a Schumpeterian process of creative destruction, implies not only continuous and non-linear economic changes, but also political, social and cultural transformations (just remember that, today, emotional relationships, elections and revolutions occur, most of all, on social networks!). Neoclassical liberals, however, assume that productive activities in the capitalist system have constant returns to scale. Even when they bow to the glaring evidence that, due to the cumulative effects of technical progress and capital accumulation, increasing returns to scale prevail in the real world, the growth model "dynamics" of neoclassical macroeconomics is still based on an aggregate production function subject to constant returns! This acquiescence arises from the fact that the neoclassical view prefers to sacrifice realism in favour of mathematical elegance and the search for equilibrium results. All in the name of theoretical abstraction.

iii) With the exception of Lewis and Rosenstein-Rodan, whose theoretical models are heavily influenced by Say's law ("every supply creates its own demand"), most developmentalists align themselves with the Keynesian hypothesis that expectations of increases in aggregate demand in the short- and long-term guide, respectively, current production and investment decisions. Even recognising that aggregate demand forges interrelations with aggregate supply, developmentalists do not renounce the canonical hypothesis that the main causality is from the former to the latter, not the other way around. Furthermore, developmentalists follow Kaldor's argument (inspired by Marx) that there are no restrictive forces on the supply side that prevent the sustainability of economic development in the very long run. When labour manifests itself as a possible restrictive factor on the supply side, the pressure of capitalist competition accelerates technical progress which, by saving labour power, makes this resource operate, in the very long run, as an "industrial reserve army" à la Marx.

Thus, most developmental economists accept the hypothesis of Prebisch, Kaldor and Thirlwall that the main restrictive factor to sustaining economic development does not come from the supply side, but from the demand side, and is associated with external contraints, that is, the balance of payments constraints. Because of this, providing a domestic production structure with the potential to generate net exportable surpluses (exports greater than imports, but not necessarily mercantilism) is an essential condition for ensuring sufficient foreign exchange flows to cover the basic international payments of any economy, without depending on external financing ("external savings"). Kaldor (1966) is right in claiming that possible supply constraints are observed in the short term, but not in the long term. In any case, recent studies confirm the Kaldorian (and therefore developmental) hypothesis that the engine of economic growth in the long term is demand and that supply forces (for example, the search for innovations by companies, through greater spending on R&D) tend to accommodate and establish dynamic feedback loops with demand forces.

In contrast, neoclassical liberal theoretical models of growth and international trade are aligned with supply-side economics. Being strongly influenced by pre-Keynesian macroeconomists (Pigou and Hicks, among others), neoclassical macroeconomics, specifically, postulates that supply-side forces determine long-term growth.

iv) For developmentalists, premature deindustrialisation is one of the structural factors responsible for the stagnation in periphery countries (especially Latin American ones) in recent decades. In the world of static and dynamic increasing returns to scale, premature deindustrialisation is a structurally bad element. If the manufacturing industry sharply reduces its share of aggregate output prematurely, it loses its power to act as the main generator and disseminator of technical progress. This ultimately leads to the interruption of the previous catching up process and to economic stagnation in the long term. This problem is almost entirely neglected by the neoclassical liberal school. Why? Because neoclassical economists give the industrial sector and high-tech services the same relative importance as agriculture and other activities characterised by lower capital intensity with respect to the aggregate impacts on long-term economic growth. The neoclassical school of thought recognises the crucial role of technological innovations in ensuring development but does not consider their impacts as differentiated by sector. This hypothesis is maintained even in endogenous growth models because in these models, technologies—measured as a stock of aggregated knowledge or human capital—although subject to increasing returns to scale, spread proportionally to all productive sectors. This paradoxical result is only possible because of the insistence with which, in neoclassical growth models (including those of endogenous growth), the economic system is seen as an aggregate production function subject to constant returns to scale (at least with respect to traditional factors such as capital and labour). Once again, realism is sacrificed in the name of the mathematical solution of equilibrium.

v) During the period in which the Bretton Woods system was in force (1944–1973), economic liberalism remained fundamentally restricted to trade transactions of goods and services and long-term capital flows. In particular, in the area of international trade, the defence of free trade was not based on the complete absence of trade barriers ("theoretical free trade"), but on the principle of multilateralism and non-discrimination ("pragmatic free trade"). Under the guise of Bretton Woods, GATT urged member countries to expand trade in goods and services, based on the principle of comparative advantage. At the time when David Ricardo (1817) formulated it, the thesis was that **some** trade is always better than **no** trade, and not that the best strategy for all countries should be to engage in unconditional free trade, as later reformulated by neoclassical scholars, notably Paul Samuelson (1948; 1949). The Bretton Woods trade and monetary arrangements, while encouraging the reduction of barriers to international trade, did not close the doors to developing countries adopting various economic policy instruments (import tariffs, production, credit and export subsidies, etc.) aimed at promoting economic development.

This flexibility changed completely after the rise of Reagan, Thatcher and the spread of neoliberalism. By defending the practice of laissez-faire in all markets—for goods, services, labour and financial capital, including short-term capital, intended for the diversification of portfolios of securities, bonds and shares—at domestic and international levels, neoliberalism became a radical ideology. There was no shortage of warnings from important dissenting voices. As early as the 1980s, economists such as Carlos Diaz-Alejandro (1985) and Hyman Minsky (1986), for example, warned that the deregulation of domestic financial markets and the liberalisation of short-term international capital flows would increase the frequency and intensity of adverse events, such as the formation and bursting of speculative bubbles and financial crises in the world economy, the consequences of which I discussed in Chapter 10.

In my judgment, the dissemination of the main neoliberal economic reforms in Latin America from the 1990s onwards was less a result of unilateral decisions by governments in the region than of external pressure from the Washington Consensus. It conditioned the restructuring with a discount on the countries' external debt, as part of the Brady Plan, on the liberalisation of domestic financial markets and the opening up of short-term capital movements. Initially without a consistent theoretical basis, the liberalisation of short-term international flows was "sold" to the countries of the continent as a panacea to eliminate the risks of exchange rate fluctuations.

Yet, it was not long before supposedly theoretical arguments appeared. Orthodox literature sought to justify external financial openness in periphery countries based on hypothetical benefits arising from supplementing their low domestic savings rate with "external savings". The warning, by Minsky (1986), that a significant part of these "external savings" flows is in the form of short- or very short-term capital, of a mainly speculative nature, is circumvented with the theory of the efficiency of financial markets. For neoclassical orthodoxy, the risk of panic and sudden stops in capital flows can be ruled out because financial markets have all the relevant information (i.e., they are efficient) to guarantee agents returns equal to the average expected by the market.

vi) In practice, the integration of Latin American periphery countries into financial globalisation was guided by the neoclassical premise of the benefits associated with the strategy of growth financed with "external savings". This strategy, adopted by the governments of Latin American countries in the last two decades, constitutes one of the target criticisms of new developmentalism, whose main merit was to have incorporated macroeconomics and macroeconomic policy into the theoretical analysis of development and stagnation.

In the case of Brazil, new developmentalism emphasises that, in addition to the "growth with external savings" strategy, two other "usual policies" contribute to the prolonging of economic stagnation. On the one hand, the failure to neutralise the Dutch disease. On the other hand, a macroeconomic policy arrangement based on a very inflexible inflation targeting regime.

I have shown in detail in Chapter 6 how these "business as usual" policies amplify exchange rate volatility and contribute to keeping the national currency tending to be overvalued in the long run. Ergo, they prolong economic stagnation indefinitely. The transmission channels are somewhat obvious. In developing countries with a high degree of openness to capital movements, monetary policy has little autonomy to preserve price stability and sustain economic growth. This is because the cycles of increases and decreases in short-term basic interest rates follow and are subordinate to global financial cycles. Due to the hegemony of the US dollar as the international reserve currency, these flows are controlled by the Federal Reserve's monetary policy. Thus, in cycles of high international liquidity, economic expansion in the United States and low US basic interest rates, the greater differential in the short-term interest rate observed in periphery countries attracts excess capital (especially short-term capital). As a result, periphery currencies tend to appreciate for as long as the international boom lasts. On the one hand, while in the short run the fall in the prices of imported goods and the competitive pressure exerted by imports contribute to anchoring inflation rates around the target of periphery countries, on the other hand, exchange rate overvaluation causes a cascade of harmful effects: it shifts a significant part of demand to imported goods (i.e., it exports jobs), artificially increases real wages and thus depresses both the expected profitability of private investments and economic growth in the long run. In other words, the overvaluation of periphery currencies accentuates and perpetuates stagnation.

There are even more harmful effects: the persistence of chronic levels of exchange rate overvaluation for long periods amplifies current account deficits. When they become unsustainable in the eyes of international investors, current account deficits trigger sudden capital flights, high uncertainty and excessive depreciation of the national currency, leading the country to a financial crisis. A vicious circle is created: Periphery countries alternate between cycles of low interest rates and overvalued exchange rates, followed by sudden capital flight, exchange rate depreciation, inflationary pressure and rising interest rates. As new developmentalism emphasises, by falling into the trap of high real interest rates and overvalued real exchange rates, periphery countries are unable to escape the tendency towards economic stagnation, even in the presence of consistent industrial and technological policies.

Furthermore, new developmentalism attributes the Dutch disease as one of the structural factors of stagnation in Latin American periphery countries. However, unlike the Venezuelan experience, pioneeringly analysed by Celso Furtado (1957), or the classic case in the Netherlands, theorised by Corden and Neary (1982), this new Dutch disease in the Latin American periphery has its origins in the wave of liberalising economic reforms adopted in the form of shock therapy (rapid trade liberalisation, opening up to the movement of short-term capital, aversion to industrial policy and other public policy mechanisms in favour of development, etc.). In fact, as new developmentalism has highlighted, the more deepened the radical liberalising reforms are, the more serious the Dutch disease becomes.

The new developmental analysis shows that the overvaluation of periphery currencies manifests itself simultaneously as a cause and effect of the worsening of this new form of Dutch disease. As a cause, the exchange rate overvaluation increases the level of domestic prices in relation to those of external trading partners (expressed in US dollars, in both cases) and reduces the competitiveness of exportable goods from the periphery, notably manufactured goods and/or services that are more technologically sophisticated. As Porcile (2021: 55) highlighted, when endorsing new developmentalism propositions, "the destruction of enterprises, activities and technological capabilities during a relatively long period of exchange rate overvaluation compromises technological learning and the dissemination of technologies (technological spillovers)". As a result, the worsening of the Dutch disease accentuates exchange rate overvaluation. In fact, the increased concentration of the export basket in primary products and industrialised goods that are intensive in natural resources (i.e., commodities) in periphery countries means that, during the boom in international prices of these products, the improvement in the terms of trade increases the inflow of foreign currency. Consequently, the national currency appreciates in real terms and reinforces the tendency towards stagnation. The appreciated real exchange rate is the link between the Dutch disease and long-term economic stagnation.

vii) Since, in my opinion, the role of economists is not restricted to developing or analysing theories on economic issues, but also to proposing solutions to economic problems and improving people's well-being, a final question arises: what can be done to escape the stagnation trap and restore the catching up trajectory in developing countries? As I argued in Chapter 8, the neoclassical liberal economists' proposals for government policies aimed at correcting market failures must be discarded. Being mere palliatives to eliminate transitory divergences in the real functioning of markets in relation to the general equilibrium supposedly achievable in the long run, these proposals would be incapable of halting stagnation and sustaining the development of periphery countries.

The recommended economic policy measures should be aligned with those discussed in Chapter 7. Let me explain why: to restore the caching up trajectory of developing countries that are stagnant, industrial policy must be conceived in a systemic way, linked to all other public policies in the microeconomic sphere (such as tax, regulatory and foreign trade policies, among others), the mesoeconomic sphere (for example, science and technology, education and training, etc.) and the macroeconomic sphere (monetary, fiscal and exchange rate policies). Under these conditions, industrial policy must be designed and integrated into national development plans. The objective of maintaining price stability must be in line with the objectives of sustaining economic growth, promoting employment and reducing social inequalities. Short-term macroeconomic policies cannot subordinate structural policies. Regardless, short-term macroeconomic policy alone will not, and has never, caused economic development.

In addition to these objectives, national development plans must include the aim of gradually replacing high carbon dioxide (CO_2) emission technologies with more efficient ones. As if the ethical reasons were not enough, the involvement of developing countries in green technologies will become an economic requirement: international pressure to adopt low-CO_2 emission technologies will mean that countries that do not adapt to the new environmental economy will be left out of the global competitive game. Since there is no rule of thumb for solving problems of such complexity, it is up to each country to adopt policies tailored to its own particularities.

Since the development and implementation of national development plans involve the mobilisation of various economic policy instruments and the coordination of government institutions, it will not be easy to put them into practice. Among the challenges facing Brazil and other developing countries, two fundamental questions serve as examples: one, how can we ensure greater autonomy for macroeconomic policies (primarily monetary, fiscal and exchange rates) in a context of broad openness to capital movements? According to what I discussed in Chapter 10, the answer is apparently simple: by adopting capital controls. And two, but how can one make the decision to adopt ad hoc capital controls if this measure can be sabotaged by the economic and political power of the agents who control the process of accumulation and revaluation of capital, currently subordinated to the logic of financial accumulation ("financialization")?[1] I do not have a simple answer to this question, but I do know that its solution is exceedingly political in nature.

Paraphrasing Keynes, neoliberalism has conquered the periphery countries of Latin America (and even more so Brazil) as completely as the Holy Inquisition conquered Spain. In this context, it is curious that the main forces resisting the adoption of national development plans are not only of an economic-financial nature, but also of a political-ideological nature. In the case of Brazil, in particular, the recovery of national development policies will depend on a clash of ideas. This will only occur when civil society actors (workers, entrepreneurs, bankers, etc.) are convinced that the state and the market are not dichotomous institutions. Both can and should act in a relatively coordinated manner, with the common goal of rebuilding the shattered nation. Only then will Brazil be able to provide its people with democracy, freedom, material wealth, social well-being and cultural diversity. And why not, happiness?

---

1 On the problem of financialization, see Bruno and Caffe (2017) and Bresser-Pereira, de Paula and Bruno (2020).

Bibliography

Abramovitz, M. (1993). "The search for the sources of growth: Areas of ignorance, old and new". *The Journal of Economic History*, Vol. 53, No. 2., June: 217–243.

Acemoglu, D., and Robinson, J.A. (2012). *Why Nations Fail: The Origens of Power, Prosperity, and Poverty*. New York: Crown Business.

Aiginger, K., and Rodrik, D. (2020). "Rebirth of industrial policy and an agenda for the Twenty-First century". *Journal of Industry, Competition and Trade*", Vol. 20 (2), Springer, June: 189–207.

Alesina, A., and Ardagna, S. (2010). "Large changes in fiscal policy: taxes versus spending." In J.R. Brown (ed.). *Tax Policy and the Economy*. Chicago: University of Chicago Press: 35–68.

Alesina, A., Barbiero, O., Favero, C., Giavazzi, F., and Paradisi, M. (2017). "The effects of fiscal consolidations: theory and evidence." Working Paper 23385. National Bureau of Economic Research.

Alesina, A., Favero, C., and Giavazzi, F. (2018). "What do we know about the effect of austerity?" *American Economic Review Papers and Proceedings* 2018, 108: 524–530.

Amsdem, Alice H. (1989). *Asia's next giant: South Korea and late industrialization*. Oxford: Oxford University Press.

Amsden, A.H. (2001). *The Rise of 'the Rest': Challenges to the West from Late-Industrializing Economies*. Oxford: Oxford University Press.

Araújo, E., and Arestis, P. (2019). "Lessons from the 20 Years of the Brazilian inflation targeting regime". *Panoeconomicus* vol. 66, Issue 1: 1–23.

Arestis, P., and Sawyer, M. (2005). "Financial liberalization and the finance–growth nexus: what have we learned?" In: P. Arestis e M. Sawyer. *Financial Liberalization Beyond Orthodox Concerns*. New York: Palgrave McMillan.

Arida, P., and Resende, A.L. (1984). "Inertial inflation and monetary reform in Brazil". Paper prepared for the Conference "Inflation and Indexation" Institute of International Economics, Washington, DC, December, 6–8, 1984. Publicado no Brasil como Texto para Discussão n. 85. Departamento de Economia: Pontifícia Universidade Católica do Rio de Janeiro (PUC/RJ), janeiro 1985.

Arthur, W.B. (1989). "Competing technologies, increasing returns, and lock-in by historical events". *Economic Journal*, Vol. 99: 116–31, March.

Auerbach, A.J., and Gorodnichenko, Y. (2012). "Measuring the output responses to fiscal policy". *American Economic Journal: Economic Policy*, vol. 4(2): 1–27.

Bacha, E. (2016). *Integrar para crescer 2.0*. Texto para Discussão no. 36. Rio de Janeiro: Iepe-Casa das Garças.

Banco Central do Brasil (2021). "Ancoragem das expectativas de inflação e condução da política monetária. Estudo Especial 112/2021. Estudos Especiais do Banco Central. Banco Central do Brasil".

Banco Central do Brasil (2021). "Ancoragem das expectativas de inflação e condução da política monetária".

Baumol, W. (1986). "Productivity growth, convergence, and welfare: What the long-run data show". *American Economic Review*, Vol. 76 (5): 1072–1085.

Berg, A. and Miao, Y. (2010). "The real exchange rate and growth revisited: the Washington Consensus strikes back?" IMF Working Paper 10/58. Washington: International Monetary Fund.

Bhagwati, J. (1958). "Immiserizing Growth". *Review of Economic Studies*, vol. 25, Issue 3, June: 201–205.

Bhagwati, J. (1978). *Anatomy and consequences of exchange control regimes*. Cambridge (Mas.): Ballinger Pub. Company.

Bianchi, P., and Labory, S. (2018). *Industrial policy for the manufacturing revolution: perspectives on digital globalization*. Cheltenham (UK): Edward Elgar.

Bonelli, R. (2015). "Comparações internacionais de produtividade na indústria e tendências setoriais: Brasil e EUA". In: N. Barbosa *et al.* (org.). *Indústria e desenvolvimento produtivo no Brasil*. Rio de Janeiro: Fundação Getúlio Vargas: 487–517.

Bresser-Pereira, L.C. (2009). "Os dois métodos e o núcleo duro da teoria econômica". *Revista de Economia Política*, vol. 29, no. 2 (14): 163–190, abril–junho.

Bresser-Pereira, L.C., de Paula, L.F., and Bruno, M. (2020). "Financialization, coalition of interests and interest rate in Brazil". *Revue de Régulation*, vol. 27: 1–24.

Bresser-Pereira, L.C. (2007). *Macroeconomia da Estagnação: Crítica da Ortodoxia Convencional no Brasil pós-1994*. São Paulo: Editora 34.

Bresser-Pereira, L.C. (2008). "The Dutch disease and its neutralization: a Ricardian approach". *Brazilian Journal of Political Economy*, vol. 28, nº 1 (109), January–March: 47–71.

Bresser-Pereira, L.C. (2009a). *"Globalização e Competição: Por que alguns Países Emergentes têm Sucesso e outros não"*. Rio de Janeiro: Elsevier.

Bresser-Pereira, L.C. (2012) "A taxa de câmbio no centro da teoria do desenvolvimento" *Estudos Avançados*, 26(75): 7–28.

Bresser-Pereira, L.C. (2019). "From Classical Developmentalism and Post-Keynesian Macroeconomics to New Developmentalism". *Brazilian Journal of Political Economy*, vol. 39, no. 2 (155): 187–210.

Bresser-Pereira, L.C. (2020). "5% do Produto Interno Bruto para o investimento público". Valor Econômico, de 02/12/2020. https://valor.globo.com/opiniao/coluna/5-do-produto-interno-bruto-para-o-investimento-publico.ghtml. Accessed on 05 December 2021.

Bresser-Pereira, L.C. (2020a). "New Developmentalism: development macroeconomics for middle-income countries". *Cambridge Journal of Economics*, Vol. 44: 629–646.

Bresser-Pereira, L.C. (2020b) "Neutralizing the Dutch disease", *Journal of Post Keynesian Economics* 43:2: 298–316. https://doi.org/10.1080/01603477.2020.1713004.

Bresser-Pereira, L.C., and Gala, P (2007) "Por que a poupança externa não promove o crescimento?", *Revista de Economia Política* 27 (1): janeiro: 3–19. http://www.rep.org.br/PDF/105-1.

Bresser-Pereira, L.C., and Gomes da Silva, C. (2009). "O regime de metas de inflação no Brasil e a armadilha da taxa de juros/taxa de câmbio", *In:* J.L. Oreiro, L.F. de Paula e R. Sobreira (orgs), *Política Monetária, Bancos Centrais e Metas de Inflação: Teoria e Experiência Brasileira.* Rio de Janeiro: FGV Editora: 21–52.

Bresser-Pereira, L.C., and Nakano, Y. (1984) "Fatores aceleradores, mantenedores e sancionadores da inflação", *Revista de Economia Política* 4(1) janeiro: 5–21.

Bresser-Pereira, L.C., and Nakano, Y. (2003). "Crescimento econômico com poupança externa?". *Brazilian Journal of Political Economy*, vol. 23, nº 2 (90), April–June: 3–27.

Bresser-Pereira, L.C., Araújo, E.C., and Peres, S.C. (2020). "An alternative to the middle-income trap". *Structural Change and Economic Dynamics*, vol. 52: 294–312.

Bresser-Pereira, L.C., Oreiro, J.L., and Marconi, N. (2014). *"Developmental Macroeconomics: New Developmentalism as a Growth Strategy"*. New York: Routledge.

Bresser-Pereira, L.C., Oreiro, J.L., and Marconi, N. (2016). *"Macroeconomia Desenvolvimentista: Teoria e Política Econômica do Novo-Desenvolvimentismo"*. Rio de Janeiro: Elsevier.

Bresser-Pereira, L.C. (2015) "The access to demand", *Keynesian Brazilian Review* 1(1) 1º. semestre: 35–43. https://doi.org/10.33834/bkr.v1i1.14.

Bulman, D., Eden, M., and Nguyen, H. (2018). "Transitioning from low-income growth to high income growth: is there a middle-income trap?" In: B. Huang, P.J. Morgan e N. Yoshino (eds). *Avoiding the Middle-Income Trap in Asia: The Role of Trade, Manufacturing and Finance*. Tokyo: Asia Development Bank Institute, 2018: 14–59.

Carneiro, R. (2002). *Desenvolvimento em crise: a economia brasileira no último quartel do século XX*. São Paulo: Editora Unesp.

Caves, R.E. (1960). *Trade and Economic Structure: Models and Methods.* Cambridge: Cambridge University Press.

Cepal (1990). *Transformación Productiva con Equidad: La Tarea Prioritaria del Desarrollo de América Latina y el Caribe en los Años Noventa*. Santiago de Chile: Naciones Unidas-Cepal.

Cepal (1994). *"El Regionalismo Abierto en América Latina y el Caribe: La Integración Económica al Servicio de la Transformación Productiva con Equidad"*. Santiago de Chile: Nações Unidas-Cepal.

Cepal (2020). *Construir un Nuevo Futuro: Una Recuperación Transformadora con Igualdad y Sostenibilidad.* Santiago de Chile: Naciones Unidas-Cepal.

Cesarin, S. (2005). "Ejes y Estrategias del Desarrollo Económico Chino: Enfoques para América Latina y el Caribe". *In:* S. Cesarin and C. Moneta (eds). *China y America Latina: Nuevos Enfoques Sobre Cooperación y Desarrollo. ¿Una Segunda Ruta de la Seda*, 3–48. Buenos Aires: BID-INTAL.

Chang, H.J. (1994). *The political economy of industrial policy*. London: McMillan Press.

Chang, H.J. (2003). *Kicking Away the Ladder: Development Strategy in Historical Perspective*. London: Anthem Press.

Chenery, H.B., and Watanabe, T. (1958). "International comparisons of the structure of production". *Econometrica*, Vol. 26, no. 4, October: 487–521.

Cimoli, M. (1988). "Technological gaps and institutional asymmetries in a North-South model with a continuum of goods". *Metroeconomica*, Vol. 39: 245–274.

Cimoli, M. and Porcile, G. (2010). "Specialization, wage bargaining and technology in a multigoods growth model". *Metroeconomica*, Vol. 61:1: 219–238.

Cimoli, M., Dosi, G. and Soete, L. (1986). "Innovation diffusion, institutional differences and patterns of trade: a North-South model. Brighton, SPRU, University of Sussex. Paper originally presented at the Conference on Innovation Diffusion, Venice, 17–21 March 1986.

Coatsworth, J.H., and Williamson, J.G. (2002). The roots of Latin American protectionism: looking before the Great Depression. NBER Working Paper no 8999. Cambridge, Ma.: National Bureau of Economic Research, June.

Corden, W.M. and Neary, J.P. (1982). "Booming sector and de-industrialization in a small open economy". *Economic Journal* vol. 92 (368): 825–848. DOI: 10.2307/2232670.

Corden, W.M. (1974). *Trade policy and economic welfare*. Oxford: Oxford University Press.

Costa, I.N. (1977). "História e demografia". *Revista de História*, Vol. 55, no. 109: 195–203. https://www.revistas.usp.br/revhistoria/issue/view/5929. Accessed on 10 February 2021.

Delfim Netto, A. (2016). "Réquiem para a função de produção agregada". Valor Econômico, 02/02/2016. https://valor.globo.com/brasil/coluna/requiem-para-a-funcao-de-producao-agregada-1.ghtml.

DeLong, J.B., and Summers, L. (2012). "Fiscal policy in a depressed economy". *Brookings Papers on Economic Activity*, Spring: 233–274.

Di Filippo, A. (2021). *El Desarrollo y la Integración de América Latina. Una Odisea Inconclusa*. Santiago de Chile: Ediciones Universidad Alberto Hurtado.

Diaz-Alejandro, A. (1985). "Good-bye financial repression, hello financial crash". *Journal of International Economics*, vol. 19, Issue 1–2, September–October: 1–24.

Diaz-Alejandro, C. (1984). "Latin America in the 1930s". In: R. Thorpe (ed.). *Latin America in the 1930s*. London: Macmillan.

Dixon, R., and Thirlwall, A.P. (1975). "A model of regional growth-rate differences on Kaldorian Lines". *Oxford Economic Papers*, New Series, Vol. 27, No. 2 (July): 201–214.

Dollar, D., and Kraay, A. (2003). "Institutions, trade and growth". *Journal of Monetary Economics*. Elsevier, vol. 50, nº 1:133–162. January.

Domar, E. (1946). "Capital expansion, rate of growth, and employment". *Econometrica*, vol. 14 (2): 137–147.

Dosi, G., and Orsenigo, L. (1988). "Coordination and transformation: an overview of structures, behaviour and change in evolutionary environments". In: G. Dosi, C. Freeman, R. Nelson, G. Siverberg, e L. Soete. *Technical Change and Economic Theory*. London: Pinter Publishers.

Dosi, G., Pavitt, K., and Soete, L. (1990). *"The Economics of Technical Change and International Trade"*. London: Harvester Wheastsheaf.

Dosi, G., Tyson, L.D., and Zysman, J. (1989). "Trade, Technologies, and Development: A Framework for Discussing Japan". *In:* J. Zysman et. al., (ed.) (1989). *Politics and Productivity*. New York: Ballinger.

Eatwell, J., and Taylor, L. (2000). *Global Finance at Risk: The Case for International Regulation*. New York: The New Press.

Eichengreen, B. (2011). *Exorbitant Privilege: The Rise and Fall of the Dollar*. New York: Oxford University Press.

Evans, P. (1992). "The State as problem and solution: Prédation, Embedded Autonomy, and Structural Change". In: S. Haggard and R.S. Kaufman. *The Politics of Economic Adjustment: International Constraints, Distributive Conflicts, and the State*. Princeton, New Jersey: Princeton University Press: 139–181.

Fajnzylber, F. (1983). *La Industrialización Trunca de América Latina*. México: Editorial Nueva Imagen.

Fajnzylber, F. (1990). *Industrialización en América Latina: de la "Caja Negra" al "Casillero Vacío"*. Cuadernos de la Cepal no. 60. Santiago de Chile: Naciones Unidas-Cepal.

Fama, E.F. (1970). "Efficient capital markets: A review of theory and empirical work". *The Journal of Finance*, Papers and Proceedings of the Twenty-Eighth Annual Meeting of the American Finance Association, vol. 25, no. 2. New York, May, 1970: 28–30.

Fazzari, S., Ferri, P., and Variato, A.N. (2020). "Demand-led growth and accommodating supply". *Cambridge Journal of Economics*, vol. 44: 583–605.

Feenstra, R.C. (2004). *Advanced International Trade: Theory and Evidence*. Princeton: Princeton University Press.

Feenstra, R.C. (1998). "One country, two systems: implications of WTO entry for China." Department of Economics, University of California, Davis.

Feldstein, M., and Horioka, C. (1980). "Domestic savings and international capital flows". *Economic Journal*, vol. 90 (358), June: 314–329.

Felipe, J., and McCombie, J.S.L. (2013). *The Aggregate Production Function and the Measurement of Technical Change: "Not Even Wrong"*. Northampton, MA: Edward Elgar Publishing, 2013.

Ffrench-Davis, R. (2015). Chile since 1999: from counter-cyclical to pro-cyclical macroeconomics. *Comparative Economic Studies*, vol. 57, no. 3: 426–453.

Fisher, I. (1907). *The Theory of Interest*. New York: The Macmillan Company, 1930.

Flam, H., and J. Flanders (1991). *Heckscher-Ohlin Trade Theory [A book containing Heckscher's and Ohlin's seminal articles]*. Cambridge (Mas.): The MIT Press, 1991.

Fleming, J.M. (1962). "Domestic financial policies under fixed and under floating exchange rates". *IMF Staff Papers* vol. 9 (3), November. International Monetary Fund: 369–380.

FMI (1994). "World Economic Outlook: A Survey by the Staff of the International Monetary Fund". Washington, DC. International Monetary Fund. October. Disponível em https://www.elibrary.imf.org/doc/IMF081/08001-9781557753854/08001-9781557753854/Other_formats/Source_PDF/08001-9781455279876.pdf. Accessed on 10 April 2021.

Friedman, M. (1956). "The quantity theory of money—a re-statement". In: M. Friedman (ed.). *Studies in the Quantity Theory of Money*. Chicago: Chicago University Press.

Friedman, M. (1963). *Inflation: Causes and Consequences*. Bombay: Asia Publishing House.

Friedman, M. (1968). "The role of monetary policy". *American Economic Review*, vol. 57: 1–17.

Fritz, B., de Paula, L.F., and Prates, D.M. (2018). "Global currency hierarchy and national policyspace: a framework for peripheral economies". *European Journal of Economics and Economic* Policies: Intervention, vol. 15, no. 2: 208–218.

Furman, J., and Summers, L. (2020). "A reconsideration of fiscal policy in the era of low interest rates". Harvard Kennedy School (Mossavar-Rahmani Center for Business & Government). Harvard University, https://www.hks.harvard.edu/centers/mrcbg/programs/growthpolicy/reconsideration-fiscal-policy-era-low-interest-rates-jason. Accessed on 10 April 2021.

Furtado, C. (1952). "Formação de capital e desenvolvimento econômico". *Revista Brasileira de Economia*, Vol. 6, no. 3, setembro.

Furtado, C. (1957). "O desenvolvimento recente da economia venezuelana (exposição de alguns problemas)". *In*: C. Furtado. *Ensaios sobre a Venezuela: Subdesenvolvimento com Abundância de Divisas*. Rio de Janeiro: Editora Contraponto: 35–118, 2008.

Furtado, C. (1959). *Formação Econômica do Brasil*. 18ª edição. São Paulo: Companhia Editora Nacional.

Furtado, C. (1961). *Desenvolvimento e Subdesenvolvimento*. Rio de Janeiro: Editora Contraponto, 2009.

Furtado, C. (1967). *Teoria e Política do Desenvolvimento Econômico*. São Paulo: Editora Abril Cultural, (edição de 1983).

Furtado, C. (1974). "Notas sobre a economia venezuelana e suas perspectivas atuais". *In*: C. Furtado. *Ensaios sobre a Venezuela: Subdesenvolvimento com Abundância de Divisas*. Rio de Janeiro: Editora Contraponto: 119–135, 2008.

Furtado, C. (1985). *A Fantasia Organizada*. 2ª edição. Rio de Janeiro: Paz e Terra.

Furtado, C. (1992). *Os Ares do Mundo*. 2ª edição. São Paulo: Paz e Terra.

Furtado, C. (1999). *O Longo Amanhecer*. 2ª edição. São Paulo: Paz e Terra.

Furtado, C. (2021). *Correspondência Intelectual: 1949–2004*. Organização, Apresentação e Notas de R.F. D'Aguiar. São Paulo: Companhia das Letras.

Gala, P. (2008). "Real exchange rate levels and economic development: theoretical analysis and econometric evidence". *Cambridge Journal of Economics* 32:273–288.

Gill, I., and Kharas, H. (2007). *An East Asian Renaissance: Ideas for Economic Growth*. Washington, DC: The World Bank.

Gilpin, R. (1987). *The Political Economy of International Relations*. Princeton: Princeton University Press.

Gomes, L. (1987). *Foreign Trade and the National Economy. Mercantilist and Classical Perspectives*. London: McMillan Press.

Graham, F.D. (1923). "Some aspects of protection further considered". *Quarterly Journal of Economics* 37: 199–227, February.

Grossman, G.M., and Helpman, E. (1990). "Trade, innovation and growth". *The American Economic Review*. Papers and Proceedings. May.

Grossman, G.M., and Helpman, E. (1991). *Innovation and Growth in the Global Economy*. Cambridge (Mas.): The MIT Press.

Guanziroli, C. (2014). "Evolución de la política agrícola brasileña: 1980–2010". *Mundo Agrário*, Vol. 15, no. 29, agosto: 1–33. https://www.mundoagrario.unlp.edu.ar/article/view/MAv15n29a07/6011. Accessed on 20 April 2021.

Hamilton, A. (1791). "Report on the subject of manufactures." *In*: H.C. Syrett (ed). *Papers of Alexander Hamilton*, Vol. 10, *December 1791–January 1792*. New York: Columbia University Press, 1966: 230–340.

Harrod, R.F. (1939). "An essay in dynamic theory". *The Economic Journal*, vol. 49 (193): 14–33.

Hausmann, R., and Hidalgo, C. (2010). "Country diversification, product ubiquity, and economic divergence". CID Working Paper No. 201. Center for International Development: Harvard University.

Hausmann, R., Hwang, J., and Rodrik, D. (2005). "What you export matters". NBER Working Paper 11905. Cambridge, MA: National Bureau of Economic Research.

Heal, G. (1998). "The Economics of Increasing Returns". Working Paper Series in Money, Economics and Finance, PW-97-20. New York: Columbia Business School (http://www.columbia.edu/cu/business/wp/).

Heckscher, E.F. (1919). "The Effect of Foreign Trade on the Distribution of National Income" *In:* H. Flam, and J. Flanders (ed.). *Heckscher-Ohlin Trade Theory*. Cambridge (Ma): The MIT Press, 1991.

Helpman, E. (1984). "A simple theory of international trade with multinational corporations". *Journal of Political Economy*, n. 92, pp. 451–471.

Helpman, E. (2011). *Understanding Global Trade*, Cambridge: Harvard University Press.

Helpman, E., and Krugman, P.R. (1985). *Market Structure and Foreign Trade*. Cambridge (Mas): The MIT Press.

Hicks, J. (1932). *The Theory of Wages*. London: Macmillan.

Hirschman, A. (1958). *The Strategy of Economic Development*. New Haven: Yale University Press.

Hirschman, A. (1968). "The political economy of import substituting industrialization in Latin America". *Quarterly Journal of Economics*, vol. LXXXII, no. 1.

Hobsbawm, E. (1994). *A Era dos Extremos: o Breve Século XX (1914–1991)*. São Paulo: Companhia das Letras.

Hoeckman, B.M., and Kostecki, M.M. (2009). *The Political Economy of the World Trading System: The WTO and Beyond*. Third edition. New York: Oxford University Press.

https://www.bcb.gov.br/conteudo/relatorioinflacao/EstudosEspeciais/EE112_ancoragem_expectativas_inflacao_conducao_politica_monetaria.pdf. Accessed on 18 November 2021.

Huang, B., Morgan, P.J., and Yoshino, N. (2018). "Introduction". In: B. Huang, P.J. Morgan, and N. Yoshino (eds). *Avoiding the Middle-Income Trap in Asia: The Role of Trade, Manufacturing and Finance*. Tokyo: Asia Development Bank Institute, 2018: 1–13.

Huang, B., Morgan, P.J, and Yoshino, N. (2018). *Avoiding the Middle-Income Trap in Asia: The Role of Trade, Manufacturing and Finance*. Tokyo: Asia Development Bank Institute.

Hume, D. (1752a). "Of money". *In:* E.F. Miller. *Essays, Moral, Political and Literary*. Indianapolis: Liberty Classics, 1952.

Hume, D. (1752b). "Of interest". *In:* E.F. Miller. *Essays, Moral, Political and Literary*, Indianapolis: Liberty Classics, 1952.

Hume, D. (1752c) "Of the balance of trade, Political discourses", *Edinburgh*, as *reprinted* in D. Hume. In: E. Rotwein (ed.). Writings on Economics, 1955.

Inter-American Development Bank (2004). *The emergence of China: opportunities and challenges for Latin America and the Caribbean*. Washington, DC: Inter-American Development Bank.

Johnson, C. (1982). *MITI* and the Japanese Miracle: The Growth of Industrial Policy, 1925–1975. Stanford: Stanford University Press.

Jones, R.W., and Neary, J.P. (1984). "The positive theory of international trade". In: *Handbook of international economics*, v. 1. Amsterdam: Elsevier.

Kahn, R. (1931). "The relation of Home investment to unemployment." *Economic Journal*, vol. 41, no. 162: 173–198.

Kaldor, N. (1957). "A model of economic growth". In: N. Kaldor. *Essays on Economic Stability and Growth*. Second Edition. London: Duckworth.

Kaldor, N. (1966). *Causes of the Slow Rate of Economic Growth of the United Kingdom: An Inaugural Lecture*. In: N. Kaldor. *Further Essays on Economic Theory*. London: Duckworth: 100–138, 1978.

Kaldor, N. (1967). *Strategic Factors in Economic Development.* Ithaca, New York: Cornell University.

Kaldor, N. (1968). "Productivity and growth in manufacturing industry: a reply". *Economica,* Vol. 35, no. 140, November: 385–391.

Kaldor, N. (1970). "The case for regional policies". In: N. Kaldor. *Further Essays on Economic Theory.* London: Duckworth: 139–154, 1978.

Kalecki, M. (1954). *Teoria da Dinâmica Econômica. Ensaios sobre as Mudanças Cíclicas e a Longo Prazo da Economia Capitalista.* São Paulo: Editora Abril, 1977.

Kelton, S. (2020). *The Deficit Myth. Modern Monetary Theory and the Birth of the People's Economy.* New York: Public Affairs.

Keynes, J.M. (1936). *The General Theory of Employment, Interest, and Money.* San Diego: Harcourt Brace Jovanovich, Publishers (1964 edition).

Keynes, J.M. (1982). *The Collected Writings of John Maynard Keynes,* in D. Moggridge, and E. Johnson (eds), vol. 27, London, Macmillan to Royal Economic Society.

Keynes, J.M. (1936). *A Teoria Geral do Emprego, do Juro e da Moeda.* São Paulo: Editora Abril, 1996.

Keynes, J.M. (1937). "The general theory of employment". *The Quarterly Journal of Economics,* vol. 51, n. 2, February: 209–223.

Koutsoyiannis, A. (1979). *Modern Microeconomics.* Second edition. London: MacMillan Education.

Krueger, A.O. (1974). "The political economy of the rent-seeking society". *The American Economic Review* 64: 291–303.

Krugman, P.R. (1979). "Increasing returns, monopolistic competition, and international trade". *Journal of International Economics,* v. 9, n. 4: 469–479, November.

Krugman, P.R. (1980). "Scale economies, product differentiation, and the pattern of trade" In: P.R. Krugman. *Rethinking International Trade.* Cambridge (Ma): The MIT Press, 1990 (originally published in *American Economic Review* 70: 950–959).

Krugman, P.R. (1981). "Intraindustry specialization and the gains from trade". *Journal of Political Economy,* 89 (5): 959–974.

Krugman, P.R. (1989). "New Trade Theory and the less Developed Countries" In: Calvo, Guillermo [ed.] (1989). *Debt, Stabilization and Development*: Essays in Honor of Díaz-Alejandro.

Krugman, P.R. (1990). "Increasing Returns and the Theory of International Trade". In: P.R. Krugman. *Rethinking International Trade.* Cambridge, Mas.: Cambridge University Press.

Krugman, P.R. (1991). *Geograph and Trade.* Cambridge (Mas.): The MIT Press.

Krugman, P.R. (1992). "Technology and International Competition: A Historical Perspective" In: Harris, M., and E.G. Moore, ed. (1992). *Linking Trade and Technology Policies.* Washington (DC): National Academy Press.

Krugman, P.R. (1984). "Import protection as export promotion: international competition in the presence of oligopoly and economics of scale" In: P.R. Krugman.

Rethinking International Trade. Cambridge, Ma: The MIT Press: 185–198 (originally published in H. Kierzkoushi. *Monopolistic Competition in International Trade*, Oxford: Oxford University Press, 1984).

Krugman, P.R. (1993). "Toward a Counter-Counterrevolution in Development Theory". Proceedings of the World Bank Annual Conference on Development Economics. Washington, DC, The World Bank: 15–62.

Krugman, P.R., Obstfeld, M., and Melitz, M. (2015). *Economia Internacional*. 10ª edição. São Paulo: Editora Pearson.

Lall, S. (2000). "The Technological Structure and Performance of Developing Country Manufactured Exports, 1985–1998". QEHWPS44. Oxford: Queen Elizabeth House, University of Oxford.

Landes, D. (1969). *The Unbound Prometheus: Technological Change and Industrial Development in Western Europe from 1750 to the Present*. Cambridge: Cambridge University Press.

Lewis, W.A. (1953). "O desenvolvimento econômico com oferta ilimitada de mão de obra". In: A.N. Agarwala e S.P. Singh (org.). *A Economia do Subdesenvolvimento*. 2ª edição. Rio de Janeiro: Editora Contraponto.

Lewis, W.A. (1954). "Economic Development with Unlimited Supplies of Labor". *The Manchester School*, Vol. 22 (2): 139–91.

Lin, J. (2009). "Answer to Chang" *In*: J. Lin, and H.J. Chang. "Should industrial policy in developing countries conform to comparative advantage or defy it? A debate between Justin Lin and Ha-Joon Chang". *Development Policy Review*, nº 27.

Linder, S. (1961). *An Essay on Trade and Transformation*. New York: Wiley.

List, F. (1841). *Sistema nacional de economia política* [tradução de Nazionaler System der Volkswirtschaftslehre]. São Paulo: Abril Cultural, 1983.

Lucas Jr., R.E. (1988). "On the Mechanics of Economic Development". *Journal of Monetary Economics* 22: 3–42. July.

Lucas Jr., R.E. (1990). "Why doesn't capital flow from rich to poor countries?" The American Economic Review, vol. 80, no. 2, May. Papers and Proceedings of the Hundred and Second Annual Meeting of the American Economic Association (May, 1990): 92–96.

Marconi, N. (2012), "The industrial equilibrium exchange rate in Brazil: an estimation". *Brazilian Journal of Political Economy*, vol. 32, No. 4, São Paulo: 656–669.

Marconi, N., Magacho, G., and Rocha, I. (2014). "Estrutura produtiva e a dinâmica econômica nos BRICs: uma análise Insumo-Produto". *Revista Economia Ensaios* no. 29 (número especial), dezembro: 119–134.

Markusen, J.R. (1984). "Multinationals, multi-plant economies and the gains from trade". *Journal of International Economics*, n. 16, pp. 205–216.

Marshall, A. (1890). *Princípios de Economia Política*. Vol. I e II. São Paulo: Editora Abril, 1982.

Martínez-García, E., Coulter, J., and Grossman, V. (2021). "Fed's new inflation targeting policy seeks to maintain well-anchored expectations". Federal Reserve Bank of Dallas. April 6, 2021. https://www.dallasfed.org/research/economics/2021/0406. Accessed on 4 December 2021.

Marx, K. (1867). *Capital: A Critique of Political Economy—The Process of Production of Capital.* Book I (Volume I). First English edition of 1887 (4th German edition changes included as indicated) with some modernisation of spelling. Translated by Samuel Moore and Edward Aveling, and edited by Frederick Engels. Moscow, USSR: Progress Publishers. Available: https://www.marxists.org/archive/marx/works/download/pdf/Capital-Volume-I.pdf.

Marx, K. (1867a). *O Capital: Crítica da Economia Política—o Processo de Produção do Capital.* Livro I. [Brazilian edition]. São Paulo: Editora Boitempo, 2013.

Marx, K. (1885). *O Capital: Crítica da Economia Política—o Processo de Circulação do Capital.* Livro II. [Brazilian Edition]. São Paulo: Editora Boitempo, 2014.

Marx, K. (1894). *Capital: A Critique of Political Economy.The Process of Capitalist Production as a Whole.* Book III (Volume III). Edited by Friedrick Engels and completed by him 11 years after Marx's death. New York: International Publishers, 1996.

Marx, K. (1894a). *O Capital: Crítica da Economia Política—o Processo Global da Produção Capitalista.* Livro III. [Brazilian edition]. São Paulo: Editora Boitempo, 2017.

Matsushita, M., Schoenbaum, T.J. e Mavroidis, P.C. (2006). *The World Trade Organization: Law, Practice, and Policy.* 2nd ed. Oxford: Oxford University Press.

Mazzucato, M. (2013). *The entrepreneurial state: debunking public vs. private sector myths.* London: Anthem Press.

McCombie, J.S.L., and Thirlwall, A.P. (1994). *Economic growth and the balance-of-payments constraint,* London: St Martin's Press.

McKinnon, R. (1991). *The Order of Economic Liberalization: Financial Control in the Transition to a Market Economy.* Baltimore: The John Hopkins University Press.

McKinnon, R.I. (1973). *Money and Capital in Economic Development.* Washington, DC: Brookings Institution.

Meade, J. (1955). *Trade and Welfare.* London and New York: Oxford University Press.

Medeiros, C.A. (2008). "Celso Furtado na Venezuela". *In*: C. Furtado. *Ensaios sobre a Venezuela: Subdesenvolvimento com Abundância de Divisas.* Rio de Janeiro: Editora Contraponto: 2008:137–156.

Medeiros, C.A. (2020). "A Structuralist and Institutionalist developmental assessment of and reaction to New Developmentalism". *Review of Keynesian Economics,* vol. 8, no. 2, Summer: 147–167.

Melitz, M. (2003). "The Impact of Trade on Intra-Industry Reallocations and Aggregate Industry Productivity." *Econometrica* 71(6): 1695–1725.

Melitz, M., and Treffler, D. (2012). Gains from Trade When Firms Matter. *Journal of Economic Perspectives,* Vol. 26, no. 2, Spring: 91–118.

Michaely, M.M., Papageorgiu, D., and Choski, A. (1991). *Liberalizing foreign trade:* lessons of experience in the developing world. v. 7. Cambridge (MA): Basil Blackwell.

Mill, J.S. (1848). *Princípios de economia política* [tradução de Principles of political economy with some of their applications to social philosophy]. São Paulo: Abril Cultural, 1983.

Minsky, H. (1982). *Can "it" Happen Again: Essays on Instability and Finance.* New York: M.E. Sharpe.

Minsky, H. (1986). *Stabilizing an Unstable Economy.* New York: McGraw Hill, 2008 (ed. original: Yale University Press, 1986).

Morceiro, P., and Guilhoto, J. (2019). "Desindustrialização setorial no Brasil". São Paulo: Instituto de Estudos para o Desenvolvimento Industrial (IEDI). https://iedi.org.br/media/site/artigos/20190418_desindustrializacao_t3rPaHz.pdf. Accessed on 29 July 2020.

Moreira, M.M. (1995). *Industrialization, Trade and Market Failures: The Role of Government Intervention in Brazil and South Korea.* London: Macmillan Press.

Mundell, R.A. (1960). "The monetary dynamics of international adjustment under fixed and flexible rates". *Quarterly Journal of Economics*, vol. 74, no. 2, 227–257.

Myrdal, G. (1957). *Teoria Económica y Regiones Subdesarrolladas.* México: Fondo de Cultura Económica (ed. 1959).

Nassif, A. (2003). *Liberalização Comercial e Eficiência Econômica: A Experiência Brasileira. PhD Dissertation.* Rio de Janeiro: Universidade Federal do Rio de Janeiro (UFRJ).

Nassif, A. (2007). "National Innovation System and macroeconomic policies: Brazil and India in Comparative Perspective". UNCTAD Discussion Paper n. 184. Geneva: United Nations Conference on Trade and Development (UNCTAD).

Nassif, A. (2010). "Brazil and India in the global economic crisis: Immediate impacts and economic policy responses". In: S. Dullien, D. Kotte, A. Márquez and J. Priewe (eds). *The Financial and Economic Crisis of 2008–2009 and Developing Countries.* New York and Geneva: UNCTAD-United Nations: 171–201.

Nassif, A. (2018). "O Brasil é um país fechado ou um país protegido?" Valor Econômico, de 03 de maio de 2018. https://valor.globo.com/opiniao/coluna/o-brasil-e-um-pais-fechado-ou-um-pais-protegido.ghtml. Accessed on 20 July 2022.

Nassif, A. (2019). "Política industrial e desenvolvimento econômico: teoria e propostas para o Brasil na era da economia digital". In: C. Feijo, and E. Araújo (orgs). *Macroeconomia moderna: lições de Keynes para economias em desenvolvimento.* Rio de Janeiro: Ed. Elsevier: 81–100.

Nassif, A., and Castilho, M. (2020). "Trade patterns in a globalised world: Brazil as a case of regressive specialization". *Cambridge Journal of Economics*, vol. 44: 671–701.

Nassif, A., Bresser-Pereira, L.C., and Feijó, C. (2018). "The case for reindustrialisation in developing countries: towards the connection between the macroeconomic regime and the industrial policy in Brazil". *Cambridge Journal of Economics*, vol. 42: 385–381.

Nassif, A., Feijó, C., and Araújo, E. (2016). "Structural change, catching up and falling behind in the BRICS: A comparative analysis based on trade patterns and Thirlwall's law". *PSL Quarterly Review*, vol. 69 n. 278 (December, 2016): 373–421.

Nassif, A., Feijo, C., and Araújo, E. (2011). *'The Long-Term "Optimal" Real Exchange Rate and the Currency Overvaluation Trend in Open Emerging Economies: The Case of Brazil'*, UNCTAD Discussion Papers no. 206, Geneva, United Nations Conference on Trade and Development.

Nassif, A., Feijó, C. and Araújo, E. (2017). A structuralist-Keynesian model for determining the "optimum" real exchange rate for Brazil's economic development process (1999–2015), *CEPAL Review*, no. 123, December, Santiago, Chile, Economic Commission for Latin America and the Caribbean (ECLAC), available at https://repositorio.cepal.org/bitstream/handle/11362/43447/4/RVI123_en.pdf.

Nassif, A., Feijó, C., and Araújo, E. (2020). "Macroeconomic policies in Brazil before and after the 2008 global financial crisis: Brazilian policy-makers still trapped in the New Macroeconomic Consensus guidelines". *Cambridge Journal of Economics*, vol. 44: 749–779.

Nelson, R.R. (1981). "Research on productivity growth and productivity differences: dead ends and new departures". *Journal of Economic Literature*, Vol. 19, no. 3, September: 1029–1064.

Nelson, R.R., and Winter, S.G. (1982). *An Evolutionary Theory of Economic Change*. Cambridge (Mas.): Harvard University Press.

North, D. (1990). *Institutions, Institutional Change, and Economic Performance*. Cambridge: Cambridge University Press.

Nurkse, R. (1951). "Formação de capital e desenvolvimento econômico". *Revista Brasileira de Economia*, Vol. 5, no. 4, dezembro.

Nurkse, R. (1951). "Problemas da formação de capitais em países subdesenvolvidos". *Revista Brasileira de Economia*, vol. 5, n. 5: 11–45.

Ocampo, J.A., and Malagón, J. (2015). "Colombian monetary and exchange rate policy over the past decade". *Comparative Economic Studies*, vol. 57, no. 3: 454–482.

Ocampo, J.A., and Parra, M. (2003). "The terms of trade for commodities in the twentieth century". *Cepal Review* 79, April.

Ohlin, B. (1924). *A Theory of Trade*. Ph.D. Dissertation. Stockholm School of Economics. In: H. Flam, and J. Flanders (ed.). *Heckscher-Ohlin Trade Theory*. Cambridge (Mas.): The MIT Press, 1991.

Ohlin, B. (1933). *Interregional and International Trade*. Cambridge (Ma.): Harvard University Press, 1968.

Palley, T. (2021). "The economics of New Developmentalism: a critical assessment". *Investigación Económica*, vol. 80 (317), Julio–Septiembre: 3–33.

Palma, G. (2005). "Four sources of de-industrialisation and a new concept of the Dutch disease". In J.A. Ocampo (ed.), *Beyond Reforms*. Palo Alto: Stanford University Press: 71–116.

Pareto, V. (1909). *Manual de Economia Política*. São Paulo: Editora Nova Cultural, 1996.

Paus, E. (2018). "The middle-income trap: lessons from Latin America". In: B. Huang, P.J. Morgan, and N. Yoshino (eds). *Avoiding the Middle-Income Trap in Asia: The Role of Trade, Manufacturing and Finance*. Tokyo: Asia Development Bank Institute, 2018: 60–105.

Pavitt, K. (1984). "Sectoral patterns of technical change: towards a taxonomy and a theory". *Research Policy* 13: 343–373.

Penrose, E. (1959). *The Theory of the Growth of the Firm*. Oxford: Oxford University Press.

Pindyck, R., and Rubinfeld, D. (2014). *Microeconomia*. 8ª edição. São Paulo: Pearson Education.

Porcile, G. (2021). "Latin American structuralism and new structuralism". In: L. Alcorta, N. Foster-McGregor, B. Verspagen, and A. Szirmai. *New Perspectives on Structural Change: Causes and Consequences of Structural Change in the Global Economy*. Oxford: Oxford University Press.

Porter, M. (1980). *Competitive Strategy*. New York: Free Press.

Porter, M. (1989). *A Vantagem Competitiva das Nações*. Rio de Janeiro: Ed. Campus.

Posner, M. (1961). "International trade and technical change". *Oxford Economic Papers*, Vol. 13: 323–341.

Possas, M.L. (1989). *Dinâmica e Concorrência Capitalista: uma Interpretação a partir de Marx*. São Paulo: Editora Hucitec.

Possas, M.L. (1996). "Competitividade: fatores sistêmicos e política industrial" In: A.B. Castro, M.L. Possas e A. Proença. *Estratégias empresariais na indústria brasileira: discutindo mudanças*. Rio de Janeiro: Editora Forense Universitária.

Prasad, E., Rajan, R., and Subramaniam, A. (2006). *"Foreign Capital and Economic Growth"*. Washington: IMF Research Department.

Prebisch, R. (1949). "El desarrollo económico de la América Latina y algunos de sus principales problemas". Santiago de Chile: Naciones Unidas-Cepal.

Prebisch, R. (1951). *Problemas Teóricos y Prácticos del Crecimiento Económico*. Santiago de Chile: Naciones Unidas/Cepal (edição de 1973).

Prebisch, R. (1959). "Commercial policy in the underdeveloped countries (from the point of view of Latin America)". *American Economic Review*, Vol. 49, no. 2, May: 251–273 (edição citada de 1958, da Cepal).

Rangel, I. (1957). *Dualidade Básica da Economia Brasileira*. In: C. Benjamin. Os Desenvolvimentistas: Obras Reunidas—Ignácio Rangel, Vol. 1. Rio de Janeiro: BNDES, 2005: 285–353.

Rangel, I. (1963). *A Inflação Brasileira*. In: C. Benjamin. Os Desenvolvimentistas: Obras Reunidas—Ignácio Rangel, Vol. 1. Rio de Janeiro: BNDES, 2005: 551–679.

Rasmussen, P.N. (1957). *Studies in Inter-Sectoral Relations*. Amsterdam: Einar Harcks.

Razin, O., and Collins, S.M. (1999). "Real exchange rate misalignments and growth". In: A. Razin, and E. Sadka (ed.). *The Economics of Globalization: Policy Perspectives from Public Economics.* Cambridge: Cambridge University Press.

Reinert, E. (2008). *"How Rich Countries Got Rich ... And Why Poor Countries Stay Poor".* London: Constable.

Resende, A.L. (2022). "A camisa de força ideológica da Macroeconomia". Versão preliminar de artigo publicado, em versão compacta, no Caderno Eu & Fim de Semana, Valor Econômico, 11/02/2022. https://valor.globo.com/eu-e/noticia/2022/02/11/andre-lara-resende-a-camisa-de-forca-ideologica-da-macroeconomia.ghtml. Accessed on 15 February 2022.

Resende, A.L. (2015). *Devagar e Simples. Estado, Economia e Vida Contemporânea.* São Paulo: Companhia das Letras.

Rey, H. 2015. *Dilemma Not Trilemma: The Global Financial Cycle and Monetary Policy Independence*, NBER Working Paper Series no. 21162, National Bureau of Economic Research, available at http://www.nber.org/papers/w21162.pdf.

Ricardo, D. (1815). "An essay on lhe influence of a low price of corn on the profits of stock". *In*: D. Ricardo (edited by P. Sraffa and M. Dobb). *Works and Correspondence of David Ricardo*. Cambridge: Cambridge University Press, V. 4, 1951–1973.

Ricardo, D. (1817). *Princípios de Economia Política e Tributação*. São Paulo: Editora Abril Cultural (edição de 1982).

Rodrik, D. (2006). "Goodbye Washington Consensus, hello Washington Confusion?" *Journal of Economic Literature*, vol. 44 (4): 973–987.

Rodrik, D. (2008). "The real exchange rate and economic growth". *Brookings Papers on Economic Activity*, 2:365–412.

Rodrik, D. (2008a). "Industrial policy: don't ask why, ask how". *Middle East Development Journal*, Demo Issue (2008): 1–29.

Rodrik, D. (2011). *The Globalization Paradox: Democracy and the Future of the World Economy*. New York: W.W. Norton & Company.

Rogers, C. (1989). *Money, Interest and Capital. A Study in the Foundations of Monetary Theory*. Cambridge: Cambridge University Press.

Romer, P.M. (1986). "Increasing Returns and Long-Run Growth". *Journal of Political Economy* 94: 1001–1037.

Ros, J. (2013). *Rethinking economic development, growth, and institutions*. Oxford: Oxford University Press.

Ros, J. (2015). "Central bank policies in Mexico: targets, instruments, and performance". *Comparative Economic Studies*, vol. 57, no. 3: 583–10.

Rosenstein-Rodan, P.N. (1943). "Problemas de industrialização da Europa do Leste e do Sudeste". In: A.N. Agarwala, and S.P. Singh (org.). *A Economia do Subdesenvolvimento*. 2ª edição. Rio de Janeiro: Editora Contraponto, 2010.

Rowthorn, R. (1975). "What remains of Kaldor's laws?" *The Economic Journal*, Vol. 85:10–19.

Rowthorn, R., and Ramaswamy, R. (1999). "Growth, trade and de-industrialization". *IMF Staff Papers*, Vol. 46, no. 1, March:18–41. Washington, DC: International Monetary Fund.

Rybczynski, T.M. (1955). "Factor Endowment and the Relative Commodity Prices". *Economica* vol. 22. *Journal of Economics*, December: 336–341.

Sachs, J.D., and Warner, A.M. (1995). "Natural resource abundance and economic growth". NBER Working Paper Series no. 5398. Cambridge, Ma.: National Bureau of Economic Research.

Samuelson, P.A. (1948). "International trade and the equalization of factor prices". *Economic Journal*, 58: 168–184.

Samuelson, P.A. (1949). "International factor price equalization once again". *The Economic Journal* 59: 181–197.

Scherer, F.M., and Ross, D. (1990). *Industrial Market Structure and Economic Performance*. Third Edition. Boston: Houghton Mifflin Company.

Schumpeter, J. (1911). *A Teoria do Desenvolvimento Econômico: uma Investigação sobre Lucros, Capital, Crédito, Juro e o Ciclo Econômico*. São Paulo: Editora Abril Cultural (edição de 1982; tradução de *Theorie der wirtschaftlichen*. Berlin: Duncker & Humblot, 1964).

Schumpeter, J. (1942). *Capitalismo, socialismo e democracia*. Rio de Janeiro: Zahar Editores, 1984.

Scott, M.F.G. (1989) *A New View of Economic Growth*, Oxford: Clarendon.

Sen, A. (2000). *Desenvolvimento econômico como liberdade*. São Paulo: Companhia das Letras.

Shaikh, A. (1974). "Laws of production and laws of algebra: The humbug production function". *Review of Economics and Statistics*, vol. 56, no. 1, February: 115–120.

Shapiro, A., and Wilson, D.J. (2019). "The evolution of the FOMC's explicit inflation target". *Economic Letter* 2019/12. San Francisco: Federal Reserve Bank of San Francisco.

Silva, J.C.A.L, Prado, L.C., and Torracca, J. (2016). "Um novo olhar sobre um antigo debate: a tese de Prebisch-Singer é, ainda, válida?". *Economia Aplicada*, Vol. 20, no. 2: 203–226.

Silva, S. (1976). *Expansão Cafeeira e Origens da Indústria no Brasil*. São Paulo: Editora Alfa Omega.

Simon, H.A. (1979). "On parsimonious explanations of production relations". *The Scandinavian Journal of Economics*, vol. 81, no. 4: 459–474.

Simonsen, M.H., and Cysne, R.P. (2009). *Macroeconomia*. 4ª. Edição. São Paulo: Editora Atlas.

Singer, H.W. (1950). "The distribution of gains between investing and borrowing countries". *The American Economic Review*, Vol. 40, No. 2, Papers and Proceedings of the Sixty-second Annual Meeting of the American Economic Association (May, 1950):473–485.

Singh, A. (2003). "Capital Account liberalization, free long-term Capital Flows, financial crises and economic development". *Eastern Economic Journal*, vol. 29 (2): 191–216.

Skidelsky, R. (1999). *Keynes*. Rio de Janeiro: Jorge Zahar Editores.

Smith, A. (1776). An Inquiry into the Nature and Causes of the Wealth of Nations. An Electronic Classic Series Publication. University Park: The Pennsylvania State University, 2005. Available: https://www.rrojasdatabank.info/Wealth-Nations.pdf.

Sobreira, R., and Oreiro, J.L. (2009). "Metas inflacionárias, fragilidade financeira e ciclo de negócios: uma abordagem pós-keynesiana". *In:* J.L. Oreiro, L.F. de Paula, and R. Sobreira (orgs). *Política Monetária, Bancos Centrais e Metas de Inflação: Teoria e Experiência Brasileira*. Rio de Janeiro: FGV Editora: 97–120.

Solow, R.M. (1956). "A Contribution to the Theory of Economic Growth". *Quarterly Journal of Economics* 70: 65–94. February.

Souza, G.S., Gomes, E.G., and Alves, E.R.A. (2020). "Uma visão da agricultura brasileira com base em dados recentes do Censo Agropecuário". *In:* J.E.R. Vieira Filho, and J.C. Gasques. *Uma Jornada pelos Contrastes do Brasil: Cem Anos do Censo Agropecuário*. Brasília: Instituto de Pesquisa Econômica Aplicada (IPEA), 2020: 39–50.

Sraffa, P. (1926). "The laws of returns under competitive conditions". *The Economic Journal*, vol. 36, no. 144, December: 535–550.

Suzigan, W., and Furtado, J. (2006). "Política industrial e desenvolvimento". *Revista de Economia Política*, Vol. 26, nº 2 (102):163–185, abril–junho.

Szirmai, A. (2012). "Industrialisation as an engine of growth in developing countries, 1950–2005". *Structural Change and Economic Dynamics*, Vol. 23: 403–420.

Tavares, M.C. (1962). "Auge e declínio do processo de substituições de importações no Brasil". In: M.C. Tavares. *Da Substituição de Importações ao Capitalismo Financeiro. Ensaios sobre Economia Brasileira*. Rio de Janeiro: Zahar Editores, 1982.

Tavares, M.C. (1985). "A retomada da hegemonia norte-americana". *Revista de Economia Política*, vol. 5 (2), abril–junho.

Taylor, J. (1993). "Discretion versus policy rule in practice". *Carnegie-Rochester Series on Public Policy*, vol. 39:195–214.

Taylor, L. (2010). *Maynard's Revenge. The Collapse of Free Market Macroeconomics*. Cambridge, MA.: Harvard University Press.

The Economist (1977). "The Dutch disease". *The Economist*, 26 November 1977: 82–83.

Thirlwall, A.P. (1979). "The balance of payments constraint as an explanation of international growth rate differences". Originally published in *Banca Nazionale del Lavoro Quarterly Review*, Vol. 32, no. 128: 45–53. Republished in *PSL Quarterly Review*, Vol. 64, no. 259, 2011: 429–438.

Thirlwall, A.P. (1983). "A plain man's guide to Kaldor's growth laws". *Journal of Post Keynesian Economics*, Vol. 5, no. 3, Spring: 345–358.

Thirlwall, A.P. (2011). "Balance of Payments Constrained Growth Models: History and Overview". PSL *Quarterly Review*, Vol. 64 (259): 307–351.

Triffin, R. (1960). *Gold and the Dollar Crisis: The Future of Convertibility*. New Haven: Yale University Press.

Tybout, J.R., and Westbrook, M.D. (1995). "Trade Liberalization and the Dimensions of Efficiency Change in Mexican Manufacturing Industries". *Journal of International Economics* 39 (0000): 53–78.

UNCTAD (2018). *Trade and Development Report 2018: Power, Platforms and the Free Trade Delusion*. New York e Geneva: United Nations Conference on Trade and Development.

Vanek, J. (1968). "The factor proportions theory: the N-factor case". *Kyklos*. 21: 749–756. October.

Varian, H. (2003). *Microeconomia: princípios básicos*. 7ª edição. Rio de Janeiro: Ed. Campus.

Verdoorn, P.J. (1949). "Fattori che regolano lo sviluppo della produttivitá del lavoro". *L'Industria*, no. 1: 45–53.

Vieira Filho, J.E.R. (2020). "Ganhar tempo foi possível?" *In:* J.E.R. Vieira Filho, and J.C. Gasques. *Uma Jornada pelos Contrastes do Brasil: Cem Anos do Censo Agropecuário*. Brasília: Instituto de Pesquisa Econômica Aplicada (IPEA), 2020: 27–38.

Wade, R.H. (1990). *Governing the Market: Economic Theory and the Role of Government in East Asian Industrialization*. Princeton, NJ: Princeton University Press [Second paperback edition, 2004].

Wade, R.H. (2015). "The role of industrial policy in developing countries". In: A. Calgagno, S. Dullien, A. Márquez-Velázquez, N. Maystre, and J. Priewe (eds.). *Rethinking development strategies after the financial crisis. Vol. I: Making the case for policy space*. 67–79. Geneva: United Nations Conference on Trade and Development.

Walras, L. (1874). *Compêndio dos Elementos de Economia Política Pura*. São Paulo: Editora Abril/Nova Cultural (1986 edition).

Wicksell, K. (1898). *Interest and Prices*, British edition. London, Macmillan, 1936.

Wicksell, K. (1901). *Lectures in Political Economy*, vol. II (British edition). London: Routledge, 1935.

Williamson J (1990). What Washington means by policy reform? In: J. Williamson. *Latin American Adjustment: How much has happened?* Institute for International Economics, Washington DC.

Williamson, J. (1995). "Estimates of FEERs". In J. Williamson (ed.). *Estimating Equilibrium Exchange Rates*. Washington, DC: Institute of International Economics.

Williamson, J. (2008). "Exchange rate economics". Working paper n° 08-3, Washington, DC: Peterson Institute for International Economics.

Wray, L.R. (1998). *Understanding Modern Money: The Key to Full Employment and Price Stability*. Edward Elgar: Cheltenham, U.K.

Young, A.A. (1928). "Increasing Returns and Economic Progress". *The Economic Journal* 152 (XXXVIII), December: 527–542.

Zysman, J. (2013). *The third globalization: can wealthy nations stay rich in the twenty-first century?* New York: Oxford University Press.

Zysman, J., Feldman, S, Kushida, K.E., Murray, J., and Nielsen, N.C. (2013). "Services with evertything: the ICT-enabled digital transformation of services". In: D. Breznitz, and J. Zysman (eds.). *The Third Globalization? Can Wealth Nations Stay Rich in the Twenty-First Century?* New York: Oxford University Press: 99–129.

Index

www.ingramcontent.com/pod-product-compliance
Lightning Source LLC
Chambersburg PA
CBHW071248230926
51849CB00001B/267
* 9 7 8 9 0 0 4 7 3 4 2 8 9 *